MICHAEL GRAVES

BUILDINGS AND PROJECTS
1982-1989

EDITED BY KAREN VOGEL NICHOLS,
PATRICK J. BURKE, AND CAROLINE HANCOCK

ESSAYS BY
ROBERT MAXWELL
CHRISTIAN NORBERG-SCHULZ

PRINCETON ARCHITECTURAL PRESS

MICHAEL GRAVES

Michael Graves was born in Indianapolis in 1934. He received his architectural training at the University of Cincinnati and Harvard University. In 1960 Graves won the Rome Prize and studied at the American Academy in Rome, of which he is now a Trustee. Graves is the Schirmer Professor of Architecture at Princeton University, where he has taught since 1962.

Graves, a Fellow of the American Institute of Architects, opened his professional practice in Princeton, New Jersey, in 1964. He has been the architect for a wide variety of projects, some of which are illustrated in this monograph, covering the years 1982-1989. A previous monograph, published by Rizzoli International, describes selected buildings and projects from 1966-1981.

Published in the United States of America by
Princeton Architectural Press
37 East 7th Street
New York, NY 10003
212.995.9620

98 97 96 95   5 4 3 2
(Second printing, 1995)

Design by
Karen Vogel Nichols, Patrick J. Burke, and Caroline Hancock

Printed in Hong Kong

Library of Congress cataloging-in-publication data:

Graves, Michael, 1934–
Michael Graves, buildings and projects, 1982-1989 / edited by
Karen Vogel Nichols, Patrick J. Burke, and Caroline Hancock ; essays
by Robert Maxwell, Christian Norberg-Schulz.
p. cm.
Includes bibliographical references.
ISBN 0-910413-13-4 (alk. paper) : $50.00 — ISBN 0-910413-17-7
(pbk. : alk. paper) : $35.00
1. Graves, Michael, 1934– . 2. Architecture, Postmodern—United
States. I. Nichols, Karen Vogel. II. Burke, Patrick J.
III. Hancock, Caroline. IV. Maxwell, Robert, 1922– . V. Norberg
-Schulz, Christian. VI. Title. VII. Title: Buildings and projects,
1982–1989.
NA737.G72A4 1989
720'.92—dc20
89-10615
CIP

CONTENTS

ACKNOWLEDGEMENTS

We would like to thank Kevin Lippert and Elizabeth Short of Princeton Architectural Press for their unending patience and perserverence throughout all phases of the writing and production of this monograph.

For several years, Bill Taylor has been responsible for most of the photography for Michael Graves, Architect, and deserves our greatest thanks for his efforts in compiling this record of the office's work.

Editorial assistance for texts and illustrations has been provided by: Laura Cerwinske, Jennifer Harlow Hayden, Cid Nelson, Laura Nelson, Carole Nicholson, Douglass Paschall, Allen Prusis, Nancy Thiel, and Lauren Westreich.

Our thanks for assistance with graphics and layout go to: Jesse Castaneda, Amy Cheun, Michelle Fornabai, John Graham, Julie Hanselmann, Anne Hicks, John Hoke, Lorissa Kimm, Mark Kelly, Selim Koder, Michael Kuhling, Cullen McCarthy, Saverio Manago, Peter Pelsinski, Jim Saywell, Tanya Uretskaya, Robert Weimer, Sarah Whiting, Ron Witte, and especially Warren Van Wees, Erica Weeder, and Wilfrid Wong, without whom we would still be faced with many blank pages.

Rome, 1981

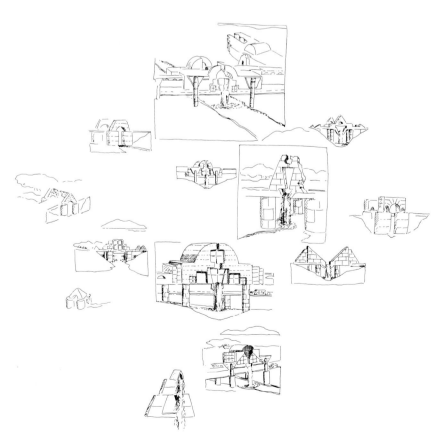

Fargo-Moorhead Cultural Bridge
Fargo, North Dakota and Moorhead, Minnesota, 1978

MICHAEL GRAVES
AND
THE LANGUAGE OF ARCHITECTURE

by Christian Norberg-Schulz

Architects' sketches tell the tale of how architecture is conceived. The drawings of the Italian Renaissance show that the building was imagined as an additive composition of elementary volumes. The choice of elements was determined by a generally accepted typology, as was the detailing. The numerous designs for centralized churches by Leonardo da Vinci offer characteristic examples.[1] During the Baroque the elements and details were basically the same, but the composition changed to become integrative, as is demonstrated by Borromini's sketches. Because of these similarities and differences in conception and means, Frankl could present the architectural history of the fifteenth, sixteenth, and seventeenth centuries as the development of recurrent types.[2] In general, I may conclude that the architect did not approach the building task in terms of *functions,* hoping that they might generate a form, but by means of a given *language,* which makes the solution generally comprehensible as part of a tradition. The analogy to spoken language is obvious; when we learn our mother's tongue, we are not taught what to say, but are given the means of expression. This "linguistic" conception of architecture was normal as late as the end of the nineteenth century. The first sketch by Martin Nyrop for the City Hall in Copenhagen (1888), for example, shows on the same sheet of paper a schematic site-plan, the composition of the volumes (main body, wings, and towers), and the detail of a typical window with subdivisions and surrounding brickwork.[3] The architect, thus, started with a vision of a hierarchy of forms, all of which have a figurative identity.

With the event of Functionalism the approach changed radically. A diagrammatic distribution of functions now became the point of departure, sometimes abstracted into a pattern of circles and connecting lines. As a supplement, spatial effects were sketched, as shown by Mies van der Rohe's perspectives of the Tugendhat and Hubbe houses.[4] The final solution was often presented as an axonometric birds-eye view, where inside and outside are hardly distinguishable. A facade in the traditional sense no longer appears. The building, thus, was conceived in terms of spatial continuity, no longer as a composition of distinct elements. The definition of "figural" parts was intentionally left out; the traditional typological units were, so to speak, forbidden and the building reduced to an abstract juxtaposition of vertical and horizontal planes. With some exaggeration it has been said that it makes no difference to turn Rietveld's drawings for the Schroder house (1923) upside-down.[5] This abstraction from reality of the individual building goes together with the loss of a commonly understood language of forms.

During the last two decades we have experienced a return to the traditional conception of architecture. This change is particularly evident in Michael Graves' sketches. In 1977 Graves abandoned the abstract Late-modern approach he had in common with the others of the "New York Five,"[6] and introduced a new method of working with "figural elements." The sketches for his own house in Princeton are characteristic, and even more so are those for the Fargo-Moorhead Cultural Center Bridge. His aims are explained in the texts accompanying the projects. Thus he says about the house: ". . . the new surfaces have been elaborated with figural elements in order to allow for a closer identification with classical and anthropomorphic sources," and about the bridge: "In its facades, the bridge employs enlarged symbolic elements of architecture such as keystones, which have been made void as windows, bringing together the two cities by providing a focus on the river and establishing it as a center. The voided keystone is also seen as a scupper which collects the sky and replenishes the river below through a waterfall which issues from its base . . . . In this way, the individual elements of the composition are seen as parts of a large narrative."[7]

Before I take a closer look at Graves' method as such, it is important to understand his aims. In the introduction to his *Buildings and Projects 1966–1981* Graves himself offers an illuminating explanation.[8] The title, "A Case for Figurative Architecture," is already significant, and in the text the issue is elaborated: "The Modern Movement based itself largely on technical expression—and the metaphor of the machine dominated its building form. In its rejection of the human or anthropomorphic representation of previous architecture, the Modern Movement undermined the poetic form in favor of nonfigural, abstract geometries . . . . While any architectural language, to be built, will always exist within the technical realm, it is important to keep the technical expression parallel to an equal and complementary expression of ritual and symbol. . . . This language, which engages inventions of culture at large, is rooted in a figurative, associational and anthropomorphic attitude. If . . . that part of our language which extends beyond internal technical requirements, can be thought of as the resonance of man and nature, we quickly sense an historical pattern of external language.

Vacation House
Aspen, Colorado, 1978

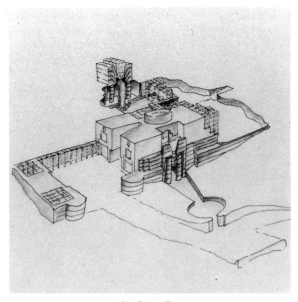

Plocek Residence
Warren, New Jersey, 1977

All architecture before the Modern Movement sought to elaborate the themes of man and landscape. Understanding the building involves both association with natural phenomena (for example, the floor is like the ground), and anthropomorphic allusions (for example, a column is like a man). . . . The cumulative effect of non-figurative architecture is the dismemberment of our former cultural language of architecture. . . . It is crucial that we re-establish the thematic associations invented by our culture in order fully to allow the culture of architecture to represent the mythic and ritual aspirations of society." The program is clear: Graves wants to substitute for non-figurative Modernism a new figurative idiom, in order to recover architecture as an expression of the "resonance of man and nature." In the texts to the projects cited above, he talks about the sky, the river, and the anthropomorphic sources, and uses the building to "collect" the content. In general, the aim is to arrive at a "poetic form" and an "architectural language," and his sketches furnish proof of his linguistic method.

As is well known, Graves' "case for a figurative architecture" is shared by several of the protagonists of Postmodern architecture and may be considered the most important issue in the quest for a more comprehensive conception of architecture. Already in the middle of the sixties, Aldo Rossi made projects based on figurative units or, in Krier's terminology, "nameable objects."[9] The works of Rossi and Krier, however, differ from those of Graves in one important respect: whereas the former intend their buildings as gross typological wholes, Graves *composes* his designs of constituent figurative parts. That is, he really works in linguistic terms, using the elements like words. His method is therefore more flexible and allows for more varied and individual solutions. The demand for a "generally understood language of form"[10] is today being furthered ever more strongly, and to help its development it is of great importance to gain a better understanding of Graves' pioneering effort. Let me therefore return to the Fargo-Moorhead project.

The main problem at Fargo-Moorhead was to span the

river, that is, to unify the two banks and the buildings upon them to form a single "place." Primarily a river separates the land into two distinct domains. At the same time, however, the two banks belong together as delimitations of a common space. A bridge brings this togetherness into presence, and makes us perceive the space as a place. In Heidegger's words: "With the banks, the bridge brings to the stream the one and the other expanse of the landscape lying behind them. It brings stream and bank and land into each other's neighborhood. The bridge *gathers* the earth as landscape around the stream."[11] We could add: it gathers the earth "under the sky." Graves' sketches show how he strove to bring together the three basic themes: the spanning of the river, the letting-through of the water, and the receiving of the sky. Different figurative elements were tried out: arch and gable, hole and cleft, vault and open fan.[12] In the final solution the span is expressed by a continuous "rustication," which in the buildings at either end is turned on the diagonal, whereas the letting-through of the water and the collection of the sky is resolved by a composite form consisting of the "voided keystone," a split vault, and several "windows." The elements partly overlap and interpenetrate in the manner of a collage. In the adjacent buildings, figurative elements are used to mark entrances and focal points. In general, the spaces are intended as a composition of centers and paths, in contrast to the flowing continuum of Modern architecture. This does not imply, however, that the Fargo-Moorhead project represents a break with Modernism. It preserves the free plan and the open form, but adds a new dimension of spatial definition and formal characterization.

The approach which is established in Graves' 1977 projects was the result of a development. From the beginning, Graves conceived the building as a kind of three-dimensional collage, and his murals serve as a condensed continuation of the imagined space, introducing fragments of our natural and built environment.[13] The building, thus, is a transition between the surrounding and the symbolic wall-decoration. The latter simultaneously offers a sense of arrival and a promise of departure; that is, it opens our eyes

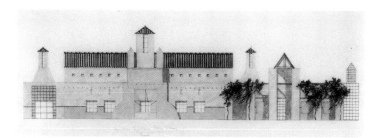

San Juan Capistrano Library
San Juan Capistrano, California, 1980

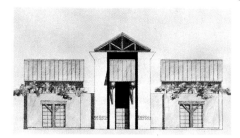

Environmental Education Center
Liberty State Park, New Jersey, 1980

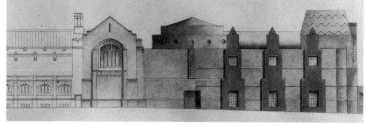

Vassar College Art Museum
Poughkeepsie, New York, 1981

to the qualities of the place. In a certain way Graves' early houses therefore already "collect" the environment and possess a value which is hardly found in the more abstract works of his contemporaries. The early houses, however, are not figurative; they are facade-less structures in the Modern tradition, and their space is flowing rather· than defined. This also comes forth in Graves' early sketches, which visualize spatial ensembles rather than compositions of distinct units.[14]

With the Schulman house in Princeton (1976) a new wish for figurative definition becomes evident. Here entrance and fireplace appear as symmetrical elements within the collage-like composition, and the body of the pre-existent house makes the whole stand forth as one comprehensive figure. Graves' own house from 1977 is also a conversion, and again the given body serves to unify the applied figural elements. It is tempting to infer that the coherence of the existing volumes in the two projects acted as a kind of catalyst to Graves' quest for a figurative architecture. The decisive step was taken with the Plocek house in Warren, New Jersey (1977). Here space has indeed become a composition of focal points and paths rather than a flowing continuum, and the built form serves both to define the spatial structure and to characterize the different parts of the building (such as basement, *piano nobile*, and attic). In general, Graves aimed at a "thematic dialogue between building and landscape," and, to achieve that, axes, symmetrical entrances, and articulate facades are reintroduced. And still, the house preserves a modern freedom of expression, as is well illustrated by the missing keystone in the street facade, which is "moved" to the garden pavilion in the back, suggesting that the house is related to the earth as well as the sky. An expectation is created by the missing stone, which is satisfied by the garden pavilion after one has walked through the house. The relation to earth and sky is also expressed internally by the vertical axis of the stair-case. In Graves' words: "The intersection of the two entry axes is marked by a stair column with its base at the lower entry level, its shaft on the main living level, and its capital in the upper story providing

light from above."[15]

But the development does not end with the Plocek house. Here, as well as in the projects for Green Brook and Aspen from 1978, the modernist collage is still predominant, although the latter house gives more emphasis to the figurative elements, introducing even wooden log-cabin construction to adapt to the locality.[16] A fully developed definition of figurative elements was realized in 1980 in three projects which, in spite of their differences due to use and context, show an analogous approach: the Red River Valley Interpretive Center in Moorhead, Minnesota; the Environmental Education Center in Liberty State Park, New Jersey; and the Public Library in San Juan Capistrano, California. The first project is particularly interesting because it is the first component of the Fargo-Moorhead Cultural Center bridge plan and shows Graves' passage from a collage-like to a "composed" solution. The result of this passage comes forth with convincing naturalness in the attractive Environmental Education Center. Here every part, large and small, possesses figural quality, and a true *building*, which is new as well as old, thus emerges. That is, historical references are evident, both in the main volumes (basilica, atrium, pergola) and in the details (roof-trusses, brackets, cornices). The library in San Juan Capistrano makes use of analogous motifs, but by means of subtle changes, Graves succeeds in creating a different, southern character. In his project for the Art History Department at Vassar College (1981), he moreover shows how his language may adapt to a Neo-gothic environment.

So far, the examples cited have been relatively small and horizontally extended buildings. How, then, does Graves' method function when the task demands a high-rise structure? The Portland Building in Portland, Oregon (1980) offers a first significant answer to the question. As a public building at the center of the downtown area, the design had to possess the quality of a true landmark. In the past, public buildings were distinguished by outspoken figural form, such as domes, towers, pediments, and columned porches.

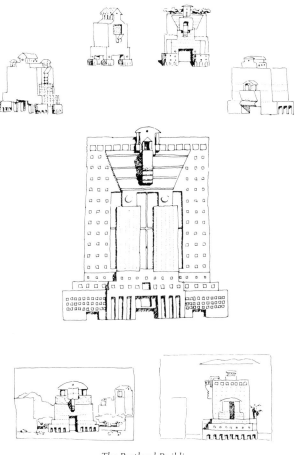

The Portland Building
Portland, Oregon, 1980

The Humana Building
Louisville, Kentucky, 1982

Modern landmarks, on the contrary, at best impress through sheer size. In Graves' solution we recognize an intended return to figural forms, with the purpose of expressing the public nature of the task. Thus he writes: "The design of the building addresses the public nature of both the urban context and the internal program. In order to reinforce the building's associative or mimetic qualities, the facades are organized in classical division of base, middle or body, and attic or head. The large paired columns on the main facades act as a portal or gate and reinforce one's sense of passage through the building along its main axis. . . . The base of the building reinforces the importance of the street as an essential urban form by providing a loggia on three sides and shopping along the sidewalk on the fourth."[17] A series of sketches illustrate Graves' quest to set these aims into work.[18] In all of them the problem consists in combining the vertical three-part division with an over-all unity of form as well as a dominant portal-motif in the middle. The means employed are figural elements, such as massive block, giant column or pilaster, giant keystone, pediment, and loggia. In the final solution, an enclosed block with intact corners, pierced by small, square windows, opens up in the middle to embrace a grandiose portal motif consisting of two colossal fluted pilasters carrying an equally colossal keystone on brackets. The fluting recalls the vertical window strips of the traditional skyscraper, whereas the keystone contains a series of horizontal band windows. Classical and modern memories are thus combined. In general, the building is simultaneously expressing the qualities of resting (loggia), standing (block), rising (pilasters), and receiving the sky

(keystone); it possesses a richness unknown in most high-rise building. Its scale is civic as well as human, and its role as an urban focus is convincing.

With the Humana Building in Louisville, Kentucky (1982), Graves realized related aims at an even larger scale, and again demonstrated the capacity of his figurative method to satisfy the circumstantial conditions. This was understood by the clients, who wrote: "The criteria are met in an extraordinary way by Michael Graves. The formal gestures of the Graves' design capture the fact that Louisville is a river city . . . . The building comes to terms in a humanistic way with the people who will enjoy its public aspects. . . . Its quiet beauty presents a form grounded in past architectural tradition, yet moving vibrantly forward into the future."[19]

At the beginning of the eighties Graves' architecture was fully developed. Accordingly, he could open the book on his work with a drawing presenting an inventory of his figures. Its title, "Rome 1981," is significant. It does not only suggest that one of Graves' main sources of inspiration are the forms of ancient Roman architecture, but also that his aim is to develop a similarly integrated and versatile language.[20] Placing the figures within a landscape of earth and sky containing hills, trees, and clouds, he moreover emphasizes the concrete character of his architecture. The forms are indeed "nameable objects" in the sense of things that we recognize and remember. The alienation from the everyday world of man, characteristic of Late-modern architecture, is thus overcome, at the same time as the art of building again

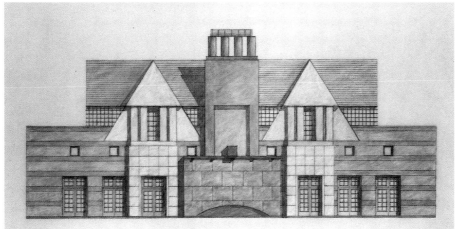

Erickson Alumni Center
West Virginia University, Morgantown, West Virginia, 1984

Henry Residence
Rhinecliff, New York, 1987

Glazer Residence
McKinney, Texas, 1983

becomes part of history.

How, then, *are* the nameable forms employed by Graves, and how are they composed? As has already been suggested, his language comprises wholes as well as subordinate parts. The former are solid or spatial or, in general, volumetric, and may be simple units such as pyramid, dome, cylinder, and cone, or composite volumes, such as basilica, arcade, bastion, and various kinds of towers. The subordinate parts are, among other things, gable, column, arch, keystone, bracket, stringcourse, cornice, and buttress. One might perhaps expect that buildings based on such conventional forms would become manifestations of a superficial historicism. Like the words of spoken language, however, the basic figural forms may be interpreted in ever new ways without losing their essential meaning. Such an interpretation, consisting in a kind of stylization, is already implied in Graves' inventory, and when the forms are set into work as a particular, concrete project, the interpretation is carried a step further to comply with the given circumstances. The keystone-motif may serve to illustrate this procedure. The keystone is part of an arch. The arch rests and rises, and in its curvature resembles the dome of the sky. Where the rising lines meet, an opening remains which is closed by the keystone. It is called a "key" because it closes at the same time as it belongs to the opening, expressing its quality as zenith and source of light. Fanning out, it receives the light, while in its resting on the arch it expresses the gravitational force of earthly matter. The keystone, thus, brings earth and sky together in one form. When the keystone is missing, light

seems to split the building apart, and its space is integrated with the "between" of earth and sky. When the stone is put back, the earth becomes cave and source, as in the garden pavilion of the Plocek house, where water flows forth under a massive arch. What is superficial, thus, is not Graves' approach, but the criticism of those who debase it for being "historicist," that is, in conflict with the modern world. It ought to be emphasized that, on the contrary, it is the historical dimension that brings Graves' buildings close to present-day life. Before I discuss this problem, however, I have to take a look at his way of putting the figurative elements together, that is, his method of composition.

Graves' sketches illustrate his procedure. An interesting combination of addition and integration is apparent. As has already been mentioned, addition is first of all known from Renaissance architecture and implies that each part preserves its completeness and individuality within the whole. Integration, on the contrary, means that the parts lose their independence to serve a unified Baroque totality.[21] In Graves' later works the elements are clearly recognizable and often emphasized, but continuities and interpenetrations nevertheless secure the integration of the whole. Out of the totality, the parts grow as articulations of the over-all image.[22] The use of surprises, such as the missing keystone in the Plocek facade, and augmentations, such as the giant pilasters and keystone of the Portland elevation, moreover contradict the general sense of classical order. We could also say that Graves never forgot Modernism's lesson of open form, although he abandoned Late-modern abstraction. In

11

Clos Pegase Winery
Calistoga, California, 1984

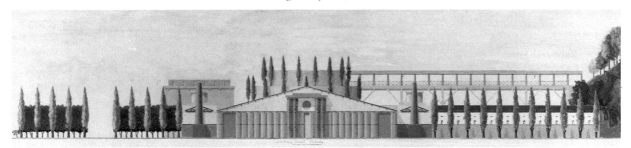

Clos Pegase Winery
Calistoga, California, 1984

general, then, Graves' architecture overcomes certain short-comings inherent in Modern architecture without losing the qualities of the free plan and the collage-like form. As has already been pointed out, his contribution consists of an improved spatial definition by means of centers and paths and of a formal characterization of the different parts of the building. To these topological and morphological improvements we may add the typological value of his projects. Graves' language is therefore complete; it comprises all the three basic dimensions of a true architectural means of expression.[23]

Michael Graves' projects from the eighties prove the fertility of his approach. In an incredibly rich series of works, ranging from small weekend houses to high-rise structures and urban ensembles, he has demonstrated that any building task may be "solved" in figurative terms and that local character may be combined with the expression of general values. A private house in the Catskill Mountains thus combines colonnade, sustaining arch, and dominant gable with rustication and log siding. The result is at the same time simple and powerful, and the house communicates with the surroundings without dissolving into them. The Henry Residence in Rhinecliff, New York is a more complex composition. An "American" symmetrical volume is squeezed between two chimney stacks, which serve as links to a round, columnar pavilion on one side, and a square, pyramidal one on the other. The many memories involved are unified by means of a complex play of symmetries in plan and elevation. Graves himself characterizes the house as "eclectic," "rural," and "picturesque." The Glazer House in McKinney, Texas is at the same time more abstract and more local in character. That is, it possesses a manifest southern flavor, at the same time as the figurative elements have a

high degree of generality, like those of the Environmental Education Center in New Jersey. Graves' ability to evoke memories and thus make the building gain a local and temporal meaning also distinguishes his Erickson Alumni Center at West Virginia University, where concrete figures such as gables, dormers, and dominant chimney stack create that particular "domestic-institutional" quality that makes life at many American colleges so pleasingly significant.

A quest for a figurative, typological architecture culminated (so far) with the highly successful Clos Pegase Winery in Napa Valley. The Californian environment and the function of wine making here induced Graves to fully exploit his Roman vocabulary in a kind of Italian-rural context. A certain degree of abstraction, however, ensures the newness of the solution. In general, the Clos Pegase Winery demonstrates that there is only *one* language of architecture: the Classical one. Classicism in fact constitutes the foundation of all historical epochs, even those that negate its anthropomorphic natural principles, such as the Gothic and the *art nouveau.* (But the language of architecture may of course sink into oblivion, as happens in Late-modern and Deconstructivist works.)

During the 1980s Graves furthermore worked out a series of urban projects, among which the towers are of particular interest (LJ Hooker Developments, Atlanta; Sotheby's Tower, New York; City Centre, Los Angeles; etc.). American memories and modes of standing and rising are here unified as a response to Sullivan's demand when writing about "The Tall Office Building Artistically Considered": "How shall we impart to this sterile pile, this crude, harsh, brutal agglomeration, this stark, staring exclamation of eternal strife, the graciousness of those higher forms of sensibility

Metropolis Master Plan
Los Angeles, California, 1988

and culture that rest on the lower and fiercer passions?" Michael Graves answers this question, thereby recovering the skyscraper as a basic expression of New World Architecture.[24] Essentially his answer is simple: Let us remember the difference between up and down!

Among Graves' urban projects, the Whitney Museum of American Art extension stands forth as a stroke of genius. Words such as "adaptation" and "context" are used today to emphasize the need for a more coherent environment. The results, however, usually entail a loss of creativity, in comparison with the stylistic symbioses of other epochs. Graves has understood the lesson of the past, and by means of a composition of differences and an ingenious act of unification, he has not only created a fascinating totality worthy of New York Pluralism,[25] but he has also "saved" Breuer's museum, one of the most hideous products of brutalist Late-modernism.

To conclude, I shall return to the questions of whether Graves' architecture suits the present situation and how it is related to the works of other contemporary architects. The "Postmodern Condition" is often described as a loss of general values, and it is asserted that forms are nothing but transitory *simulacra*.[26] This nihilistic attitude obviously reflects certain aspects of the present state of affairs. The world we live in no longer consists of locally rooted ethnic domains, but has become an open multitude of fragments of the most various origin. The word "deconstructivism" is often used in this connection, and a total relativism of meaning seems to be a necessary consequence. But the nihilistic attitude is evidently not in agreement with the aims of Postmodern architecture. When Robert Venturi in 1966 initiated the new development,[27] he wanted a meaningful architecture which

should express the "complexities and contradictions" left out by Modernism; his successors have again and again emphasized that architecture ought to "affirm and reestablish the inherent order of things."[28] The question, then, is whether the concepts of "meaning" and "order" make sense in the present world. Fortunately there are also thinkers who open up the way towards a reconquest of meaningful forms:[29] Heidegger's conception of *thing* is of particular interest here.[30] Rather than the reflection of an *idea* (which can never be grasped as such), Heidegger understands the thing as the "gathering of a world." The meaning of a thing or form thus consists in what it gathers. As examples he analyzes nameable things such as "jug" and "bridge." I have already quoted part of his description of the bridge, which shows that Heidegger intends "gathering" in a very concrete sense. The description or "saying" of a thing is possible because it has a name which belongs to language. Language "contains" the world, and is called by Heidegger the "House of Being." It serves to reveal things as they are, to interpret something that remains in relation to the here and now.

Although language, and in particular poetic language, is the original means of expression, it does not exhaust the disclosure of meaning. Meaning or truth also has to be "set into work." Human life takes place between earth and sky, and architecture as an art is the means to render this condition visible. An architectural figure is a nameable thing which gathers earth, sky and the between of human life in a certain way. It reveals how life takes place and helps man to understand and master his condition. The basic figures are archetypes, which have to be interpreted over and over again in ever new ways. Graves' Louisville clients intuited that when they said that his solution was "grounded in the past, yet moving into the future." Architecture is therefore always old and new; it is historical in the sense that it forms part of the story of how man found a foothold "on earth under the sky." It is not historicist, however, if one with this term intends a superficial play with borrowed forms.

We understand that the Postmodern quest for meaning in general and Michael Graves' language in particular have an existential foundation. We also realize that the demand for a contemporary language of architecture is the crucial issue of the present. In a world which no longer consists of distinct domains and traditions, language becomes our rescue. In spite of many aberrations and superficial whims, the architecture of the last decade proves that such a language is on the way. In this development, American architecture is of particular interest. America is, because of its pluralistic situation, "the primitive and precious model of what is to change the condition of many over the globe" (Thomas Paine), and its architecture has from the very beginning given pride of place to language.[31]

Michael Graves' works form part of the American tradition, and represent a significant contribution to the recovery of the language of architecture. The complete nature of his designs is in this context important. Whereas a Postmodern architect like Rossi gives almost exclusive attention to typology, and the Late-modernists still remain within the limits of spatial or structural effects, Graves has understood that architecture comprises the dimensions of space and form as well as type. Thereby he comes closer than perhaps anyone else to the nature of the classical language, which for centuries gave Western architecture a foundation and allowed even minor talents to realize a meaningful expression. What we need today, however, is not a revival of the classical language, but a new means of expression built on the same timeless foundation. "Individual voices speaking a commonly understood language"[32] is what Postmodernism should mean. Graves' language is, in fact, both personal and impersonal. It is not there to be copied but to teach us the existential basis and the general dimensions of our field. The most important contribution of Graves, however, consists in the works his language has made possible. His buildings show that it is still possible to express by means of a poetic form the inherent order of things in relation to the realities of the contemporary world.

1. W. Lotz, "Das Raumbild der italienischen Architekturzeichnung der Renaissance," Mitteilungen des kunsthistorischen Instituts in Florenz (Düsseldorf, Juli 1936).

2. P. Frankl, Die Entwicklungsphasen der neueren Baukunst (Leipzig: 1914). American edition: Principles of Architectural History (Cambridge, Mass., 1968).

3. Millech, Danske arkitekturstromninger 1850–1950 (Kobenhavn, 1951), 212.

4. W. Tegethoff, Die Villen und Landhausprojekte von Mies van der Rohe (Essen, 1981).

5. C. Norburg-Schulz, "Casa Schröder," Il mondo dell'architettura (Milan, 1986).

6. Richard Meier, Peter Eisenman, Charles Gwathmey, John Hejduk.

7. Michael Graves Buildings and Projects 1966–1981, eds. K.V. Wheeler, P. Arnell, and T. Bickford (New York: Rizzoli International, 1982), 97, 111.

8. Ibid., 11ff.

9 D. Porphyrios, ed., "Leon Krier," Architectural Design Profile (London, 1984).

10. R.A.M. Stern, "Modern Traditionalism," in Robert A.M. Stern Buildings and Projects 1981–1985, ed. Luis F. Rueda (New York, 1986).

11. M. Heidegger, "Building Dwelling Thinking," in Poetry, Language, Thought, ed. A. Hofstadter (New York: Rizzoli International, 1971), 152.

12. Graves, op. cit. 116–17.

13. Ibid., 47, 214–15.

14. Ibid., 39, 69, 85.

15. Ibid., 119.

16. Ibid., 145ff.

17. Ibid., 195.

18. Ibid., 198.

19. P. Arnell and T. Bickford, eds, A Tower for Louisville (New York: Rizzoli International, 1982), 7.

20. Graves studied at the American Academy in Rome from 1960 to 1962.

21. C. Norberg-Schulz, Intentions in Architecture (London: Allen & Unwin, 1963).

22. "Michael Graves: The Humana Building," in GA Document 14 (Tokyo: A.D.A. Edita, 1985), 15.

23. C. Norberg-Schulz, The Concept of Dwelling (New York: Rizzoli International, 1985), Ch. VI.

24. C. Norberg-Schulz, New World Architecture (New York: Princeton Architectural Press, 1988).

25. C. Norberg-Schulz, "The Prospects of Pluralism," in New York Architecture (Deutsches Architeckturmuseum, Frankfurt a. M., 1989).

26. J.-F. Lyotard, The Postmodern Condition (Manchester, 1984). M. Perniola, La societá dei simulacri (Bologne, 1980).

27. R. Venturi, Complexity and Contradiction in Architecture (New York: Museum of Modern Art, 1966).

28. Stern, op. cit., 6.

29. Such as Heidegger, Bachelard, Gadamer, Bollnow.

30. Heidegger, "The Thing," Poetry, op. cit.

31. C. Norberg-Schulz, New World Architecture, op. cit.

32. Stern, op. cit.

1982–1989

PROJECT ASSISTANTS

The following people have worked in Michael Graves' office and have contributed to the projects shown here.

DEAN ACQUAVIVA • MARY JANE AUGUSTINE • MATTHEW BAIRD • SHEILA BAN • JOSEPH BARNES • RAYMOND BEELER • RONALD BERLIN • LYNDA BLEILER • MERYL BLINDER • GUSTAVO BONEVARDI • WENDY BRADFORD • SUSAN PIKAART BRISTOL • THEODORE BROWN • PATRICK BURKE • JANE BURNSIDE • BARBARA BUSECK • PAULA BUSHONG • SUSAN BUTCHER • CHRISTOPHER CALOTT • LAURENCE CAPO • JENNIFER CARLISLE • PAMELA CARTER ROWE • JESSE CASTANEDA • RICO CEDRO • AMY CHEUN • CHRISTOPHER CHILDERS • ADINA CHOUE-QUET • GRETCHEN CHRISTIE • CHRISTINA CHUN • WILLIAM COCHRANE • DAVID COLEMAN • FREDERICK COOKE • MICHAEL CRACKEL • ROGER CROWLEY • WENDY CSATARI • SEAN CULLEN • JOHN DIEBBOLL • MEGAN DOWNER • GEORGE DOWNS • DAVID DYMECKI • MARK DZEWULSKI • LINDA WHELAN EVANS • LISA FISCHETTI • NATALIE FIZER • IAN FLEETWOOD • AMY FORSYTH • CAROLYN FOUNTAIN • YOSSI FRIEDMAN • PIERRE FUHRER • JOSE GARCIA • NANCY GARNER • LYNNE GEISON • LINDA GERACE • REBECCA GODSHALL • GEORGIA JUNE GOLDBERG • NICHOLAS GONSER • JOSE GONZALEZ • JOHN GRAHAM • CAROLINE GREEN • JAMES GREENBERG • PAUL GRESHAM • ALEXEY GRIGORIEFF • THOMAS HANRAHAN • JULIE HANSELMANN • MARY HARRIS • YVONNE HARRIS • MAXIMILLIAN HAYDEN • ANNE HICKS • GAVIN HOGBEN • JOHN HOKE • TYLER LEE HOLMES • LAWRENCE HONES • ANN JOHNSTON • MICHELLE JUSTICE • PAUL KATZ • MARK KELLY • KEVIN KENNON • ELIZABETH KILKENNY • LORISSA KIMM • RANDALL KING • MIKE KINSEY • LINDA KINSEY • KIRAN KIPATDIA • SELIM KODER • MICHAEL KUHLING • RONALD LAMOREAUX • GARY LAPERA • ROBERT LEACH • MARGARET LEAVER • LEE LEDBETTER • ALEX LEE • LISA LEE • LAURIE LOCKWOOD • HERBERT LONDENSKY • JUDITH MCCLAIN-TWOMBLY • CAROL MCCOLLOUGH • WENDY MCCOLLOUGH • ANDREW MCNABB • KEITH MCPETERS • STEPHANIE MAGDZIAK • SAVERIO MANAGO • ROBERT MARINO • MARY MARTELLO • LESLIE MASON • JANE MAYBANK • MIMI MEAD • DON MENKE • JOAN MERCANTINI • VICTORIA MEYERS • HARUHISA MIKAMI • TIMOTHY MONTAQUE • ELIZABETH MORE • PATRICK MULBERRY • MARK NADEN • PETER HAGUE NEILSON • CID NELSON • GERALDINE NELSON • LAURA SUE NELSON • KAREN VOGEL NICHOLS • SANDRA NICHOLS • CAROLE NICHOLSON • RONALD NORSWORTHY • DEBRA O'BRIEN • NICHOLAS OWENS • SHARON PACHTER • STEPHEN PANZARINO • TRACY PANZARINO • STUART PARKS • DOUGLASS PASCHALL • CLEMENT PAULSON • JASON PEARSON • PETER PELSINSKI • ANN PENDLETON • JAMES PRICCO • ALLEN PRUSIS • CHARLYN RAINVILLE • MARYANN RAY • EMILY REEVES • ERIC REGH • PAT RICCIO • BARRY RICHARDS • JULIET RICHARDSON-SMITH • MILES RITTER • PIM ROBBERRECHTS • DAVID ROCKWOOD • K. WHITNEY ROGERS • WILLIAM ROSE • ANITA ROSSKAM • THOMAS ROWE • ROSLYN RUBESIN • DANIEL RUIZ • JAMES SAPP • JAMES SAYWELL • CLETUS SCHOMMER • ROSEMARY SCOPELLITI • DOUGLAS SHANEFIELD • DAN SHEPPERD • MALLORY SHURE • STEVEN SIVAK • HOKE SLAUGHTER • ROGER SMITH • TERENCE SMITH • VINCENT SNYDER • CRAIG SPANGLER • TAUNYA VAN DER STEEN • SERGIO STEUER • MICHELLE STIVELMAN • DONALD STRUM • SUZANNE STRUM • JOE SULLIVAN • JAMISON SUTER • LINDSAY SUTER • SANDRA SWIK • LESLIE SYLVESTER • KEAT TAN • RENE TAN • WILLIAM TAYLOR • DAVID TEETERS • NANCY THIEL • KIRSTEN THOFT • ERIC THOMPSON • CRAIG THOMSON • MARTHA THORP • EDWARD TUCK • PETER TWOMBLY • TANYA URETSKAYA • BARBARA VAN DER WEE • WARREN VAN WEES • SUSAN VIK • JANE VOGEL • ELIZABETH WAKEFIELD • CINDY WALKER • ERICA WEEDER • ROBERT WEIMER • LESLEY WELLMAN • RUTH WELLS • LAUREN WESTREICH • SARAH WHITING • GREGG WIELAGE • ANA WILLIAMSON • TONY WILSON • JULIA WIRICK • RONALD WITTE • FREDERICK WOLF • ALEXANDER WONG • WILFRID WONG • ROSS WOOLLEY • ELLEE WYNN-BRISCOE • ADAM YARINSKY • MEHRDAD YAZDANI • DAVID YUGUCHI • MARY CHUNG YUN • CHRISTIAN ZAPATKA • PAMELA ZIMMERMAN

ASSOCIATED ARCHITECTS AND DESIGNERS

The following associated architects or interior designers have worked with Michael Graves, Architect on the projects represented in this monograph.

ACOCK SCHLEGEL ARCHITECTS • AKAMATSU & SUGANO ARCHITECTS AND ENGINEERS • AUSTIN HANSEN FEHLMAN • BECKSTOFFER & ASSOCIATES • EMMANUEL BESNARD BERNADAC AND XAVIER PARIS • BRYANT & BRYANT, AIA • CHERRY + WELSH • COCO & BALDASSANO, ARCHITECTS • ED2 INTERNATIONAL • FUKUWATARI & ARCHITECTURAL CONSULTANTS • GRUEN ASSOCIATES • THE GRUZEN PARTNERSHIP • GSAS ARCHITECTS/ PLANNERS • HAMANO INSTITUTE • RAYMOND HUFF • ISD • RAYMOND J. JAMINET AND PARTNERS • JESTICO + WHILES • S. VIC JONES & ASSOCIATES • KOBER CEDERGREEN RIPPON • KOBER RIPPON ASSOCIATES • VLASTIMIL KOUBEK, AIA • KOZO KEIKAKU ENGINEERING • LANGDON WILSON • ALAN LAPIDUS P.C. • LORENZ & WILLIAMS, INC. • MELTON HENRY • MONACELLI ASSOCIATES • MORRIS ARCHITECTS • MORRIS*AUBRY ARCHITECTS • RAPP AND FRENCH • REYNA/CARAGONNE ARCHITECTS • HILDEGARD A. RICHARDSON AIA • RICHARDSON BUTLER ASSOCIATES • RAY ROUSH • S.C.A.U. • SEKISUI HOUSE, LTD. • SHIMIZU CORPORATION • CARL A. STRAUSS & ASSOCIATES • JOHN CARL WARNECKE & ASSOCIATES • SETH WARNER • WILSON AND ASSOCIATES • ZENITAKA CORPORATION

INDEX OF PROJECTS

SAN JUAN CAPISTRANO LIBRARY
SAN JUAN CAPISTRANO, CALIFORNIA

South facade detail

The city of San Juan Capistrano established architectural design guidelines which required new buildings to follow the indigenous Spanish mission style. This requirement prompted Graves to examine the properties and attributes of this style as a generic type. Transformed from its Renaissance beginnings, in part because of the climate, the Spanish mission style is characterized by its treatment of light. Light is also a central issue in the design of a library.

Graves used light monitors and clerestories to filter natural light into the building. In strategic locations, these light filters help orient and guide the visitor within the plan. Typical of the generic style, the library is organized around a central outdoor courtyard, whose surrounding peristyle screens the interior from the intense daylight. The courtyard, with its fountains and picturesque cypress trees, is a place of repose at the center of the building. This organization also allows several elements of the program to retain their own identities, without sacrificing a sense of overall unity. The children's wing is located on one side of the courtyard, the adult reading room and bookstacks on the second, the auditorium on the third, and garden gazebos on the fourth. Graves has designed a future expansion of the library which will replace the gazebos.

View from the south

Courtyard

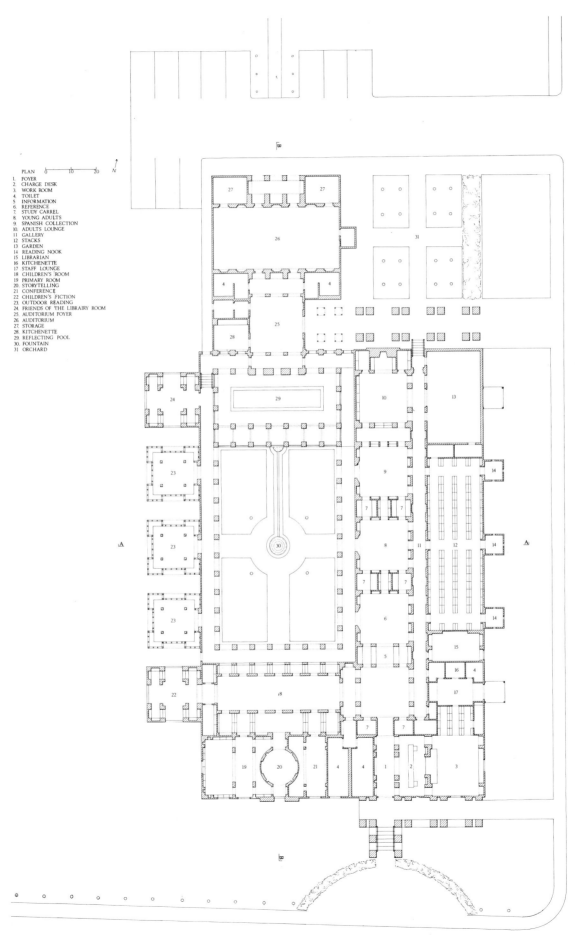

PLAN   0   10   20   N

1. FOYER
2. CHARGE DESK
3. WORK ROOM
4. TOILET
5. INFORMATION
6. REFERENCE
7. STUDY CARREL
8. YOUNG ADULTS
9. SPANISH COLLECTION
10. ADULTS LOUNGE
11. GALLERY
12. STACKS
13. GARDEN
14. READING NOOK
15. LIBRARIAN
16. KITCHENETTE
17. STAFF LOUNGE
18. CHILDREN'S ROOM
19. PRIMARY ROOM
20. STORYTELLING
21. CONFERENCE
22. CHILDREN'S FICTION
23. OUTDOOR READING
24. FRIENDS OF THE LIBRARY ROOM
25. AUDITORIUM FOYER
26. AUDITORIUM
27. STORAGE
28. KITCHENETTE
29. REFLECTING POOL
30. FOUNTAIN
31. ORCHARD

Plan

Entrance

Reading alcoves from the street

Courtyard loggia

View to courtyard

Gallery

Reference room

Periodicals room

Reading room

Reading room

Children's story room

1982

ENVIRONMENTAL EDUCATION CENTER
LIBERTY STATE PARK
JERSEY CITY, NEW JERSEY

Entry

The Environmental Education Center at Liberty State Park in New Jersey was designed as a "wildlife interpretive center" for the study and exhibition of the indigenous wildlife and environmental context of the park. The building's central auditorium and three linked galleries are used for conferences and exhibitions. A mural, located in the lobby, recollects the former industrial landscape from which the natural park land is being reclaimed.

The building is organized to suggest a reciprocal relationship between architecture and landscape. Entering the complex through paired pavilions, the visitor can choose to enter the building on one side or, on the other side, to take a meandering path which tours a series of descriptive pavilions and environmental sculptures installed in the marsh. The character of the architecture is derived from indigenous park structures built of exposed heavy timber construction.

Roadway facade

1 ENTRY PORCH
2 ENTRY HALL
3 RECEPTION
4 EXHIBITION
5 AUDITORIUM
6 SITE ORIENTATION PAVILION
7 MEETING ROOM
8 STAFF OFFICE
9 TOILET
10 STORAGE
11 KITCHENETTE
12 JANITOR
13 PROJECTIONIST

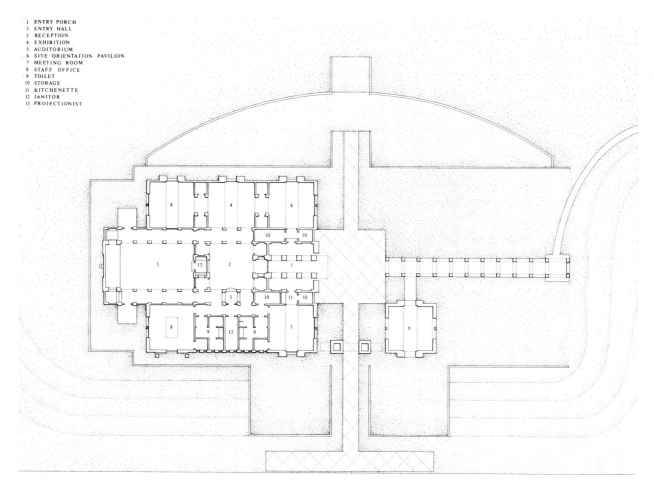

ENVIRONMENTAL EDUCATION CENTER

N   0 4 8   16

Plan

Industrial Landscape mural

Auditorium

Entry

Nature walk pavilion

North facade with birdhouse

1982

PLOCEK RESIDENCE
WARREN, NEW JERSEY

View from the street

The Plocek residence is sited on a heavily wooded, steeply sloping hillside in suburban New Jersey. The three stories of the house are expressed in the street facade whose articulation recalls the classical tripartite division of rusticated base, *piano nobile* or main living floor, and attic story. The house is entered at the lower level through a gate pulled forward from the street facade and also at the main level through the east facade adjacent to the parking court.

The house is experienced as a series of layers organized along the two primary axes of entry whose intersection is marked by a central "stair column." The column's large wooden framed capital at the upper story is capped by a skylight which allows natural light to penetrate the center of the house. Second floor bridges with full height metal railings wrap around the stair column and reinforce its reading as an object in the center of the plan.

The house is furnished with built-in cabinetry, freestanding furniture, lamps and rugs designed by Graves. The mural above the fireplace terminates the main east-west axis of the house. Entitled "Archaic Landscape," it recollects the general themes of the architecture and also refers to the natural landscape of the hillside beyond.

South and west facades

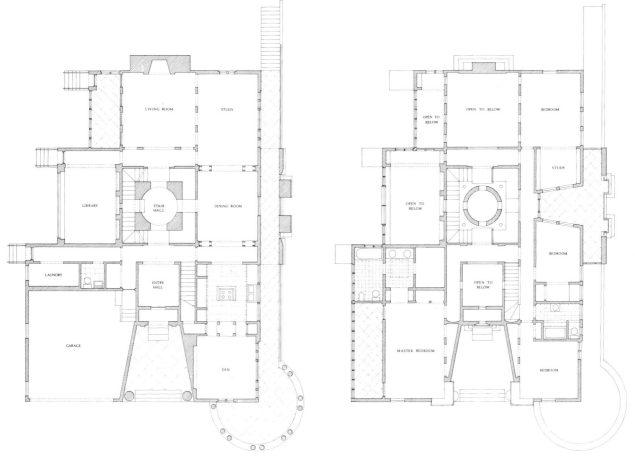

First floor plan   *Second floor plan*

Street facade

Entry court facade

Living room

Foyer

Lower level stair hall

Stair column from second floor

Stair column detail

Living room from second floor bridge

Dining room

Kitchen, breakfast counter

Kitchen

THE HUMANA BUILDING
LOUISVILLE, KENTUCKY

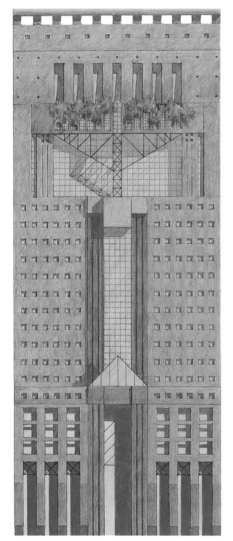

Main Street elevation

South elevation

The Humana Building, a 26-story office tower located in downtown Louisville, was designed as the corporate headquarters for Humana, a company specializing in health care. In contrast to the tendencies of modern architecture, evident in the plazas of several surrounding developments, the Humana Building occupies the whole site, helping to re-establish the street edge as an essential urban form. The building's orientation to the Ohio River, and its attempt to mediate the difference in scale between the small townhouses on one side and a skyscraper on the other, reinforce its contextual relationship with this particular city and site. Within the outdoor loggia, which acts as the entrance to the building, a large waterfall fountain refers to the nearby falls of the Ohio River, where the city of Louisville was founded in the 19th century.

The 525,000 square foot building includes two parking levels below grade, a large public fountain and retail shops on the first floor, Humana's offices, and a conference center. The building's formal organization reflects its division into these significant parts. The lower portion, six floors high, is devoted to public space and to Humana's executive offices. General offices are located in the body of the building. The conference center occupies the 25th floor, with access to a large outdoor porch overlooking the city and the river beyond.

View from Main Street

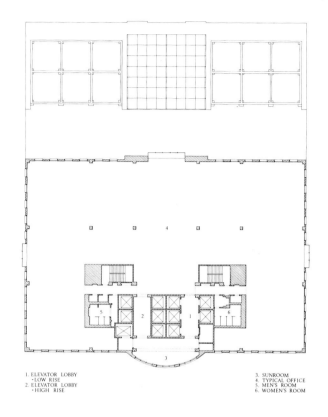

1. ELEVATOR LOBBY
   - LOW RISE
2. ELEVATOR LOBBY
   - HIGH RISE
3. SUNROOM
4. TYPICAL OFFICE
5. MEN'S ROOM
6. WOMEN'S ROOM

Typical office floor plan

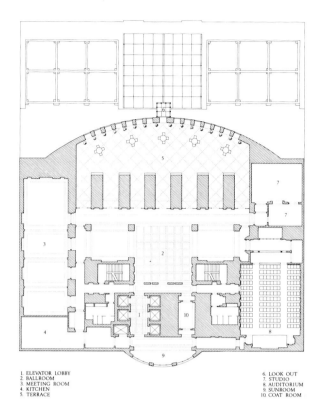

1. ELEVATOR LOBBY
2. BALLROOM
3. MEETING ROOM
4. KITCHEN
5. TERRACE
6. LOOK OUT
7. STUDIO
8. AUDITORIUM
9. SUNROOM
10. COAT ROOM

Conference center plan

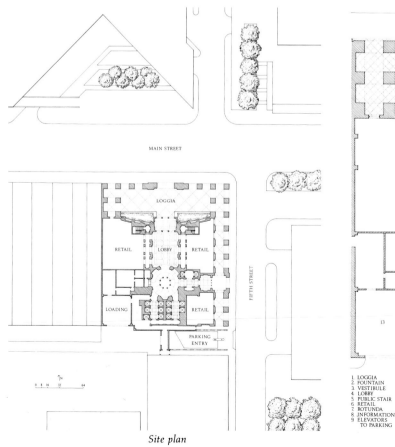

Site plan

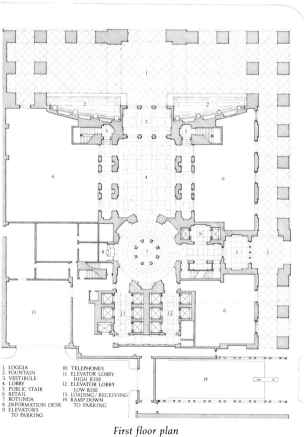

1. LOGGIA
2. FOUNTAIN
3. VESTIBULE
4. LOBBY
5. PUBLIC STAIR
6. RETAIL
7. ROTUNDA
8. INFORMATION DESK
9. ELEVATORS
   TO PARKING
10. TELEPHONES
11. ELEVATOR LOBBY
    HIGH RISE
12. ELEVATOR LOBBY
    LOW RISE
13. LOADING / RECEIVING
14. RAMP DOWN
    TO PARKING

First floor plan

View from the south

View from Main Street

View from the south

View from the north

Entrance loggia

Fifth Street loggia

Entrance loggia

Twenty-fifth floor terrace

Twenty-fifth floor balcony

Twenty-fifth floor terrace

Southwest corner

Auditorium

Entrance lobby

First floor rotunda

Elevator lobby

Stair between executive floors

Sixth floor reception

1982

MATSUYA DEPARTMENT STORE
TOKYO, JAPAN

Preliminary elevation

Model view from the Ginza

The existing Matsuya Department store is located on the Ginza, the heart of the primary shopping district of Tokyo. The building's facade was originally designed in a Beaux Arts style and later refaced in steel and glass. Because of deterioration of the existing facade, Graves was asked to prepare a feasibility study, including redesigning the exterior and renovating the interior escalator and stair cores. The project was not built.

The character of the proposed facade was derived from traditional Japanese stone and masonry buildings. The building was organized so that the extensive show windows and entry doors of the ground floor visually supported the *piano nobile*, which would have contained special functions, such as meeting rooms, exhibition galleries, and sales areas requiring natural light. The upper portion of the new facade would have offered flexibility within sales floors through the use of small windows. Banners, which are traditional on the Ginza, would have hung from upper level steel roof sheds, identifying special events held in the store.

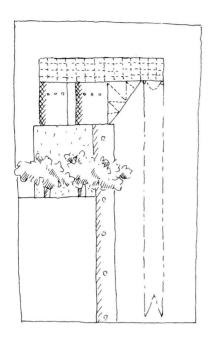

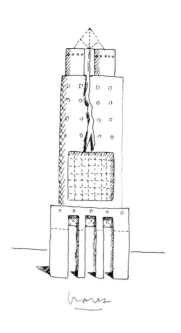

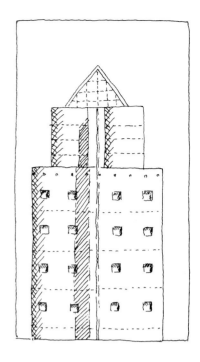

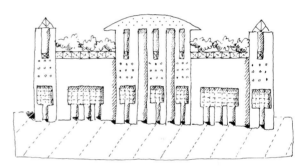

Elevation studies

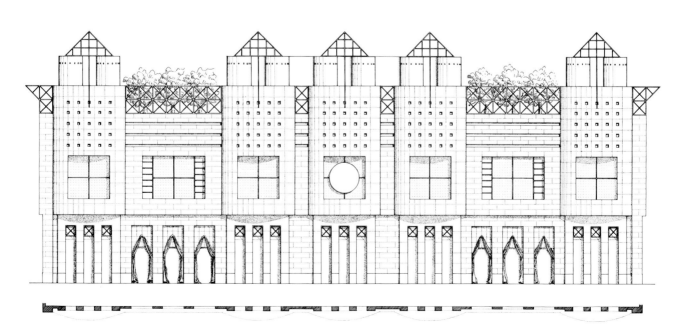

Street elevation and plan

1982

SUNAR HAUSERMAN SHOWROOM
DALLAS, TEXAS

Textile pavilion entrance

The Dallas showroom is organized to allow visitors to maintain a sense of place and orientation while viewing SunarHauserman's extensive collection of furniture groups and systems. Linear galleries and "hinge" rooms help establish hierarchy in the plan and guide the visitor through the exhibition space. The large display room is seen as the central figure in the composition because of its size, location, and the articulation of its walls. The simplicity of this room is distinct from the idiosyncracies of its perimeter and intensify its reading as a central figure. Its primary axis is terminated by a wall mural in the conference room that recaptures significant elements of the architectural themes of the showroom. Two separate pavilions containing the textile collections are located within the large central room. Skewed in plan and draped with fabric, the two pavilions appear as distinct, romantic, picturesque elements within a larger landscape.

Textile pavilion

Textile pavilion

Textile pavilions

Reception room

1. ENTRANCE
2. RECEPTION
3. OFFICE SYSTEMS DISPLAY
4. TEXTILE PAVILLION

5. OFFICE
6. CONFERENCE
7. KITCHEN

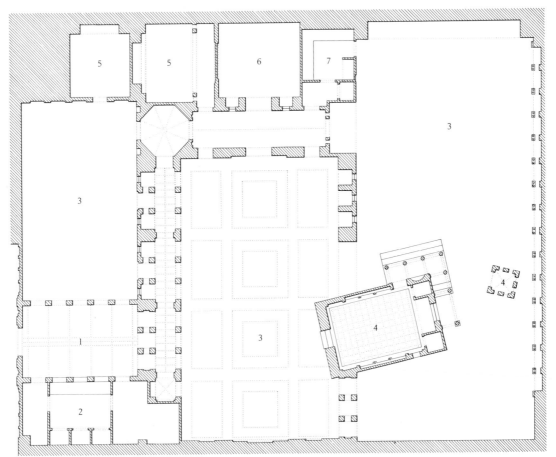

Plan

Gallery adjacent to furniture display room

1982

SUNAR HAUSERMAN SHOWROOM
CHICAGO, ILLINOIS

"Easel" construction

In 1982, Graves renovated the SunarHauserman furniture showroom in Chicago, which he designed in 1979. The renovation involved a major expansion including a new primary axis of entry which re-organized the composition, formally linking the old and new sections.

Large display spaces for furniture systems contrast with the smaller scale of rooms containing office and domestic furniture. Casement fabrics designed by Graves for SunarHauserman are draped along the perimeter arcades, indicating the boundary between inside and outside. As a continuation of the 1979 scheme for the showroom, the corridor wall is articulated to resemble an exterior facade.

In 1985, Graves added a large room for wall systems displays and audio-visual presentations.

Textile display

Entrance

Entrance

Textile display

Textile sample room

1. ENTRANCE
2. RECEPTION
3. OFFICE SYSTEMS DISPLAY
4. TEXTILE ROOM
5. FABRIC ROOM

6. OFFICE
7. CONFERENCE
8. PROJECTION PAVILLION
9. KITCHEN
10. STORAGE

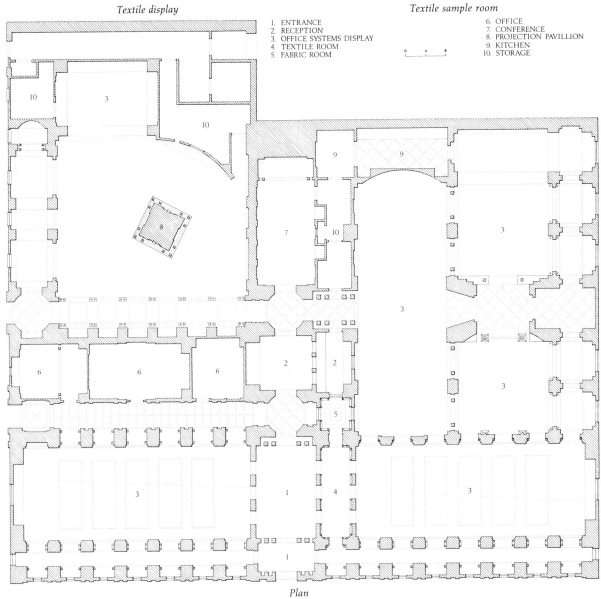

Plan

Furniture display room, 1985

Conference room

1982

REPUBLIC BANK AND TEXAS THEATER
SAN ANTONIO, TEXAS

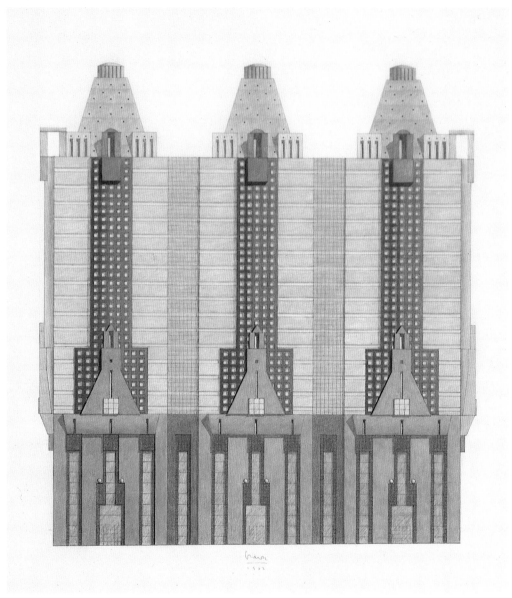

St. Mary's Street elevation

The design of the Republic Bank building was commissioned by the San Antonio Conservation Society as a feasibility study accommodating extensive commercial development of the site, while preserving the historic Texas Theater, which was scheduled for demolition. Graves' scheme was not executed. Four office towers totaling one million square feet were planned to be built in phases in an L shape around the theater. Designed as identical vertical towers, the buildings would have also merged horizontally, offering the greatest flexibility for planning tenant space. Bank offices would have occupied a special building in the corner. Terraces, open to the sun and to the view of the scenic San Antonio River, were proposed for the roof of the theater's auditorium. The proposed exterior materials were native limestone and glazed terra cotta. The articulation, materials, and colors were chosen to reflect the traditions of the local architectural context.

Model view from the river

Elevation studies

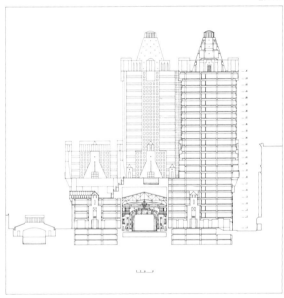

Section through theater

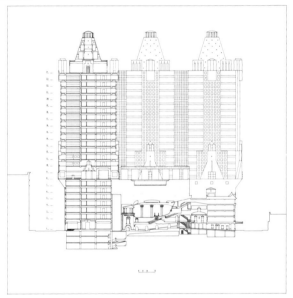

Section through theater

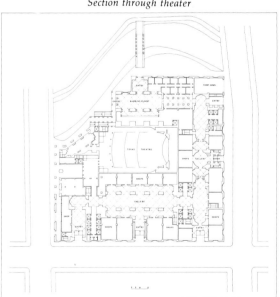

Ground floor plan

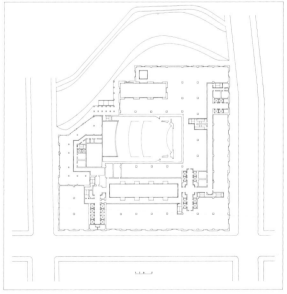

Second floor plan

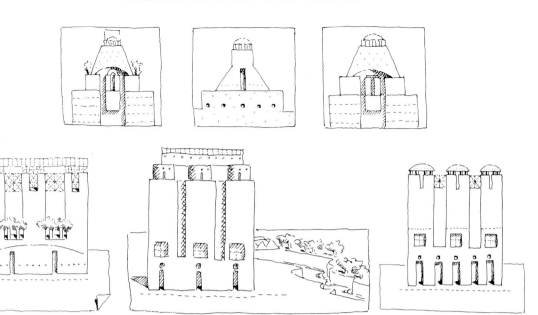

Elevation studies

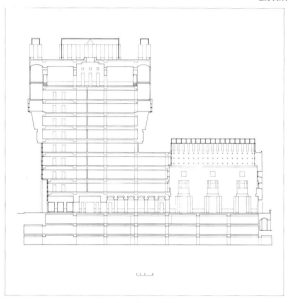

Section through bank

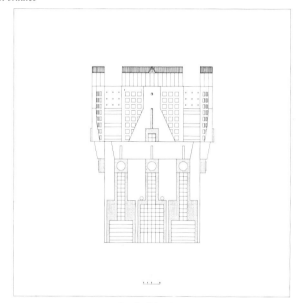

Bank elevation

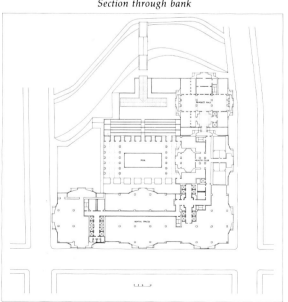

Eighth floor plan

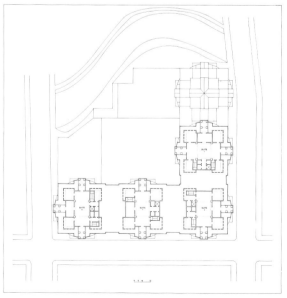

Penthouse plan

MUSEUM OF ART AND ARCHAEOLOGY
EMORY UNIVERSITY
ATLANTA, GEORGIA

Egyptian gallery

This project involved the renovation of one of the original buildings on the Emory University campus, a three-story marble-clad structure designed in 1916 by the Pittsburgh architect, Henry Hornbostel. Originally built as a law school, the building was renamed Michael C. Carlos Hall. The renovated building is listed on the National Register of Historic Places. No exterior changes were permitted other than two new fire stairs that were designed to be compatible with the original facades.

The renovation program consisted of two main components: the Museum of Art and Archaeology, and teaching spaces and faculty offices for the Departments of Art History and Anthropology. Because of a difference in floor levels between the two sides of the building, the museum is organized on one side and the departmental offices and classrooms on the other. In the museum, storage and preparation workshops are located at the basement level. The first floor is divided into several galleries for the permanent installation of the Archaeology Collection. Graves designed special exhibition cases and vitrines for each of these rooms. Floors are stenciled with plans of related architectural structures, such as the Acropolis in Athens and the Egyptian Temple of Ramses II. The floor stencils reinforce the themes in the collections and refer to the floors in Henry Hornbostel's architecture building at Carnegie Mellon University, which are inlaid with plans of significant architectural monuments. A narrow and dramatically lit curving stair connects the first floor of the museum with the more neutral galleries on the second floor, which are used for temporary exhibitions.

Museum entrance

South stair addition

East stair addition

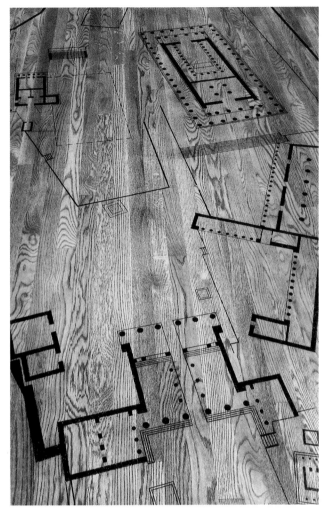

Floor stencil, the Acropolis

Michael C. Carlos Gallery of Greek Art

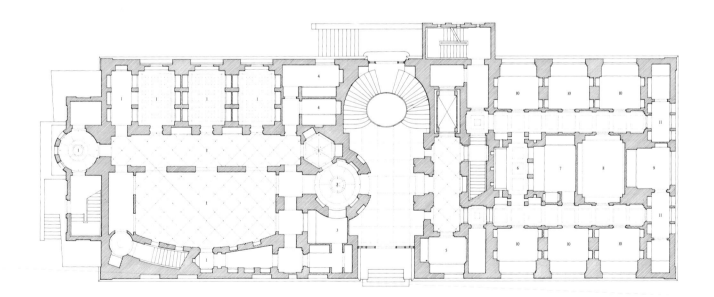

MUSEUM OF ART & ARCHAEOLOGY

1 ARCHAEOLOGY EXHIBITION
2 FOYER
3 RECEPTION
4 ADMINISTRATION OFFICE

DEPARTMENT OF ANTHROPOLOGY

5 KITCHEN
6 RECEPTION
7 SECRETARIES
8 CONFERENCE ROOM
9 DEPARTMENT CHAIRMAN
10 FACULTY OFFICE
11 ASSISTANT OFFICE

First floor plan

Temporary exhibition gallery

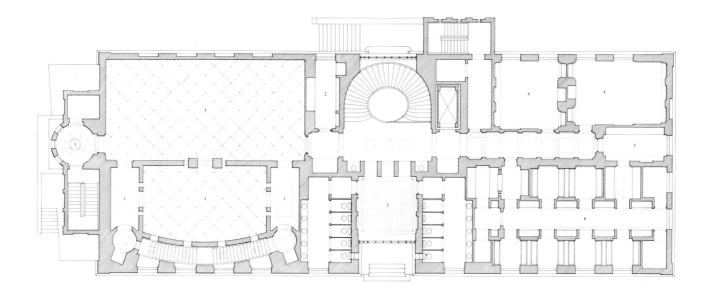

MUSEUM OF ART & ARCHAEOLOGY

1 ART EXHIBITION

DEPARTMENT OF ART HISTORY

2 EQUIPMENT ROOM
3 LOUNGE
4 CLASSROOM
5 PHOTO ROOM
6 SLIDE LIBRARY

Second floor plan

First floor circular gallery

Second floor circular gallery

Egyptian gallery

Egyptian gallery

ST. JAMES TOWNHOUSES
CINCINNATI, OHIO

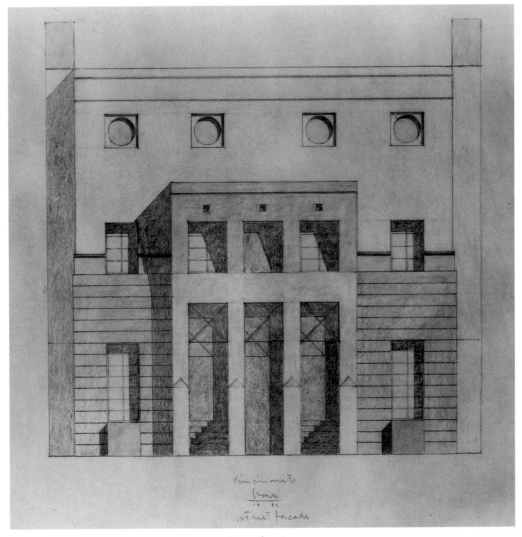

Street elevation

A Cincinnati developer commissioned Graves to design a series of two-family townhouses to be built in the St. James residential section of Cincinnati. The project was not executed. The site was a large infill lot in a neighborhood of multiple-family dwellings built in the late 19th and early 20th centuries. The existing houses were clad primarily in stucco and brick with limestone detailing. The proposed housing followed the general configuration, scale, and polychromatic values of the existing neighborhood. Terra cotta rustication was proposed for the base of the buildings, and cream-colored stucco above. Each unit would have been identified by a large front porch and second story window.

Street view

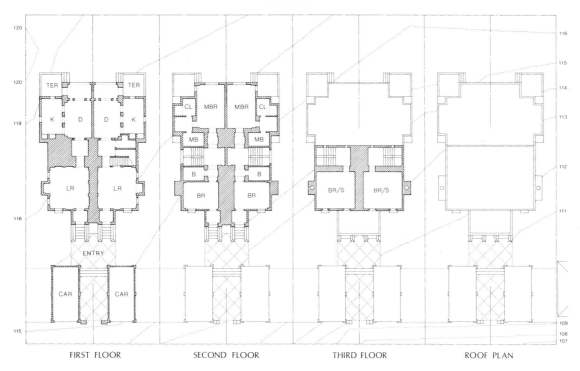

FIRST FLOOR   SECOND FLOOR   THIRD FLOOR   ROOF PLAN

Combined site and floor plans

Street elevation

THE NEWARK MUSEUM
MASTER RENOVATION PLAN
NEWARK, NEW JERSEY

Garden entry elevation

The master renovation plan for The Newark Museum encompasses new public facilities, as well as the expansion of support space in all four of the Museum's main buildings. Acquisition of an adjacent YWCA building in 1982 provided the opportunity for the Museum to be enlarged and improved throughout. By emphasizing a clearly organized connection of the buildings, Graves' design enables visitors to orient themselves easily to the expanded complex.

Fundamental to the plan are three major skylit courts, linked by gallery passages. The existing museum court remains at the center of the composition, while a new three-story skylit sculpture court connects the Main Museum, North Wing and the Ballantine House. The sculpture court also serves as the entrance to new exhibition galleries in the North Wing. Graves also designed a skylit lobby for the new side entry to the South Wing, formerly the YWCA. The new space includes offices, a library, the Education Department's Junior Museum, a Mini-Zoo, Arts Workshop, and the Lending Collections, as well as a 300-seat auditorium in what was previously a gymnasium. The new side entry leads visitors down to the auditorium and up to the Junior Museum and other activities in the Education Department.

The Museum's North Wing was renovated for exhibition of the permanent collection in newly designed galleries. Exhibitions of American painting and sculpture are located on the first two floors, Oriental Art on the third floor, and Decorative Arts within the connection to the Victorian Ballantine House. The Ethnology and Science collections remain on the second and third floors of the original museum building.

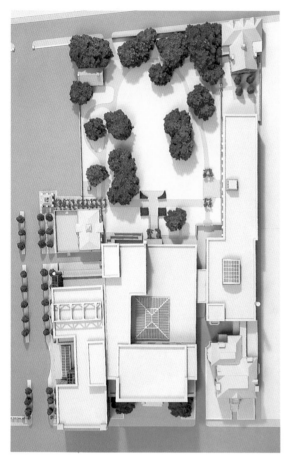

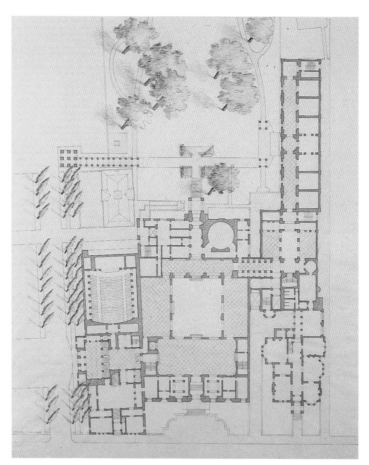

Model overhead view

Site plan

Model view of street elevation

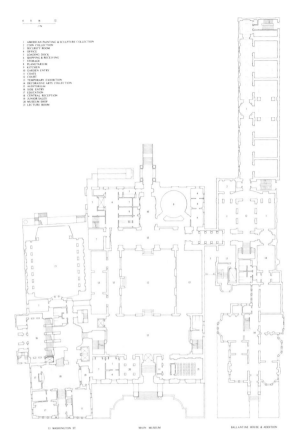

First floor plan

Second floor plan

South Wing entrance

Garden entrance lobby

South Wing entrance lobby

Auditorium

Asian Art gallery

American Art gallery

Atrium

TEA SERVICE

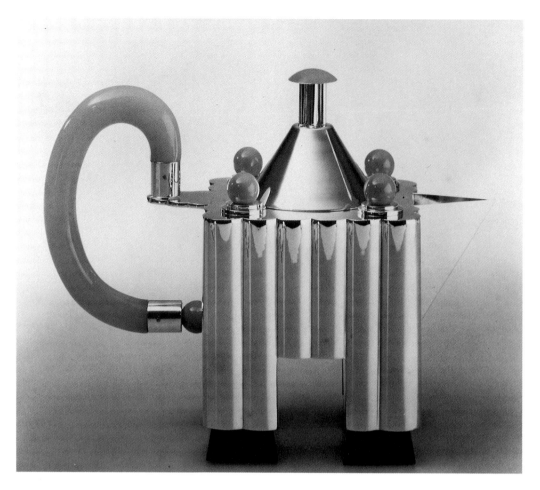

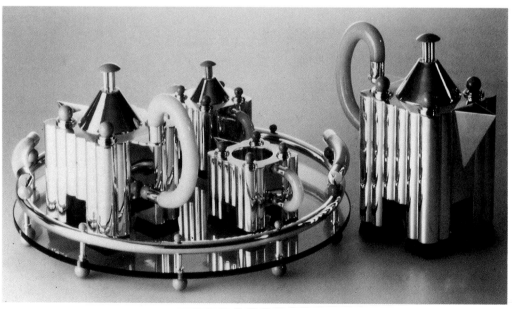

The tea service is the result of an experimental project carried out by Alessi under the name "Programma 6." The project began in 1980 and was completed in 1983 with the introduction of limited edition sterling silver tea services designed by eleven internationally known architects.

BLOOMINGDALE'S SHOPPING BAG

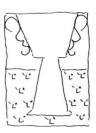
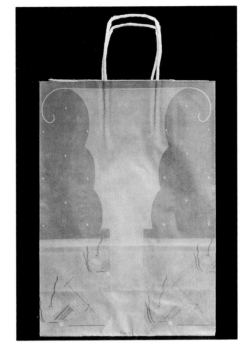
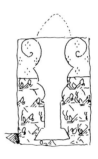

The shopping bag was designed for Bloomingdale's spring and summer collections. In the center of the composition is a large vase which recalls the use of the bag as a vessel or container. The color and decoration of the background reflects the seasonal themes.

GENTLEMEN'S QUARTERLY AWARD

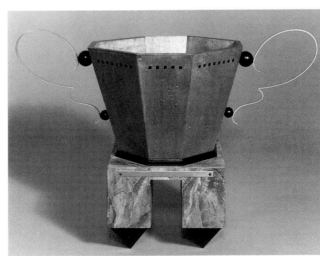

This trophy, commissioned by *Gentlemen's Quarterly* magazine for an annual awards program, was designed in the form of a traditional loving cup. The cup is made of a variety of materials, including birds eye maple, ebony, stainless steel, and *faux marbre*.

LAMPS

Ceramic table lamp

Yamagiwa table lamp

Ceramic table lamp

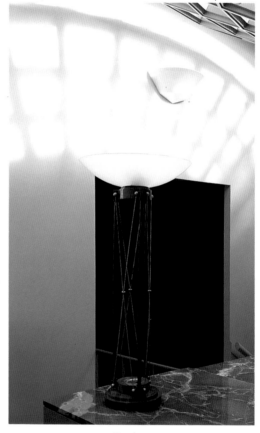

"Ingrid" floor lamp

Torchere

The tradition of artificial interior light originated in torches and lanterns. The small table lamp designed for Yamagiwa in Tokyo uses the lantern as its archetype. The lamp provides two different kinds of light; while the top, or crown, offers a soft ambient glow through its alabaster shade, the four gridded sides offer brighter illumination for reading. Two ceramic table lamps in the form of pavilions or small *palazzi* offer light from both the top and the sides.

The other two lamps illustrated here are derived from the tradition of the torch. Both were designed for the Plocek residence. The standing "Ingrid" lamp, named for Mrs. Plocek and produced by Sawaya & Moroni, has an onyx shade and a mahogany base inlaid with ebony and brass. The table lamp has a glass shade and a wood base painted in *faux marbre*.

LIGHTING FIXTURES

Ceiling mounted fixture

Pendant fixture

Wall-mounted lantern, Humana Building terrace

Wall-mounted lanterns, Humana Building passage

Graves has designed several lighting fixtures to be mounted to architectural surfaces. Included are a wall-mounted lantern which is available in several sizes, a ceiling-mounted light with opalescent shade, and a pendant fixture. The fixtures are manufactured by Baldinger Architectural Lighting.

FURNITURE

SunarHauserman side chair and table

The chairs and tables illustrated here were designed to be used in either the conference room or the dining room. The bench, which is made in two sizes, was originally designed for the Diane Von Furstenberg boutique in New York. Instead of being based on a machine aesthetic—which has characterized much of modern furniture—these chairs, tables, and benches attempt to follow a craft tradition. They are all made of birds eye maple veneer with ebony inlays. Though the various elements of this furniture, such as the legs, seats, and backs, have been abstracted, they ultimately refer to the zoomorphic and anthropomorphic beginnings of the imagery of furniture. By continuing these ancient figurative themes in furniture, Graves allows the pieces to be seen both as contemporary and within historical memory.

Bench for Diane Von Furstenberg boutique

Dining chair

Dining chair

1982

"FIRE" STAGESETS AND COSTUMES
LAURA DEAN, CHOREOGRAPHER
THE JOFFREY BALLET, NEW YORK

Costume studies

Cartoon for stageset

The ballet "Fire" was conceived and choreographed by Laura Dean for the Joffrey Ballet, loosely based on the theme of the bacchanal. The bacchanal was originally a celebration of the first harvest and its dances have been thought to be the setting for the first "theater." The stageset attempts to describe these ritual acts pictorially and to establish a dialectic between the original outdoor surroundings of the bacchanal and the indoor performance on the stage. The literal foreground space of the stage where the dancers perform and the virtual backdrop of the stageset offer an orthodox spatial sequence. However, these traditional spatial roles are transferred or even reversed when the artifacts represented in the background seem to be propelled into the foreground of the stage by the dancers' engagement with them.

In addition to representing foreground and background, the stageset is composed as a diptych, its division reinforcing the choreographer's interest in experimenting with the "partnering" or pairing of male and female dancers. The altar, one of the more literal elements of the composition, is paired with the most ephemeral figure, the empty easel, on opposite sides of the central dividing columns. Two small pavilions occupy the middle ground of the stageset. The roof of one is cleft, the other erect, further developing the association of female and male figures.

Costume studies

Costume details

Dancers in costume

Performance

"A SOLDIER'S TALE"
GEULAH ABRAHAMS, CHOREOGRAPHER

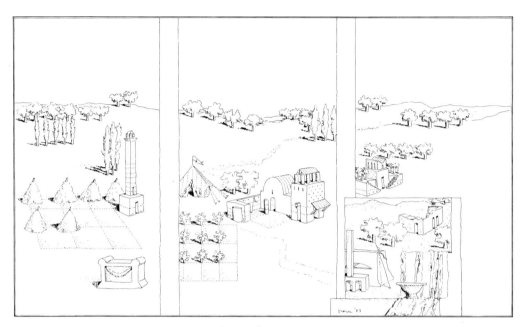

Cartoon for stageset

Performance

The dance piece, "A Soldier's Tale," was choreographed by Geulah Abrahams based on the musical work of the same title composed by Igor Stravinsky. The stagesets designed by Graves included a backdrop, and several large objects such as a bed, a pavilion, and a table and chairs, which represent specific elements within the story's narrative.

ALCANTARA TEXTILE PAVILION
MILAN, ITALY

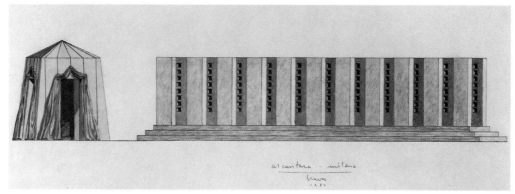

Elevation study

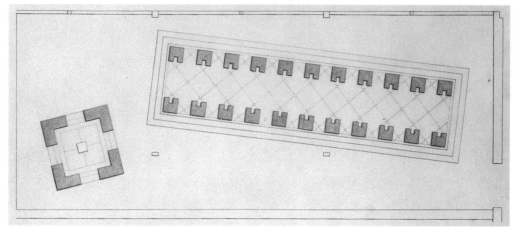

Plan

Installation

The textile display pavilion was designed for an exhibition at a major trade fair in Milan. The main structure was seen as a colonnade whose inner face contained small openings allowing fabric samples to be displayed. At the end, a tent-like structure displayed larger draped examples of selected fabrics.

1983

RIVERBEND MUSIC CENTER
CINCINNATI, OHIO

Roof detail with statues

The J. Ralph Corbett Pavilion at the Hulbert Taft, Jr. Center for the Performing Arts, called Riverbend, was designed as the summer home for the Cincinnati Symphony Orchestra. It is an outdoor performance facility for the orchestra as well as popular music and, occasionally, opera and dance. The design took a fresh approach to assembling many people under one roof. In its simplicity the scheme summons thoughts of a congregation under a tent, a building by a river, or a pavilion in a park. The building seats 5,000 people under cover and approximately 8,000 on the surrounding grassy hill. Nonetheless, a level of intimacy is achieved by the tent-like form of the roof and the garden arcade or pergola which establishes the boundaries of the lawn. Public food concessions and restrooms are located at the lower level of the pergola, facing the entry court and parking. Within the pavilion, the stagehouse provides stage and wing space as well as dressing rooms, a green room, and a terrace overlooking the Ohio River.

Eight figurative statues representing musical muses were placed along the cornice of the pavilion to establish a frontal facade and reinforce the theme and narrative of the building. The statues were developed from *grisaille* paintings by the artist Edward Schmidt. Though rendered like classical sculptures in the round, their flat, billboard-like construction of porcelain enamel panels reveals their modernity.

View from pergola

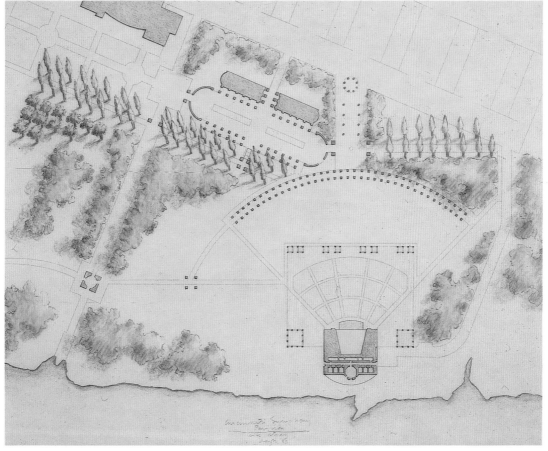

Site plan

Character studies

J. Ralph Corbett Pavilion

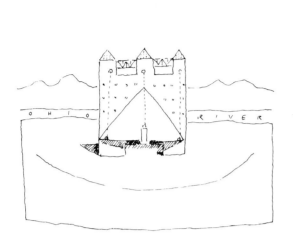
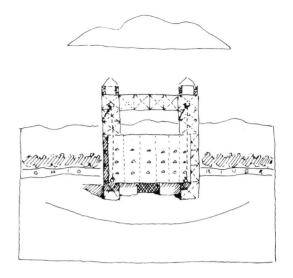

Character studies

J. Ralph Corbett Pavilion

Lower level pergola and stair tower

Upper level pergola

River facade detail, green room

View from Ohio River

1983

PORTICO SQUARE TOWNHOUSES
PHILADELPHIA, PENNSYLVANIA

Garden elevation study

Garden elevation study

The complete renovation of two adjoining townhouses in Philadelphia was proposed. In the project, which was not built, Graves reorganized the unit plans as one- and two-bedroom apartments which would have been entered from a central corridor. At the rear of the buildings, a large studio would have been added to the two-bedroom apartments, acting as a new architectural element in the garden.

View from the garden

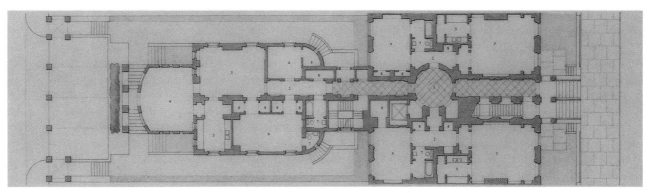

First floor plan

GLAZER FARMHOUSE AND STUDIO
McKINNEY, TEXAS

Courtyard

This small farm complex, which was never built, was designed to provide a summer and weekend retreat for a husband and wife who spent the majority of their time in Dallas. Their avocations were farming, pottery, and painting. The program included a farmhouse and two studios. The buildings, which assumed a rural, agrarian character, were designed to be built by local workmen using vernacular techniques and local construction materials.

The site plan accommodated an existing shed on the western edge of the property. To the east was an orchard and to the south, a pond. The buildings created an outdoor "room" facing south, enclosed on three sides by a pergola. This large outdoor area offered spatial release from the small interior rooms. The courtyard included a fireplace for a barbecue which acted as a hearth in the outdoor room. The location of a proposed greenhouse encouraged a perspectival view of the farmland, the pond, and the rolling hills beyond.

Courtyard elevation study

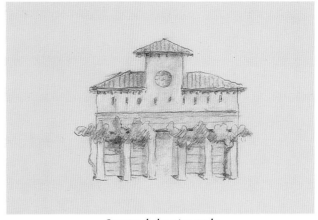

Courtyard elevation study

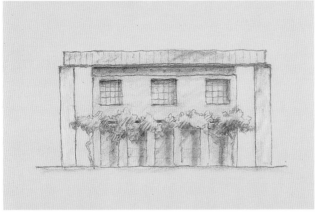

Preliminary courtyard elevation of house

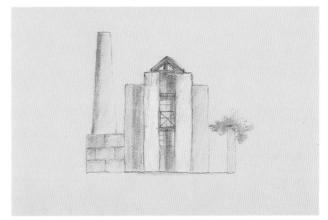

Preliminary south elevation of house

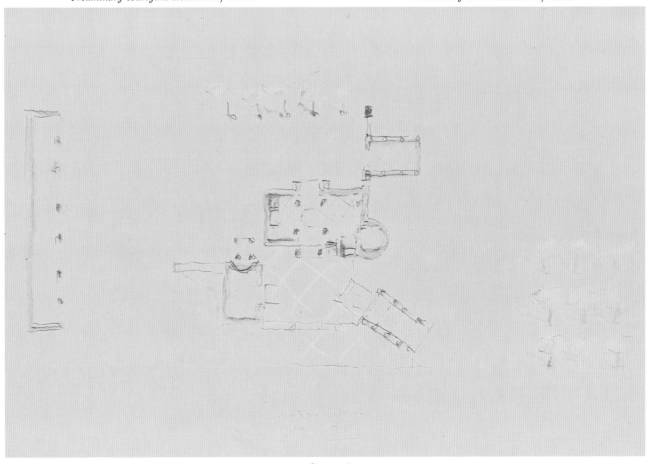

Site parti

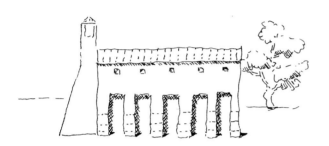

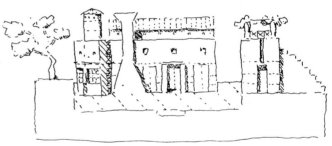

Character studies

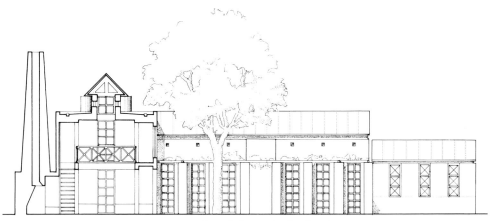

Section A through house, Studio elevation

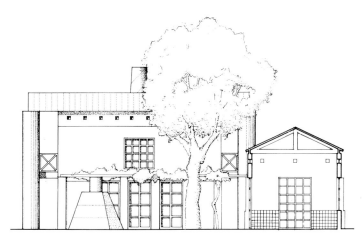

Section D through studio, House elevation

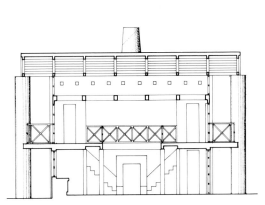

Section B through house

1 CARPORT
2 STUDIO
3 STORAGE
4 LIVING ROOM
5 KITCHEN
6 BARBECUE

1 OPEN TO BELOW
2 BALCONY
3 LOFT
4 STORAGE

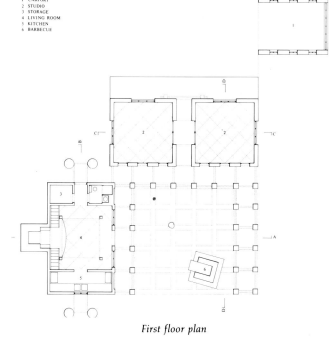

First floor plan

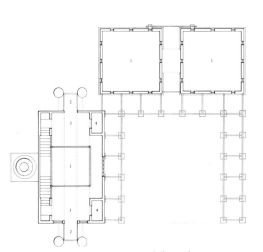

Second floor plan

Courtyard elevation of house

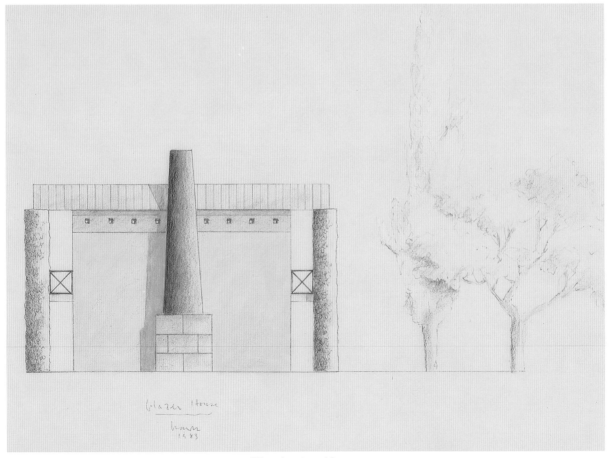

West elevation of house

Model view from the southeast

Model view from the north

COURTYARD INSTALLATION
DEUTSCHES ARCHITEKTURMUSEUM
FRANKFURT, GERMANY

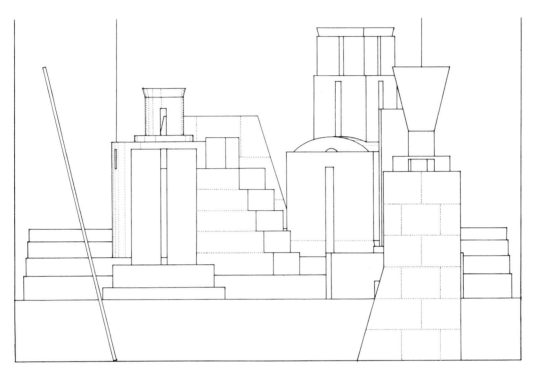

Courtyard elevation

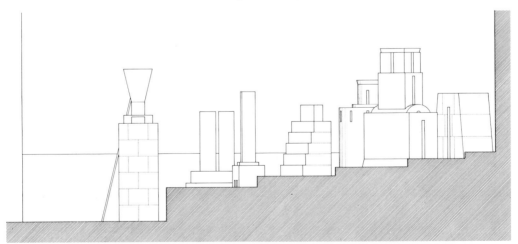

Courtyard section

One wing of the museum of architecture in Frankfurt, West Germany is lined with small, narrow, outdoor courtyards for special installations. Several architects were asked to design installations to commemorate the opening of the building. The courtyard assigned to Graves terminates one of the museum's major corridors. Graves designed a series of small archaic pavilions and placed them on a steeply rising ground, accentuating the corridor's sense of perspective. The ground was rendered as a rock outcropping, to form a romantic or picturesque setting for the idealized architectural fragments.

Courtyard study

Courtyard installation

1983

CENTER FOR THE VISUAL ARTS
OHIO STATE UNIVERSITY
COLUMBUS, OHIO

Rotunda

Graves participated in an invited competition for the Center for the Visual Arts at Ohio State University. His design for the new facility, accommodating the University's innovative and experimental visual arts programs, was not chosen for further development.

Graves proposed that the Center for the Visual Arts be sited at the entrance to the campus, adjacent to existing performing arts buildings. The design was organized around a central rotunda which would have acted as the formal, public entrance to the complex and would have provided orientation to the building's activities. Establishing a reciprocity between interior and exterior spaces, the rotunda would have linked the main exhibition galleries with an outdoor courtyard to the west. The exhibition galleries would have allowed for both traditional and developing forms of art. Their sizes, proportions, and equipment would have made possible new combinations of visual and performing arts. The independent west wing would have housed a center for advanced study in the visual arts, including studios for visiting fellows, an art and technology laboratory, and teaching space.

On the east side of the site, the proposed Fine Arts Library would have completed the figure of the "Oval"—the main public space of the campus. Two new entry pavilions would have formed a gate to the Oval. One would have served as an orientation area for the library, and the other would have contained a campus information kiosk.

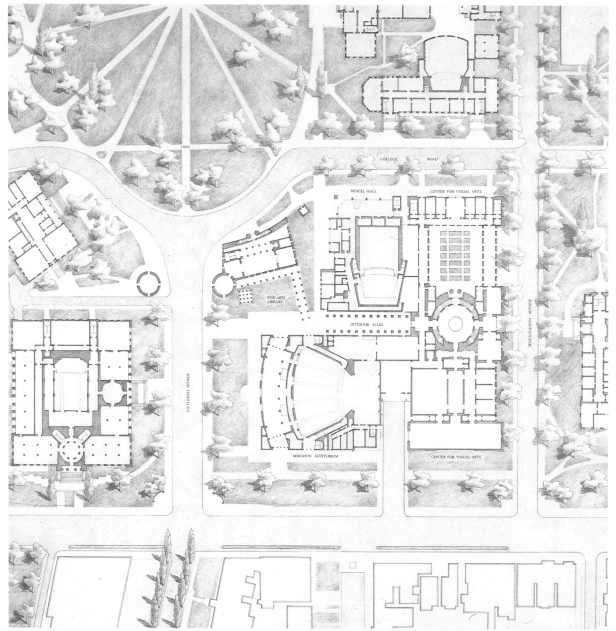

Site plan

Model view from the Oval

OHIO STATE UNIVERSITY VISUAL ARTS CENTER

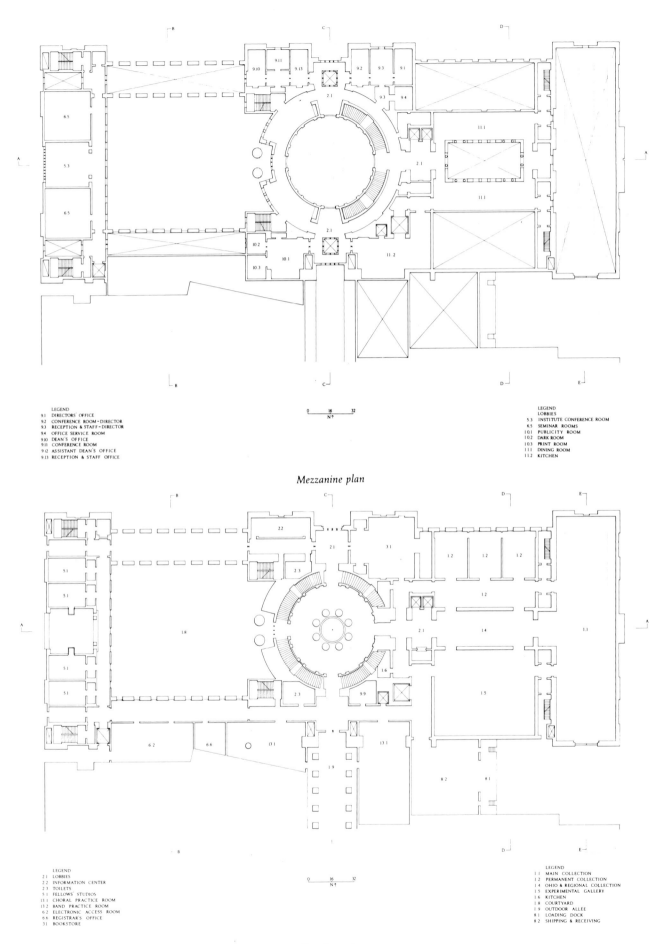

Mezzanine plan

LEGEND
9.1 DIRECTORS' OFFICE
9.2 CONFERENCE ROOM - DIRECTOR
9.3 RECEPTION & STAFF - DIRECTOR
9.4 OFFICE SERVICE ROOM
9.10 DEAN'S OFFICE
9.11 CONFERENCE ROOM
9.12 ASSISTANT DEAN'S OFFICE
9.13 RECEPTION & STAFF OFFICE

LEGEND
LOBBIES
5.3 INSTITUTE CONFERENCE ROOM
6.5 SEMINAR ROOMS
10.1 PUBLICITY ROOM
10.2 DARK ROOM
10.3 PRINT ROOM
11.1 DINING ROOM
11.2 KITCHEN

0   16   32
N↑

LEGEND
2.1 LOBBIES
2.2 INFORMATION CENTER
2.3 TOILETS
5.1 FELLOWS' STUDIOS
13.1 CHORAL PRACTICE ROOM
13.2 BAND PRACTICE ROOM
6.2 ELECTRONIC ACCESS ROOM
6.6 REGISTRAR'S OFFICE
3.1 BOOKSTORE

LEGEND
1.1 MAIN COLLECTION
1.2 PERMANENT COLLECTION
1.4 OHIO & REGIONAL COLLECTION
1.5 EXPERIMENTAL GALLERY
1.6 KITCHEN
1.8 COURTYARD
1.9 OUTDOOR ALLEE
8.1 LOADING DOCK
8.2 SHIPPING & RECEIVING

0   16   32
N↑

First floor plan

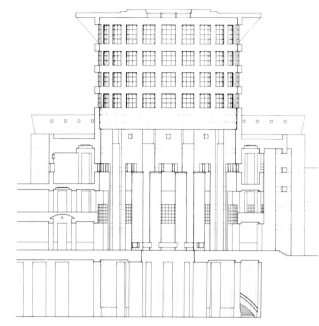

Section through rotunda

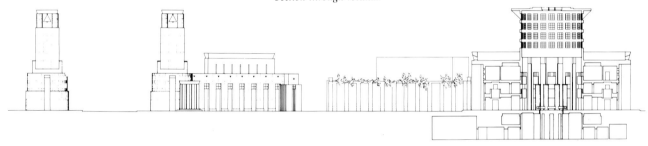

Longitudinal section

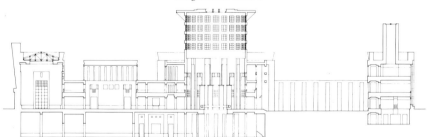

Cross section

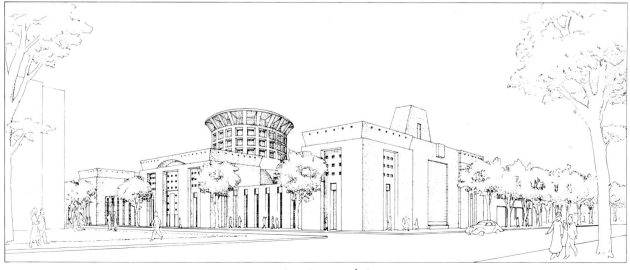

View from Seventeenth Avenue

College Road elevation

High Street elevation

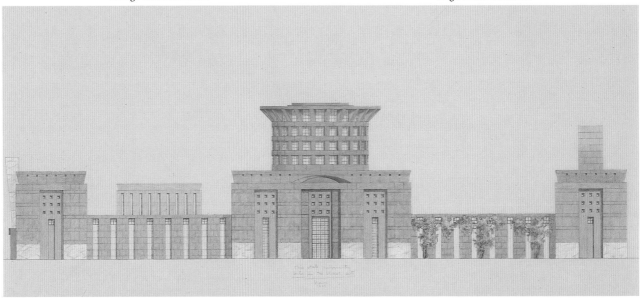

Seventeenth Avenue elevation

Model view from Seventeenth Avenue

Character studies

Model view from Seventeenth Avenue

1983

PRIVATE RESIDENCE
HOUSTON, TEXAS

Site model

The program for this large residence in an affluent suburb of Houston included typical family living quarters—such as a living room, dining room, kitchen, breakfast room, and bedrooms—as well as special outbuildings for servant and guest quarters, a greenhouse, and a poolhouse. A large formal garden, swimming pool, and tennis court were also provided. The project was not built.

Rather than isolate the house in the center of its site, which is done in many American suburbs, Graves attempted more complex inter-relationships of building to building and building to landscape. The house and its site were organized so that activities requiring different levels of privacy were distinguished by access, form, and orientation to the natural light.

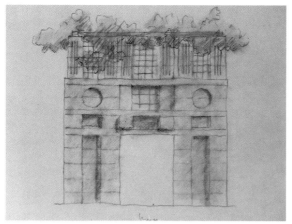

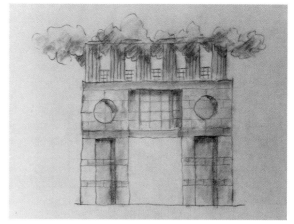

Entry pavilion study　　　　　*Entry pavilion study*

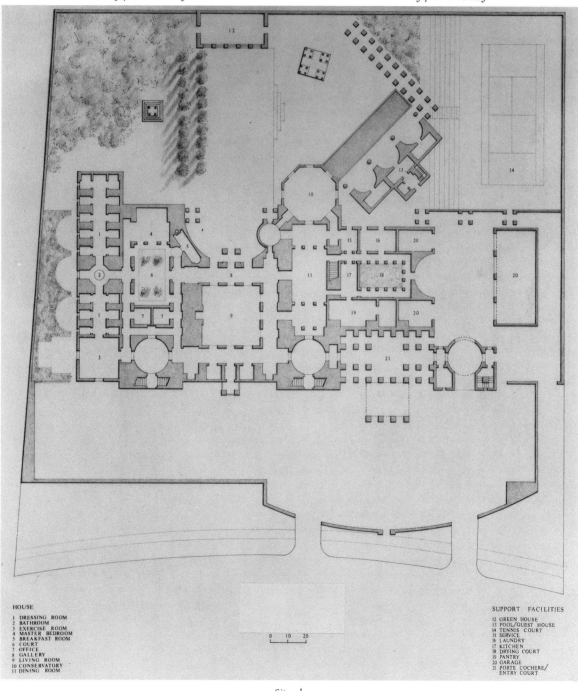

HOUSE
1 DRESSING ROOM
2 BATHROOM
3 EXERCISE ROOM
4 MASTER BEDROOM
5 BREAKFAST ROOM
6 COURT
7 OFFICE
8 GALLERY
9 LIVING ROOM
10 CONSERVATORY
11 DINING ROOM

SUPPORT FACILITIES
12 GREEN HOUSE
13 POOL/GUEST HOUSE
14 TENNIS COURT
15 SERVICE
16 LAUNDRY
17 KITCHEN
18 DRYING COURT
19 PANTRY
20 GARAGE
21 PORTE COCHERE/
    ENTRY COURT

0　10　20

Site plan

Street elevation study

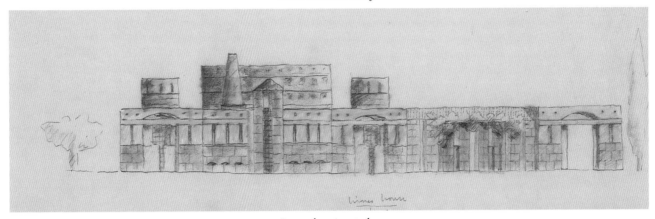

Street elevation study

Model view from the garden

Preliminary street elevation

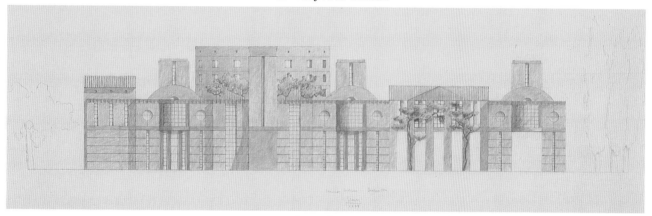

Street elevation

Model view from the street

1983

ALEWIFE CENTER
CAMBRIDGE, MASSACHUSETTS

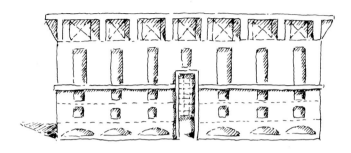

Elevation studies

Alewife office building and Building 29

The Alewife Center Master Plan, never executed, organized a series of 100,000 - 150,000 square foot office buildings along an outdoor circulation spine which terminated in a hotel and health club at the edge of an existing pond. Parking for 1,800 cars was accommodated on several underground levels throughout the 17-acre site. A pedestrian walkway through the site was intended to connect a major subway stop to the west with the residential neighborhood and public playing fields to the east.

The proposed first phase of the project was a four-story, 98,000 square foot speculative office building. Rather than basing this building on the abstract and often alienating symbols characteristic of much of modern office development, Graves saw its design as a large urban house or *palazzo*. The facades of the building were organized in a traditional three-part horizontal division of base, middle, and top, differentiated by changes in material, color, and window openings. The dark red masonry base of the building would have given the impression of ample support for the weight of the building above. The upper levels, finished in cream-colored stucco, were made to appear lighter than the base because of their material, color, and increased use of glass. An attic story or cornice, relieved with generous windows, marked the top of the building. The building would have been entered through a colonnade facing the driveway and parking lots and forming the first side of a future courtyard.

The project also included renovation of the facades of an adjacent industrial building, called Building 29, used for offices and workshops.

Court elevation

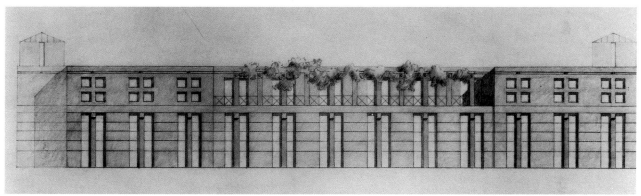

Building 29 street elevation

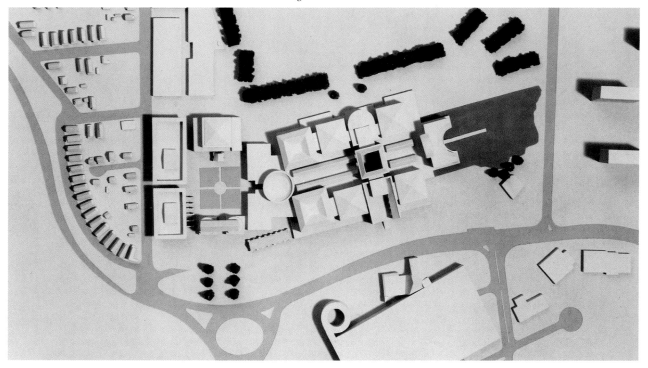

Master plan site model

1984

CARRIAGE HOUSE RENOVATION
NEW YORK, NEW YORK

Foyer

Library

Plan

This project involved the complete renovation of the upper floor of a two-story carriage house. The apartment is entered through a new entrance foyer in the form of a rotunda located at the top of an existing staircase. The rotunda is disengaged from the side walls so that it is perceived as a free-standing object within the space. To one side of the rotunda are the library and the living room, oriented to the street. To the other side are the kitchen and the dining room. A gallery or corridor leads from the kitchen and dining area to private studies and bedrooms. Beyond the master bedroom at the end of this gallery is an outdoor terrace designed as a garden room with lattice walls.

Library and entrance rotunda from the living room

Living room

Living room

1986

GRAVES RESIDENCE
PRINCETON, NEW JERSEY

Entry courtyard

View from garden

Michael Graves' residence is a converted warehouse that was built in 1926 by Italian stonemasons who were constructing various masonry buildings at Princeton University. It was built in a typical Tuscan vernacular style using hollow clay tile, brick, and stucco. The L-shaped building, originally divided into many storage cells, is being renovated in stages. The recently completed north wing, entered through an outdoor courtyard that was once a truck dock, includes a living room, dining room, and library with a garden terrace on the first floor, and a master bedroom and study on the second floor.

Garden elevation

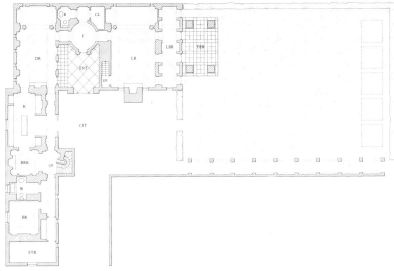

First floor plan

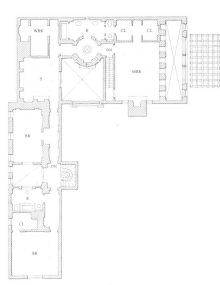

Second floor plan

Dining room

Second floor rotunda

Living room view to garden

Dining room

Master bedroom

Living room

1984

GLENDOWER COURT TOWNHOUSES
HOUSTON, TEXAS

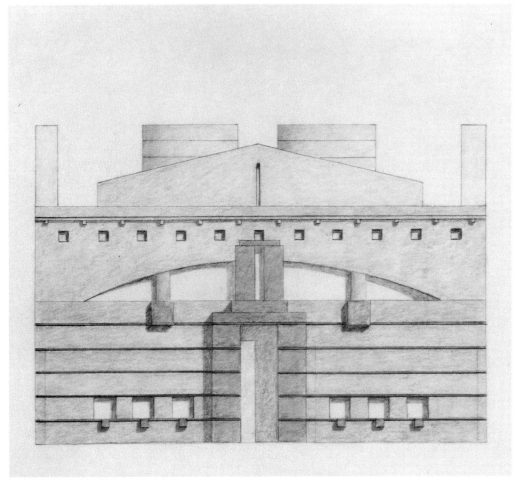

Street elevation

Along Glendower Court in suburban Houston, Texas, a developer assembled a number of sites for two-family houses, the prevailing pattern of development in the neighborhood. These houses, never built, were seen primarily as street facades on infill sites. Since several houses were planned for the same neighborhood, various facade options were designed. Each unit was required to have a two-car garage. Wooden garage doors would have been painted and banded with molding in an effort to present them as part of the rusticated base of the house. The entries to the two units would have been combined as one outdoor courtyard with a major portal on the street, thereby diminishing the sense of extensive garages by emphasizing the front door. A second outdoor courtyard within the center of each townhouse would have provided light to the surrounding rooms in the interior.

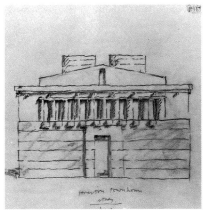

Elevation study

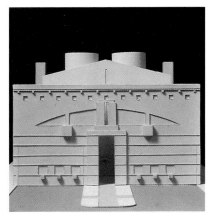

Model view from the street

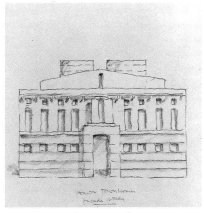

Elevation study

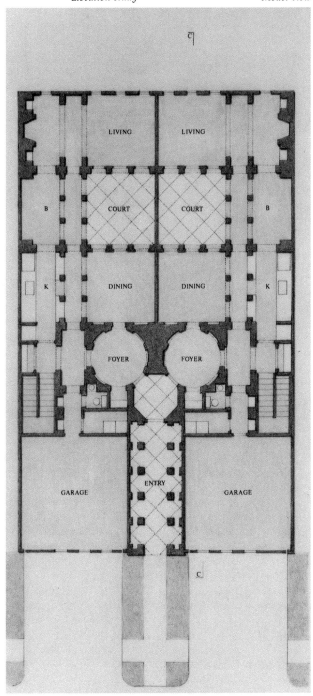

First floor plan

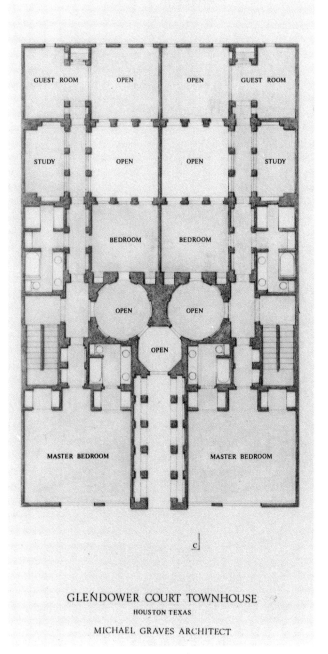

GLEŃDOWER COURT TOWNHOUSE
HOUSTON TEXAS

MICHAEL GRAVES ARCHITECT

Second floor plan

1984

GLENDOWER COURT RESIDENCE
HOUSTON, TEXAS

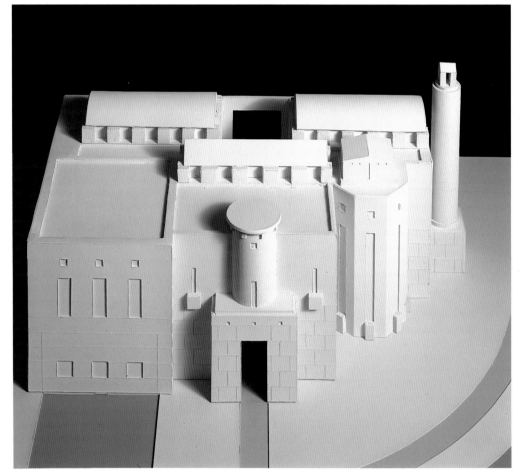

Model

In a suburb of Houston containing both single-family and two-family houses, a developer purchased a corner site characterized by the curvilinear street pattern. Graves designed a speculative house for this site; the project was not built.

In the proposed design, an open courtyard in the center of the house would have secured the family's privacy from the street and provided light to the rooms surrounding it. The organizational strategy of the plan placed the primary social rooms, such as the living room, dining room and breakfast room, in an *enfilade* against the rear property line. Picturesque spaces attached to this rectilinear block of rooms followed the curve of the street. These special elements, which included the front entrance, the study, and the fireplace, would have provided this large house with a more intimate and domestic scale.

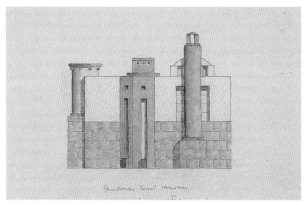

Side elevation

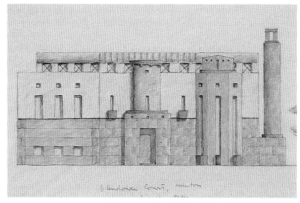

Entrance elevation

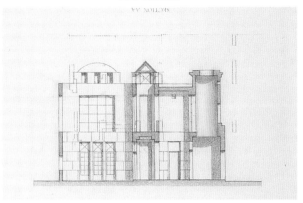

Section AA

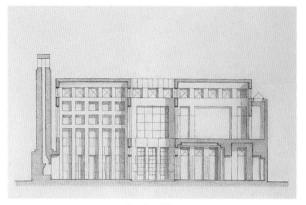

Section BB

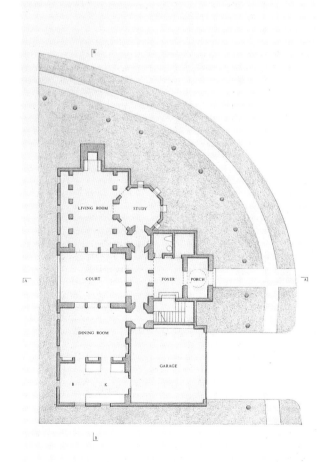

First floor plan

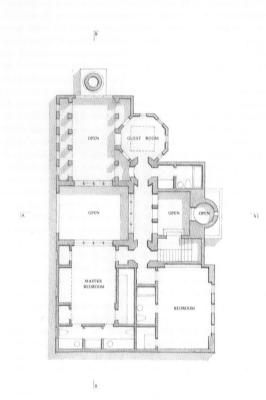

Second floor plan

1984

MIXED USE DEVELOPMENT
STAMFORD, CONNECTICUT

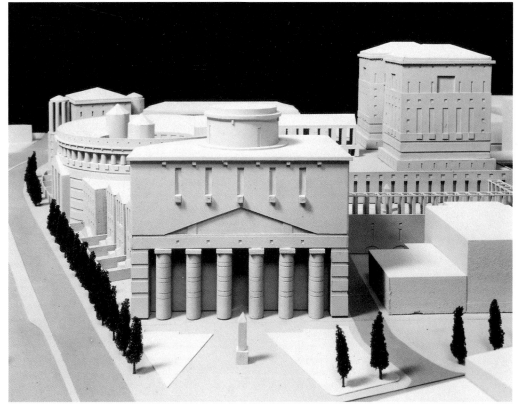

Model, Municipal Office Building

The master plan for a mixed use development encompassing two blocks in downtown Stamford, Connecticut included offices, stores, apartments, a municipal office building, and parking for 1900 cars. Two schemes were prepared based on similar programs of use, but with differing site configurations, according to the availability of specific parcels of land. The project was suspended at the conclusion of the master plan phase.

Both schemes for the master plan addressed the scale and function of the local context. Existing buildings surrounding the site contain retail shops at street level and offices above. The proposed development retained this pattern at the street and in a series of linked public spaces through the center of these large blocks. In the first scheme, a major pedestrian axis was established between an existing public park to the west and an enlarged public square to the east. Small-scale housing units faced the park along Washington Street. An outdoor rotunda, with a retail base and five stories of offices above, established the west end of the internal east-west axis. A skylit pedestrian arcade would have extended eastward to the retail base of the 15-story twin office towers which faced the public square.

In contrast to many of the other office developments in the area which expose their parking garages continuously along the street edge, these schemes returned the street perimeter to public use, through the placement of retail stores, housing, and the municipal building. Parking was distributed across the entire site, one level below grade, and through the center in multi-level garages. The upper decks of the central parking structures were used as terraces, parks, and an outdoor recreation space accessible from adjacent office buildings.

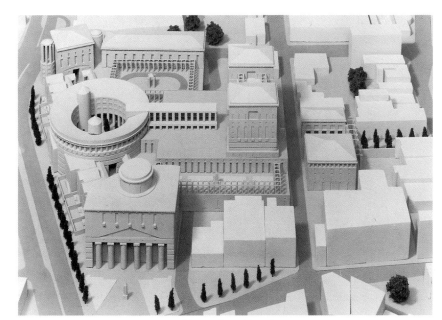

Model view from Main Street

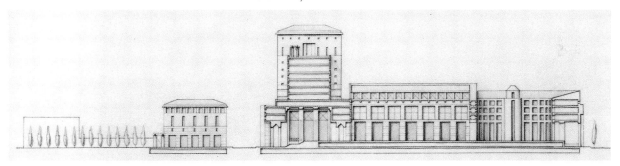

East-west section

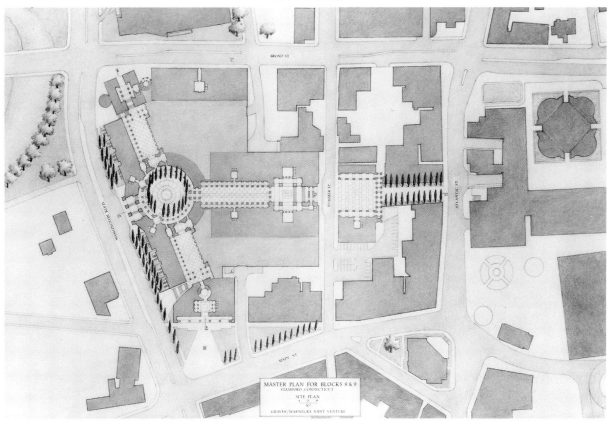

Site plan

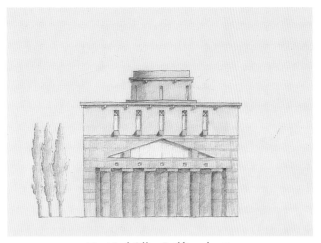

Municipal Office Building elevation

Office building elevation

Model view from Washington Street

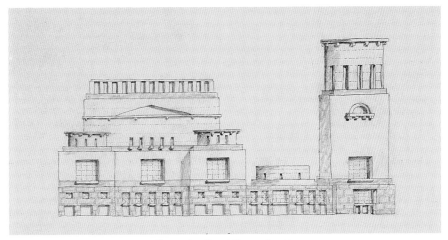

Alternative Broad Street elevation

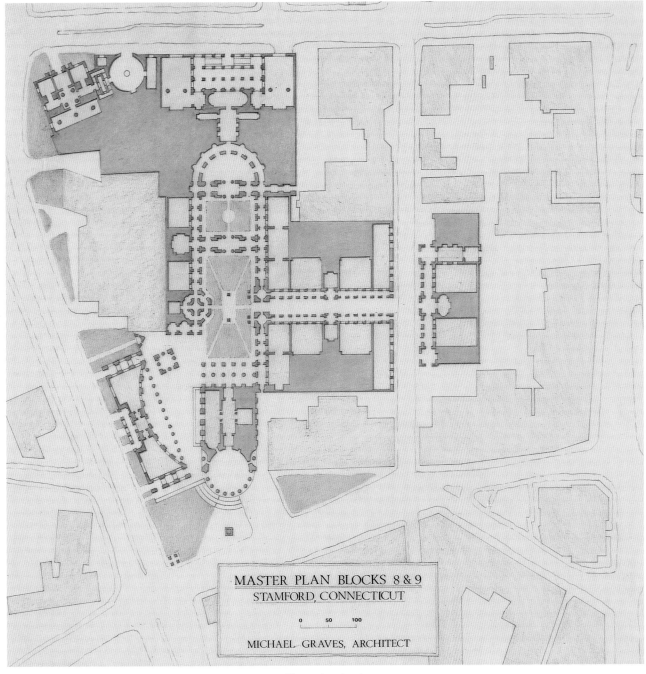

MASTER PLAN BLOCKS 8 & 9
STAMFORD, CONNECTICUT

0   50   100

MICHAEL GRAVES, ARCHITECT

Alternative site plan

CASTELLI LEONE FOLLY

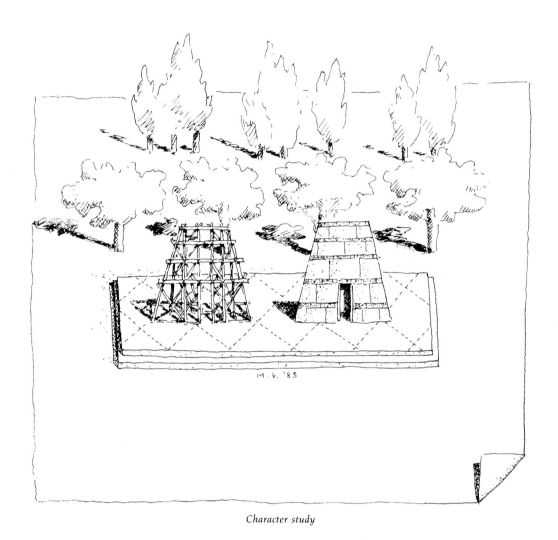

Character study

This garden folly was designed for an invitational exhibition at the Leo Castelli Gallery in New York which included the work of numerous architects. The folly places two fundamental and divergent forms of habitation, the solid enclosure and the porous or framed enclosure, on a single slab in the garden. Placing them side by side identifies their parallel beginnings and the ambiguous dialectic between them. The two forms represent archetypal polarities of construction and formal composition.

Both formal types are metaphorical representations of conditions found in the landscape. The solid enclosure probably originated as a replication of the cave; its character provides protection, security, and a clear sense of boundary. The framed enclosure is a fragile remembrance of the solid enclosure and may be the antecedent of the columniated temple. However, the two types emerge from opposite formal concepts. The solid is composed in a subtractive manner, as the sculptor working in stone subtracts or excises his material. The frame is composed in an additive manner, as the sculptor working in steel combines material to form his composition. Neither the enclosed form nor the framed form is pure, as each carries the sense of its opposite. The portal or door, for instance, interrupts the continuity of the solid; and the structural members of the frame clearly enclose its space, resulting in a sense of boundary.

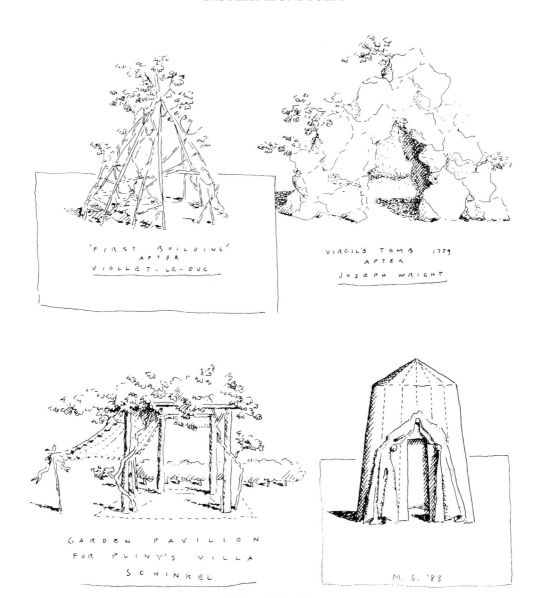

'FIRST BUILDING'
AFTER
VIOLLET-LE-DUC

VIRGIL'S TOMB 1779
AFTER
JOSEPH WRIGHT

GARDEN PAVILION
FOR PLINY'S VILLA
SCHINKEL

M. G. '83

Referential sketches

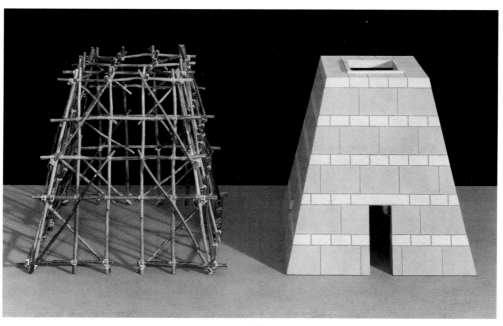

Model

1984

ERICKSON ALUMNI CENTER
WEST VIRGINIA UNIVERSITY
MORGANTOWN, WEST VIRGINIA

Elevation study

Garden elevation

The Erickson Alumni Center is designed for alumni banquets, receptions, and meetings. The building also includes the offices of the West Virginia University Alumni Association.

Located on a sloping site on a college road at the edge of the campus, the Alumni Center is developed on two levels. Built into the slope of the hillside are two stories of offices and meeting rooms overlooking a double height banquet hall. The banquet hall opens onto a large terrace for outdoor events. In character, the Alumni Center is seen as a large house, an inviting and familiar place for alumni returning to the campus. Elements such as the dormers, the fireplace and chimney, and the garden lattice help establish the domestic character of the architecture.

Entrance facade

Garden facade

Section through entrance and banquet hall

Site and ground floor plan

Banquet hall

Garden facade detail

Entrance

1984

CLOS PEGASE WINERY
NAPA VALLEY, CALIFORNIA

Winery entrance facade

Aerial view from the east

The Clos Pegase Winery, located near Calistoga in the Napa Valley of California, takes its name and its thematic organization from the myth of Pegasus, which is the subject of a significant painting by Odilon Redon in the owner's art collection. The initial project, which involved collaboration with the New York artist, Edward Schmidt, included a winery with public winetasting and more private winemaking functions, a residence for the owner, and a sculpture park in which to hold outdoor events and display the owner's sculpture collection. The winery and residence were completed. Plans for the sculpture park were suspended.

The master plan organized the site along an axis of water emanating from the "grotto of Pegasus" at the summit of the knoll and concluding in the winery's two formal ponds. The public areas for the winery and sculpture garden were located on one side of the axis, while the more private winemaking functions were located on the other side. The residence, located on the "private" side, is protected from public and production activities, with views of the vineyards to the south and east. The winery building is organized as two main wings with separate entrances. The offices and public winetasting rooms are located in one wing, which is entered from a large public portico. The other wing includes the winemaking functions and is entered from the working court and delivery area.

In the master plan, the sculpture garden was an integral part of the winery's design. The procession through the sculpture gardens would have begun in a circular building at the rear of the winery. This building, stepped in section, would have been seen as symbolic mountain—the mountain of Pegasus—and would have been used for visitor orientation, parties, and outdoor winetastings. In location and character, the building stood between the natural landscape and the other winery buildings. As garden architecture, it would have embodied the dual themes of the project: those of landscape and building, and of work and pleasure. The interior would have been embellished by a continuous painted frieze depicting the seasonal cycle of winemaking.

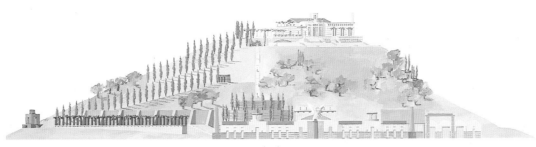

South elevation

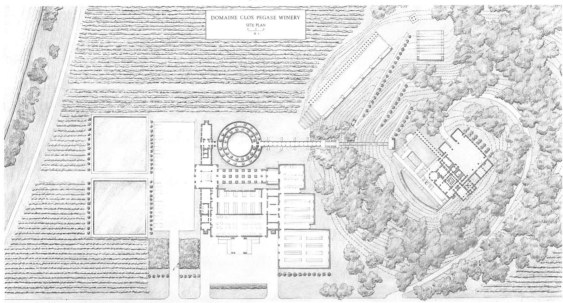

Master site plan

Master plan model view from the south

Winery entry portico study

Winery working court elevation study

Winery entry portico study

Winery working court elevation study

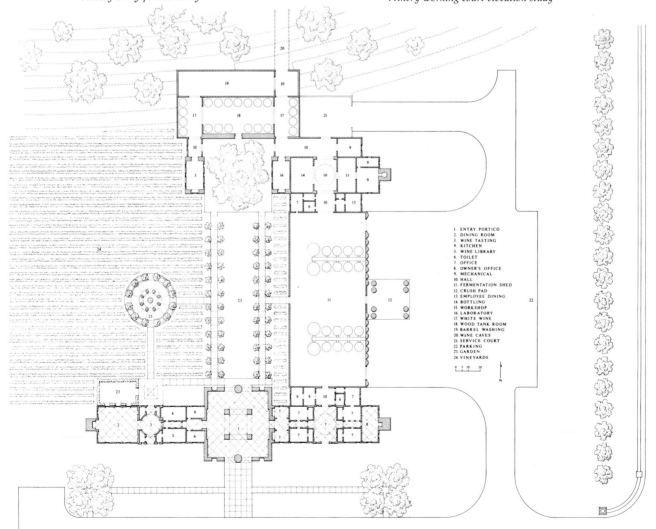

1. ENTRY PORTICO
2. DINING ROOM
3. WINE TASTING
4. KITCHEN
5. WINE LIBRARY
6. TOILET
7. OFFICE
8. OWNER'S OFFICE
9. MECHANICAL
10. HALL
11. FERMENTATION SHED
12. CRUSH PAD
13. EMPLOYEE DINING
14. BOTTLING
15. WORKSHOP
16. LABORATORY
17. WHITE WINE
18. WOOD TANK ROOM
19. BARREL WASHING
20. WINE CAVES
21. SERVICE COURT
22. PARKING
23. GARDEN
24. VINEYARDS

Winery plan

Winery entrance elevation study

Winery working court elevation

Master plan model, view from the east

Winery entry portico

Winery view from the southeast

Winery working court facade

Winery working court

Winery view of fermentation shed from entry portico

Winery tasting room and wood tank room

Winery courtyard

Winery, window detail

Winery fermentation shed

Winery public foyer

Winery public foyer

Winery fermentation room

Residence, model view from the south

Residence, model view from the east

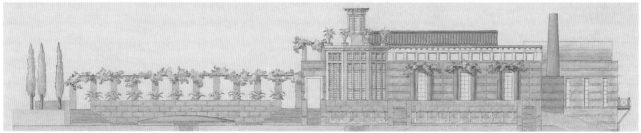

Residence, south lawn elevation

RESIDENCE KEY

1 ENTRY COURT
2 GARAGE
3 ENTRY
4 DINING ROOM
5 ATRIUM
6 WINTER GARDEN
7 LIVING ROOM
8 STUDY
9 MASTER BEDROOM
10 JAPANESE BATH
11 WALLED GARDEN
12 POTTERY STUDIO
13 WORKING COURT
14 BREAKFAST ROOM
15 KITCHEN
16 GUEST BEDROOM
17 BEDROOM
18 POOL
19 FLOWER AND
   VEGTABLE GARDEN
20 ORCHARD

RESIDENCE PLAN

SECOND FLOOR PLAN

Residence plan

Residence, living room terrace

Residence, view from the pool

CANAL PLAZA
CHANDLER, ARIZONA

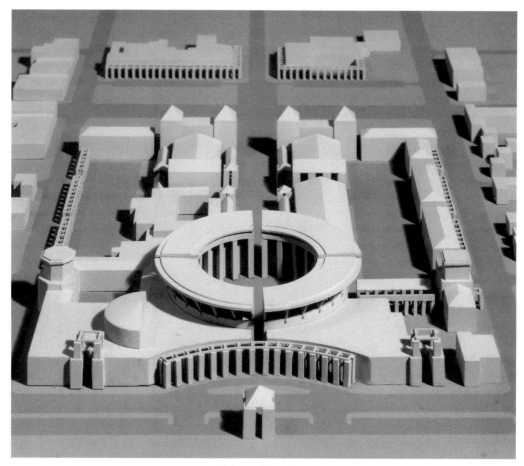

Model view from the east

The proposed redevelopment of downtown Chandler, Arizona would have used the canal located under Commonwealth Avenue as the major symbolic theme. The organization provided by the canal's axis and its major cross street would have allowed the construction to be phased, while giving a sense of civic unity to the entire project. This project was a feasibility study and was never realized.

Graves proposed that four quadrants surrounding the new public plaza be built separately to house the City Council Chambers, a police building, a public library, and offices. Throughout the development, retail activities were located at the sidewalk level, while offices and residential units existed above. Proposed development adjacent to the new central plaza would have continued this pattern of retail and commercial use along the axis of the re-established canal. Pergolas throughout the site would have unified new and existing buildings, masked parking structures, and provided shade from the intense southwestern sun.

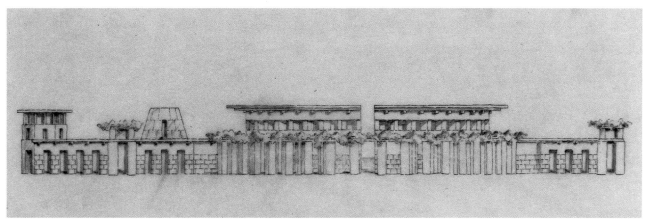

Delaware Street elevation

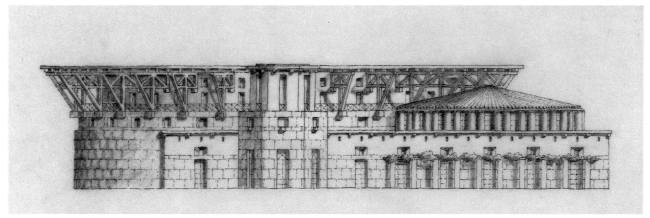

Boston Street elevation

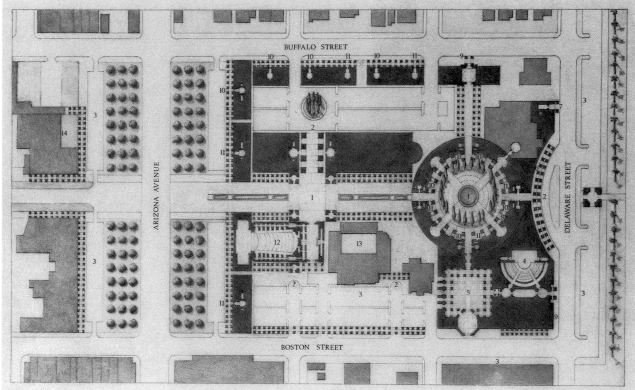

1 CANAL PLAZA
2 AUTOMOBILE DROP OFF
3 PARKING
4 COUNCIL CHAMBER
5 COURTYARD

6 EXISTING CITY HALL
7 MUNICIPAL OFFICES
8 RESTAURANT
9 COMMERCIAL

10 COMMERCIAL /OFFICE
11 COMMERCIAL /RESIDENTIAL
12 AUDITORIUM
13 ADULT CENTER
14 SAN MARCOS HOTEL

Site plan

DIANE VON FURSTENBERG BOUTIQUE
NEW YORK, NEW YORK

Foyer

This clothing boutique for Diane Von Furstenberg, before it was demolished, was located in the Sherry Netherland Hotel on Fifth Avenue in New York City. The project included major interior renovations and the replacement of an existing storefront which was out of character with the rest of the street facade. The new facade sensitively conformed to the historical character of the hotel and introduced the commercial themes of the boutique.

The boutique carried women's fashion lines designed by Diane Von Furstenberg as well as accessories and related products. The store had a very small ground floor and an expanded mezzanine level. The first of two major ground floor rooms opened volumetrically onto the second floor, providing a visual connection between floors and relieving the perception of confinement one might otherwise have experienced in such a small shop. The second room, with fabric draped tent-like from the ceiling, gave the feeling of a bazaar. This made the space more ephemeral and lighter, compensating for its deep position in the plan and lack of daylight. The second floor was used for modelling and presenting specialty garments. The character of the entire shop, except for the tent room, was imagined as a cabinet. Its detailing and composition thus contributed to the ambiance of the shop as a fine wardrobe.

Shop entrance

Facade detail

Second floor display

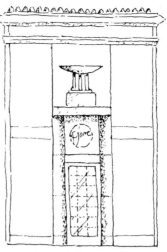

Entry elevation studies

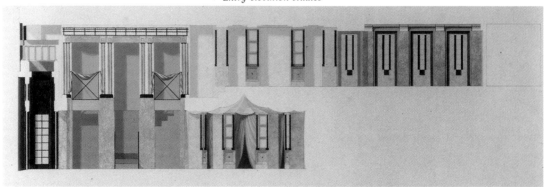

Section

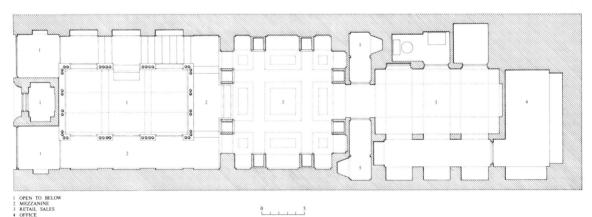

1 OPEN TO BELOW
2 MEZZANINE
3 RETAIL SALES
4 OFFICE
5 DRESSING ROOM

0   5

Second floor plan

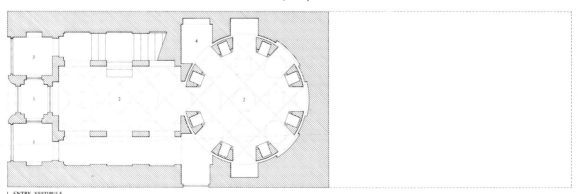

1 ENTRY VESTIBULE
2 RETAIL SALES
3 DISPLAY WINDOW
4 DRESSING ROOM

0   5

First floor plan

Column detail

Accessories cabinet

Tent room

JENCKS RESIDENCE FIREPLACES
LONDON, ENGLAND

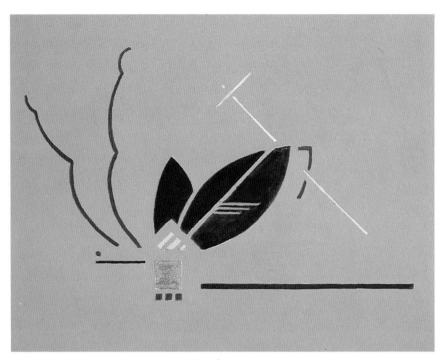

Stencil pattern

"Spring" fireplace

"Winter" fireplace

Charles Jencks, a historian and architect, designed a "thematic" residence in London. He asked Graves to design two fireplace walls, one to symbolize "winter", and the other "spring." Busts of representative figures were placed on columns above the mantel of each fireplace. The walls behind were painted and stenciled in colors and patterns that reinforced the seasonal themes.

1984

STAGE CURTAIN

The stage curtain for the Kentucky Center for the Performing Arts in Louisville establishes a "wainscot" within the proscenium opening by the change in color and use of pattern. The dark blue color of the base of the curtain and the wave-like character of the pattern make reference to the Center's site at the edge of the Ohio River. The upper portion of the curtain is cream-colored and seen as more ephemeral than the base.

FOLDING SCREEN

The Rizzoli bookstore and gallery in New York commissioned a number of architects to design folding screens for an exhibition. Graves' screen is made in the form of a stone arcade or loggia with more ephemeral lengths of fabric draped across its head.

THE GREAT GATSBY
ILLUSTRATIONS

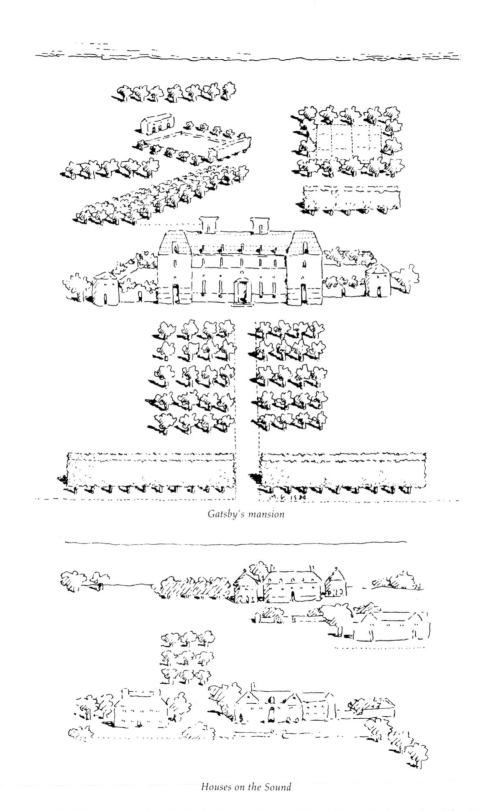

Gatsby's mansion

Houses on the Sound

Graves provided illustrations for a limited edition printing of *The Great Gatsby* produced by Arion Press. His pen and ink drawings are used throughout the printed text to illustrate various scenes and artifacts described in the book. A terra cotta relief depicting Gatsby's mansion on Long Island Sound was inset into the cover of a box containing a special edition of the book.

Myrtle's dog

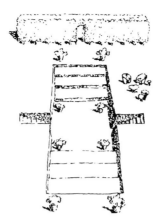

Sunken Italian garden

Cocktails in the garden

Gatsby's gorgeous car

Gatsby's blue gardens

Cemetery

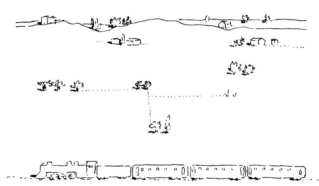

Long Island Railroad

Gatsby's gardens

Nick's weatherbeaten bungalow

1985

GRAND REEF MASTER PLAN
GALVESTON, TEXAS

Condominium tower elevation

The master plan for this large resort development, which was never realized, encompassed the entire East Beach section of Galveston, including approximately 450 acres of privately-owned property and adjacent city park land. The overall concept placed condominiums and resort hotels along the beach front, incorporating two existing medium-rise condominiums. Twelve new 14-story condominium towers would have been arranged in a large crescent facing the Gulf of Mexico. The buildings were spanned by a continuous covered "bridge" containing restaurants and a public walkway. The Grand Reef Crescent, as a large figural gesture, would have established a recognizable image for the entire complex.

Located immediately behind the Crescent, a commercial and retail strip development was proposed, making reference to the "Strand"—the major shopping street in downtown Galveston. In the center of the site, small-scale housing units would have surrounded an 18-hole golf course designed by Robert Trent Jones. A clubhouse at the east end of this course would have led to a second 18-hole championship golf course within city park land.

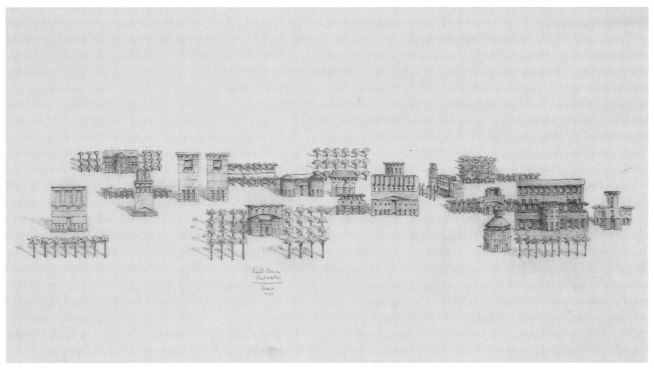

Hotel character studies

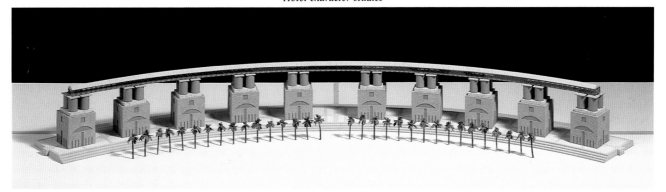

Condominium crescent model

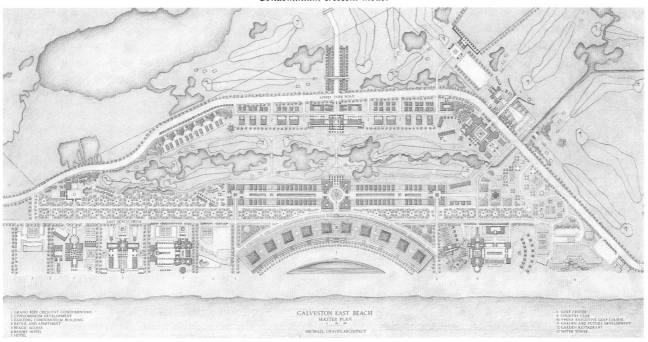

Site plan

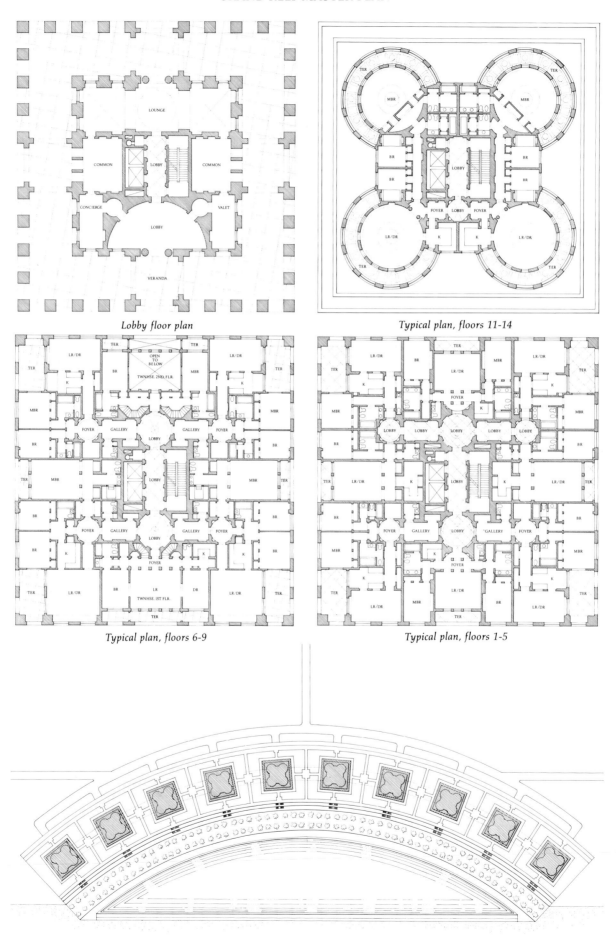

Lobby floor plan

Typical plan, floors 11-14

Typical plan, floors 6-9

Typical plan, floors 1-5

Condominium crescent site plan

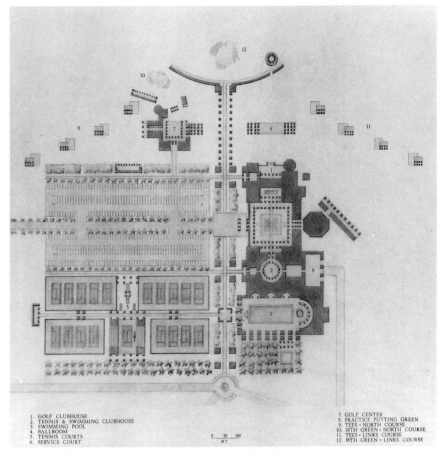

1. GOLF CLUBHOUSE
2. TENNIS & SWIMMING CLUBHOUSE
3. SWIMMING POOL
4. BALLROOM
5. TENNIS COURTS
6. SERVICE COURT
7. GOLF CENTER
8. PRACTICE PUTTING GREEN
9. TEES - NORTH COURSE
10. 18TH GREEN - NORTH COURSE
11. TEES - LINKS COURSE
12. 18TH GREEN - LINKS COURSE

Golf and Racquet Club plan

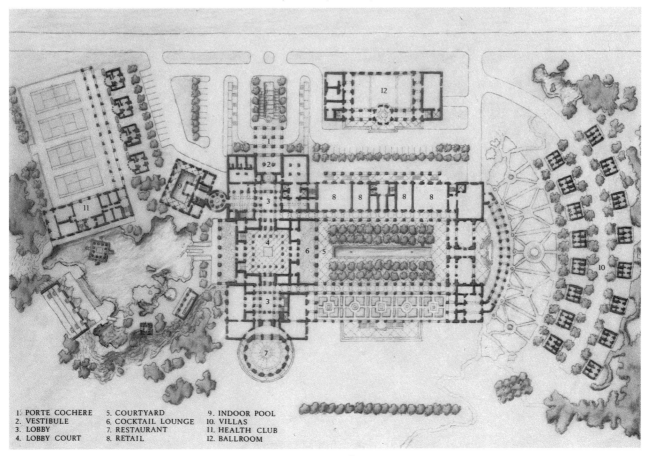

1. PORTE COCHERE
2. VESTIBULE
3. LOBBY
4. LOBBY COURT
5. COURTYARD
6. COCKTAIL LOUNGE
7. RESTAURANT
8. RETAIL
9. INDOOR POOL
10. VILLAS
11. HEALTH CLUB
12. BALLROOM

Hotel site plan

PHOENIX MUNICIPAL GOVERNMENT CENTER
PHOENIX, ARIZONA

Preliminary master plan model

The project for the Phoenix Municipal Government Center resulted from a two-stage design competition involving a master plan for a twelve-block area in the center of the city, and a more detailed scheme for a civic center, including a new City Hall, City Council Chambers, Municipal Courts, and Water and Wastewater Building. Graves was not chosen as the architect for the project. In both stages of the competition, Graves proposed a mixture of civic and commercial buildings within the government mall area, to provide a diversity of use that would ensure active urban life. Located at the intersection of Washington Street and 4th Avenue, the four municipal buildings would have surrounded an open civic square, whose form and character were derived from the history and climate of Phoenix.

The periphery of the proposed buildings conformed to the existing street edges, while the facades along the square were distinctly juxtaposed with the city grid, thereby emphasizing their civic importance as monuments in the city. Loggias, covered arcades, and courtyards provided passages through this downtown area to the more private lobbies and offices of nearby commercial buildings. The square itself was organized as a series of courtyards, arcades, gardens, fountains, and pools. The various water elements were used thematically throughout the scheme, referring to the founding of Phoenix in the desert.

The City Council Chambers was proposed as the formal and symbolic center of Graves' scheme. The building, pyramidal in shape, represented the unity of the program. Water would have flowed from its top to an elevated fountain above the portico, and finally to the palm court at its base. The building and its function would thus have been linked by the theme of water as the life-giving force of the city. Visitors could have ascended the building, internally or externally, to a column supporting the Phoenix statue.

The proposed Council Chambers was flanked by City Hall and the Municipal Courts Building. City Hall conformed to the street edges of Washington, Jefferson, and 3rd Avenue, engaging the new square on its western face through a curved colonnade—an open, collective gesture to the citizens of Phoenix. In front of the colonnade, protected from the sun by a canvas canopy, an amphitheater would have been used casually by employees and the general public or for public assembly on formal occasions.

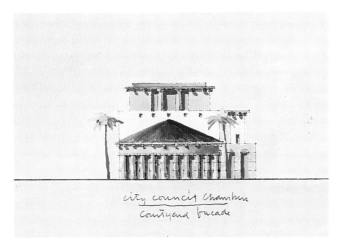

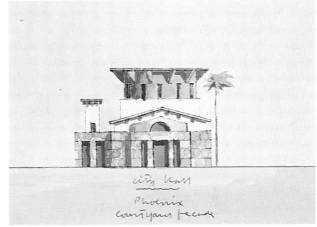

City Council Chamber and City Hall, preliminary courtyard elevations

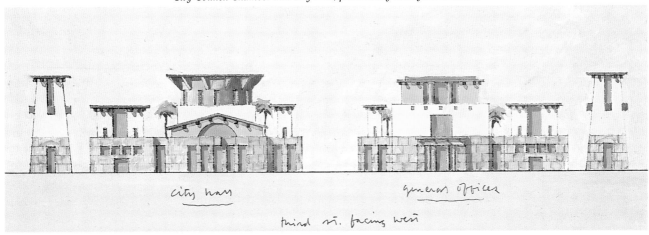

City Hall, Third Avenue elevation study

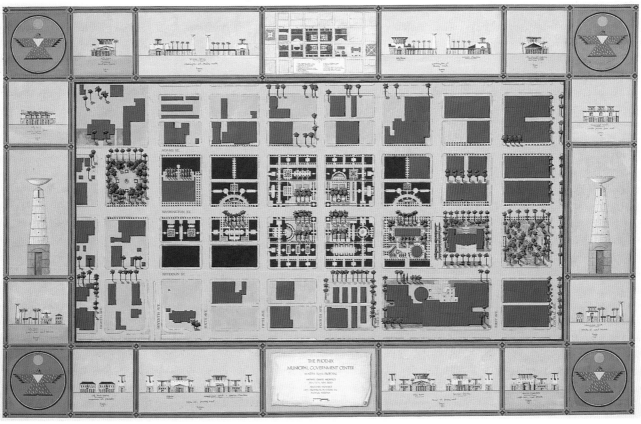

Preliminary master plan

Model view of City Hall

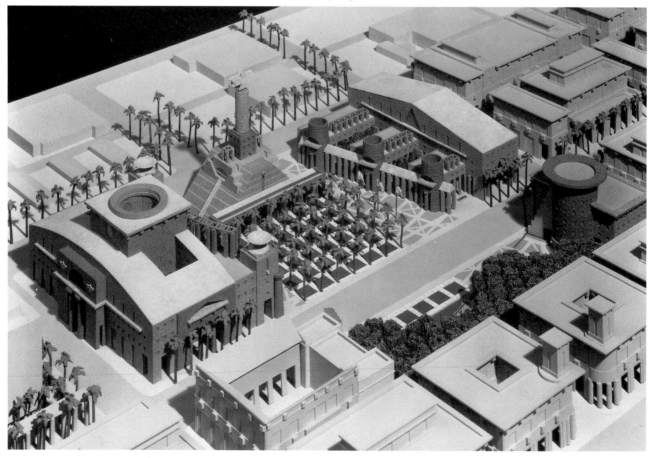

Model view of Civic Square

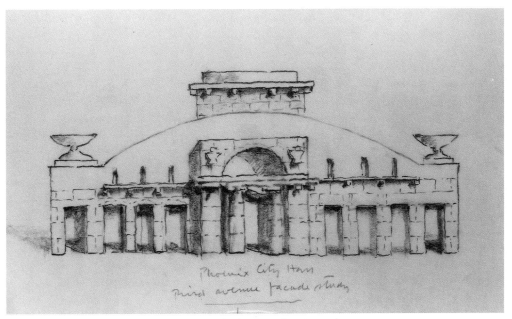

City Hall, Third Avenue elevation study

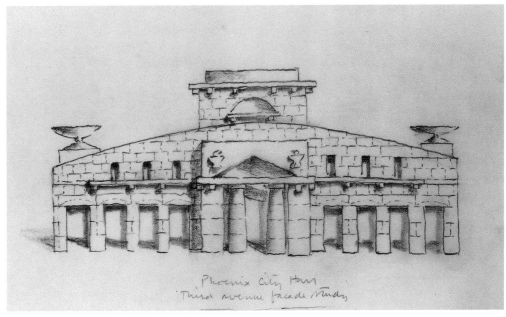

City Hall, Third Avenue elevation study

Municipal Water Building, elevation study

City Council Chambers, elevation study

Model view of Civic Square

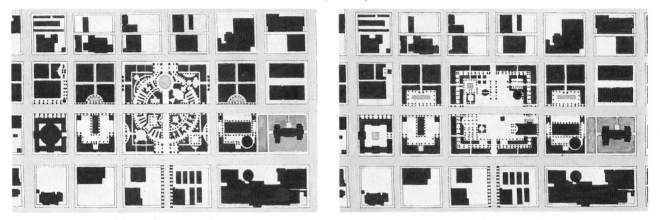

Master plan parti study *Master plan parti study*

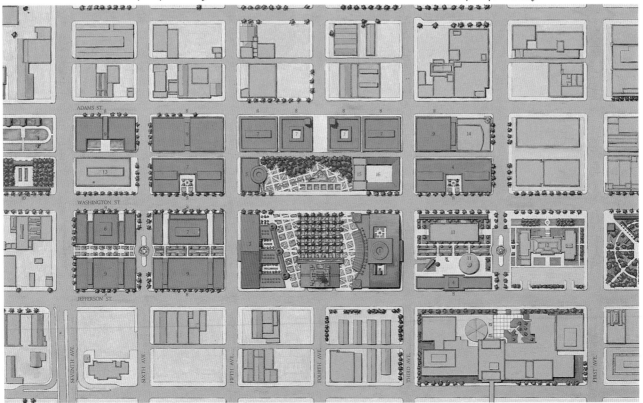

Master plan

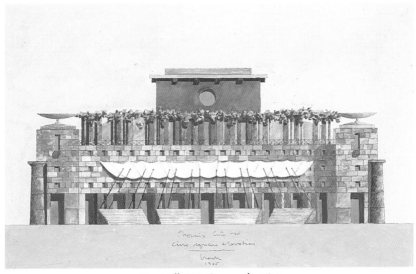

City Hall Civic Square elevation

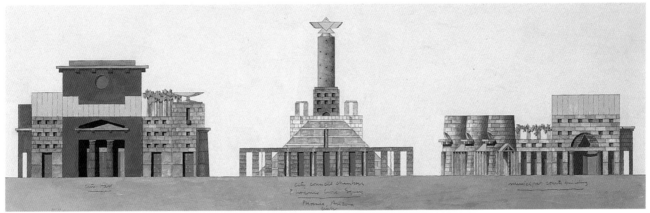

Civic Square elevation

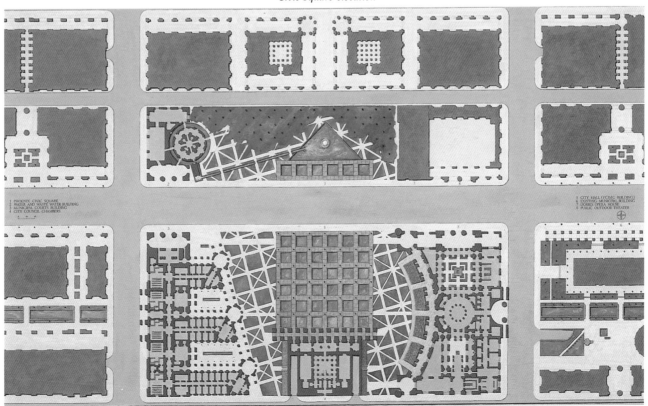

Site plan

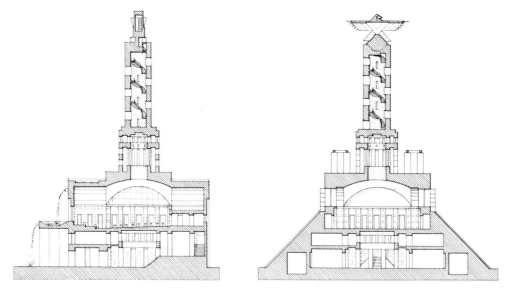

City Council Chambers sections

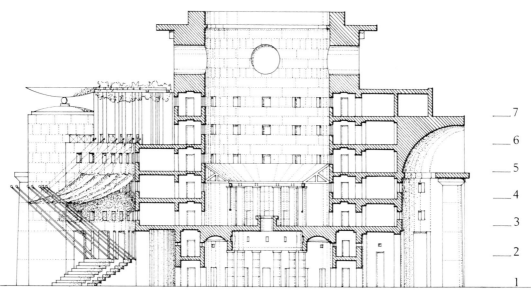

City Hall cross section

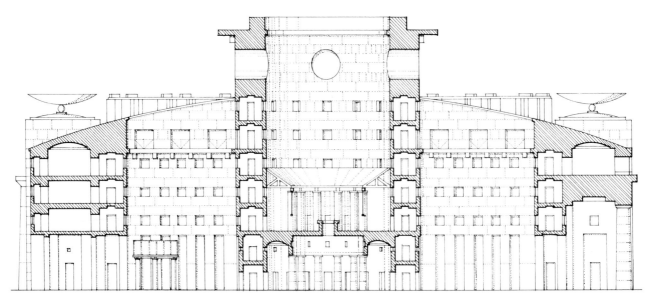

City Hall longitudinal section

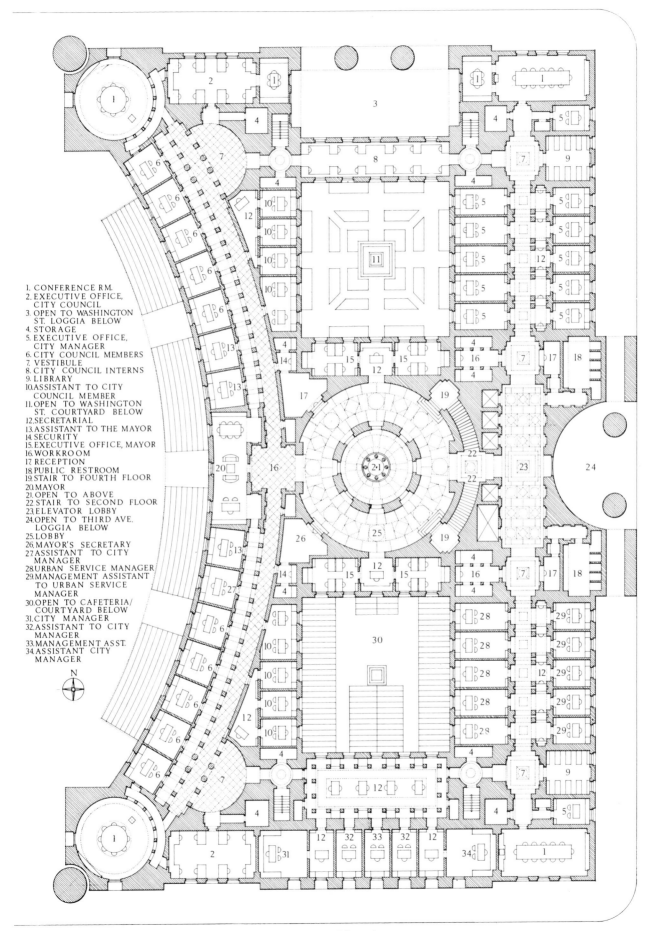

1. CONFERENCE RM.
2. EXECUTIVE OFFICE, CITY COUNCIL
3. OPEN TO WASHINGTON ST. LOGGIA BELOW
4. STORAGE
5. EXECUTIVE OFFICE, CITY MANAGER
6. CITY COUNCIL MEMBERS
7. VESTIBULE
8. CITY COUNCIL INTERNS
9. LIBRARY
10. ASSISTANT TO CITY COUNCIL MEMBER
11. OPEN TO WASHINGTON ST. COURTYARD BELOW
12. SECRETARIAL
13. ASSISTANT TO THE MAYOR
14. SECURITY
15. EXECUTIVE OFFICE, MAYOR
16. WORKROOM
17. RECEPTION
18. PUBLIC RESTROOM
19. STAIR TO FOURTH FLOOR
20. MAYOR
21. OPEN TO ABOVE
22. STAIR TO SECOND FLOOR
23. ELEVATOR LOBBY
24. OPEN TO THIRD AVE. LOGGIA BELOW
25. LOBBY
26. MAYOR'S SECRETARY
27. ASSISTANT TO CITY MANAGER
28. URBAN SERVICE MANAGER
29. MANAGEMENT ASSISTANT TO URBAN SERVICE MANAGER
30. OPEN TO CAFETERIA/ COURTYARD BELOW
31. CITY MANAGER
32. ASSISTANT TO CITY MANAGER
33. MANAGEMENT ASST.
34. ASSISTANT CITY MANAGER

N

City Hall third floor plan

1985
HOTEL AND SPORTING CLUB
PRINCETON, NEW JERSEY

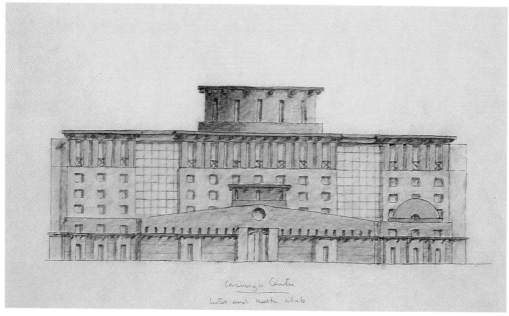

Hotel elevation

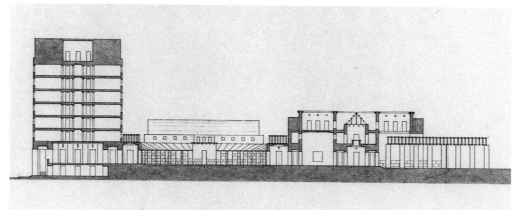

Section through hotel

The program for this feasibility study, never realized, included a hotel and sporting club located within a larger mixed use development along Route One, south of Princeton, New Jersey. Rather than treating these two facilities as separate buildings, the design unified them in a single composition, centered on a circular entry court and a restaurant shared in common. On the ground floor, a cross axis would have connected the lobbies to the parking lot on the south side and the outdoor recreational facilities on the north side.

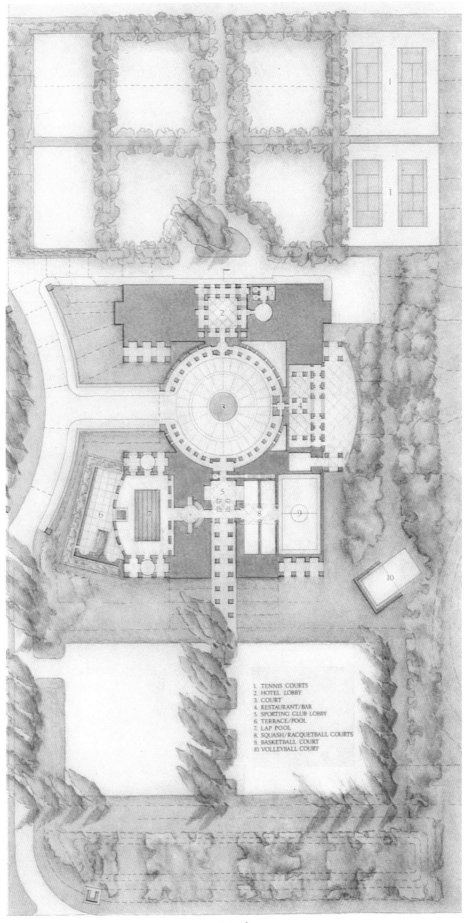

1. TENNIS COURTS
2. HOTEL LOBBY
3. COURT
4. RESTAURANT/BAR
5. SPORTING CLUB LOBBY
6. TERRACE/POOL
7. LAP POOL
8. SQUASH/RACQUETBALL COURTS
9. BASKETBALL COURT
10. VOLLEYBALL COURT

Site plan

COLUMBUS CIRCLE REDEVELOPMENT
NEW YORK, NEW YORK

Model view from Columbus Circle

In 1985, as a result of the imminent completion of a major convention center in New York, the city offered the site of the existing Coliseum for sale to developers. Interested developers were asked to submit not only their bids and programs of use but also architectural designs. Graves' scheme was designed in conjunction with the Gruzen Partnership. The development team proposed a large mixed use development for the site, including major retail space at the base, offices and a hotel at the middle level, and apartments in two high rise towers. Total square footage was approximately 2,300,000 square feet. The development team was not chosen for the project.

The tripartite division of the building would have articulated its various uses and would have helped integrate the building within the surrounding urban context. The building's base would have reinforced the curve of Columbus Circle and been similar in height to neighboring structures. The twin apartment towers, though larger in size, would have symbolically referred to many of the West Side residential buildings facing Central Park. Major retail shops, restaurants, spaces for entertainment, and other similar activities would have been located at the base of the building. This would have brought new life to the neighborhood, as well as continuing the urban pattern already established in the nearby Lincoln Center district.

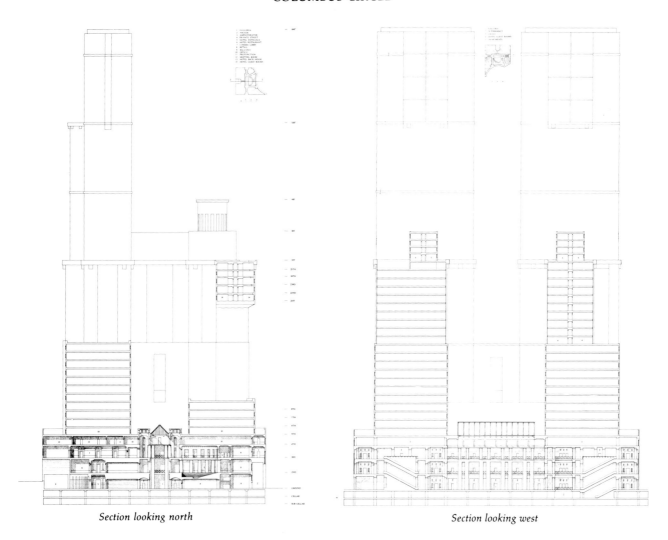

Section looking north

Section looking west

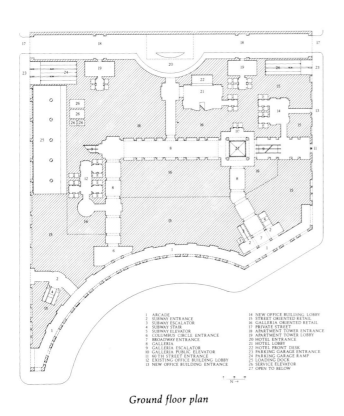

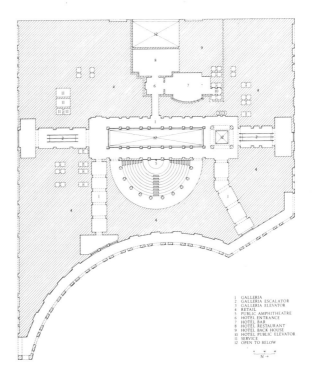

Ground floor plan

Second floor plan

East elevation study

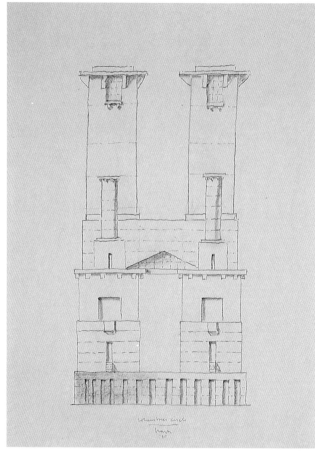

East elevation study

East elevation study

East elevation study

View from Central Park

CHAMBER MUSIC HALL ADDITION
SAN FRANCISCO CONSERVATORY OF MUSIC
SAN FRANCISCO, CALIFORNIA

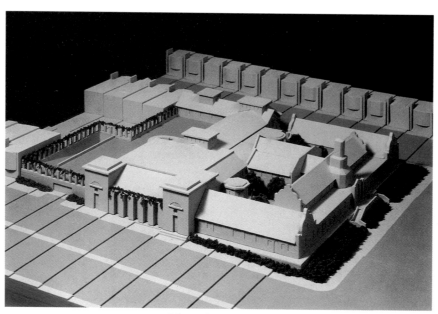

Model view from 19th Avenue

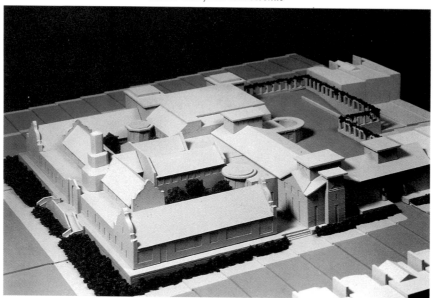

Model view from Ortega Street

When Graves was commissioned to prepare plans for the proposed addition to the San Francisco Conservatory of Music, the school was planning to increase its curriculum for the study and performance of chamber music. The expansion program included a 100-seat chamber music hall, rehearsal rooms, practice rooms, and support facilities. After several years of study the project was suspended.

The plan of the original building was compromised by previous additions which contradicted existing circulation patterns. The proposed addition would have restructured this circulation, provided a variety of sectional treatments allowing natural light to penetrate the interior of the complex, and created a continuous street edge. Although the main pedestrian entry would have remained on Ortega Street, the new chamber music hall and existing concert hall would have shared a new public lobby on 19th Street. The style of the existing building is Spanish Colonial. The addition, with its stucco walls and red clay tile roofs, would have continued the original aesthetic.

Main lobby

Chamber Music Hall

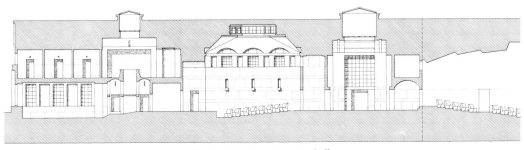

Section through performing halls

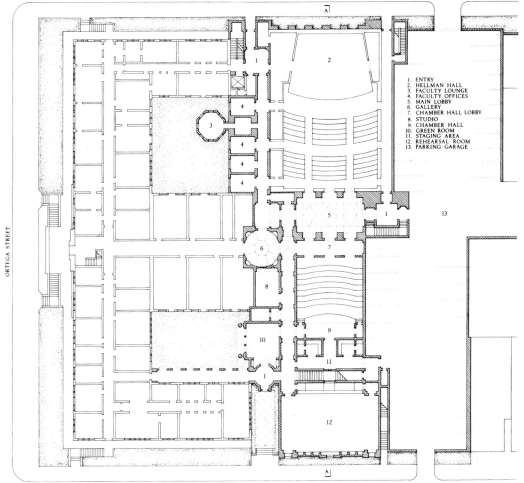

1. ENTRY
2. HELLMAN HALL
3. FACULTY LOUNGE
4. FACULTY OFFICES
5. MAIN LOBBY
6. GALLERY
7. CHAMBER HALL LOBBY
8. STUDIO
9. CHAMBER HALL
10. GREEN ROOM
11. STAGING AREA
12. REHEARSAL ROOM
13. PARKING GARAGE

ORTEGA STREET

Site plan

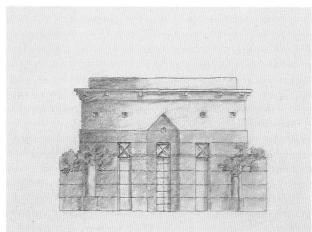

Preliminary rotunda studies

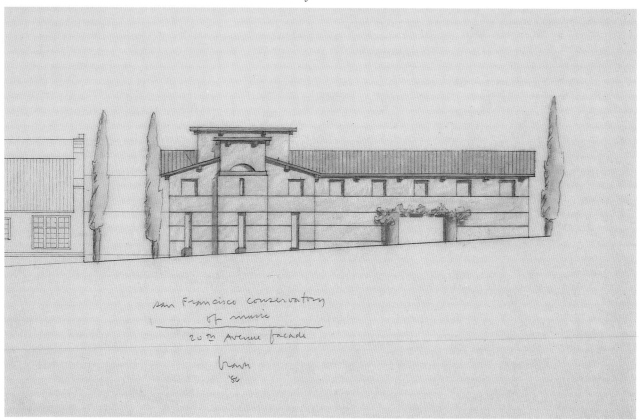

20th Avenue elevation study

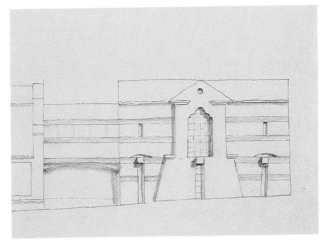
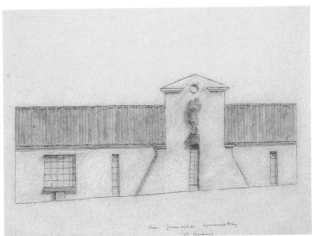
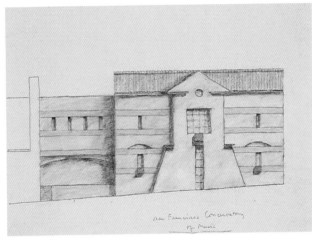

20th Avenue elevation studies

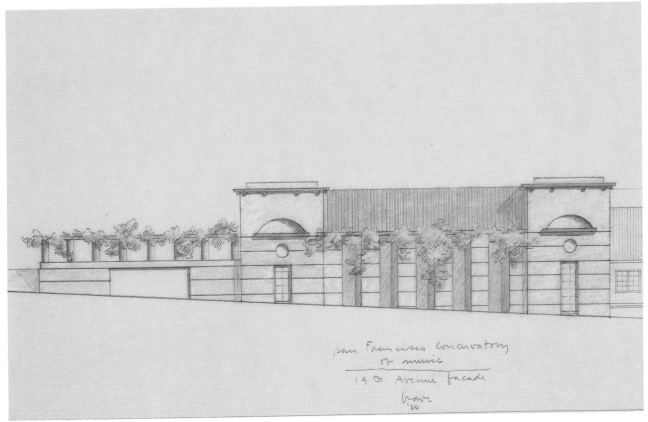

19th Avenue elevation study

1985

AVENTINE
MIXED USE DEVELOPMENT
LA JOLLA, CALIFORNIA

Model view from the south

Model view from the north

The project called Aventine is located on a twelve-acre site, which is the northernmost parcel in University Center, a large mixed-use development in La Jolla, California. The master plan for Aventine includes a 400-room hotel, speculative office building, three theme restaurants, and a health club with outdoor swimming pool. The project totals 482,500 square feet. A major parking garage built into the steeply sloping hillside extends under several of the buildings.

The buildings overlook a large formal pool. They are sited to take advantage of the views and to allow sunlight to penetrate to the center of the site, where major recreational activities are located. Though the buildings have their own individual compositional character, the commonality of their architectural language and materials allows Aventine to be seen as a unified ensemble.

Character studies

South elevation

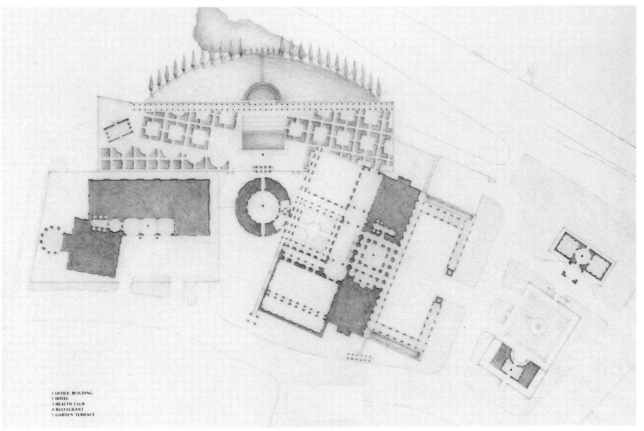

1 OFFICE BUILDING
2 HOTEL
3 HEALTH CLUB
4 RESTAURANT
5 GARDEN TERRACE

Site plan

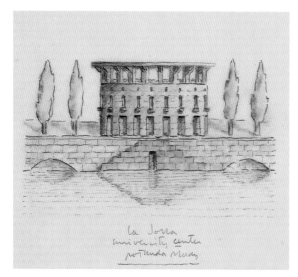

Health Club rotunda studies

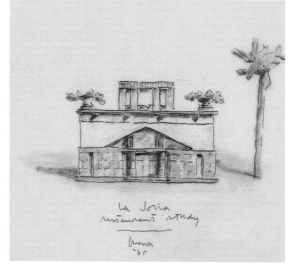

Restaurant studies

Hotel from the south

Health Club rotunda studies

Health Club rotunda studies

Office building from the south

1985

SOTHEBY'S TOWER
NEW YORK, NEW YORK

Preliminary model view from York Avenue

This project includes the renovation of Sotheby's auction house, the addition of one office floor for Sotheby's and the construction of a 27-story residential tower above. The tower will include approximately 280 apartments and a health club. The building is divided into three parts: the cultural and commercial base of Sotheby's, and the two-part residential tower. The lower portion of the tower's facade will contain balconies and masonry decoration on a diagonal grid. The upper portion of the building is distinguished by greater areas of glass and corner apartments with large windows offering views of Manhattan and the East River.

At the center of the building, supported by the base of Sotheby's, is an emblematic figure or object. This figure repeats the gray-green color of the building's base, creating a visual link between the auction house and the residential tower. The figure, however, is primarily a symbolic gesture whose form is an abstraction of a *palazzo*-like house or of the kind of artifact or furniture auctioned at Sotheby's. Traditionally there has been a strong relationship between building and furniture, in that furniture makers have given architectural forms to their cabinets, vitrines, commodes, and other objects. In the Sotheby's facade, the emblematic figure recognizes that equivocal relationship and represents both the auction house and the residence.

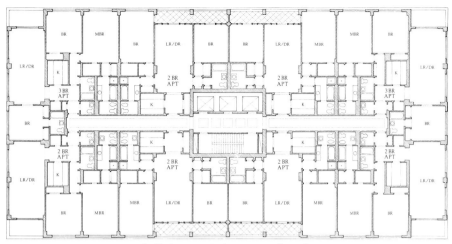

Preliminary typical apartment floor plan

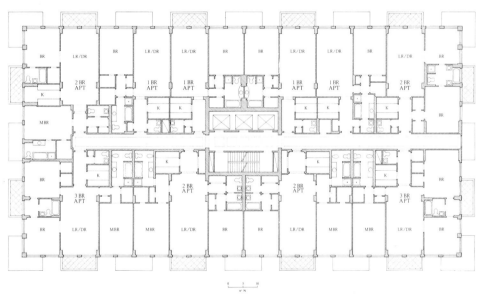

Preliminary typical apartment floor plan

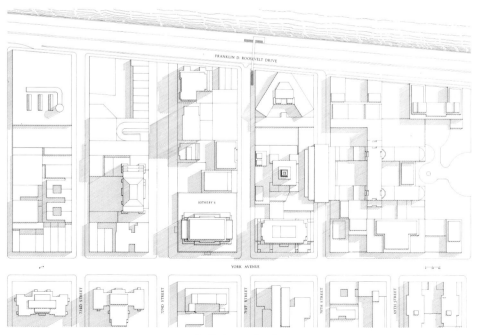

Preliminary site plan

177

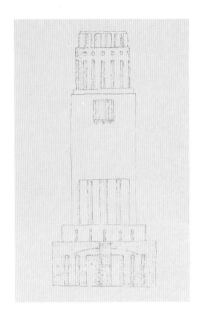

Preliminary model study

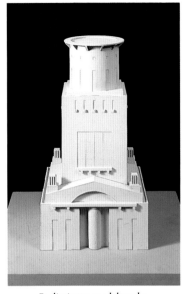

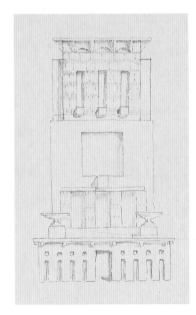

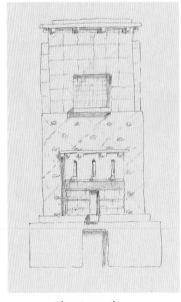

Elevation studies

Preliminary model view from York Avenue

1986

PRIVATE RESIDENCE
CATSKILL MOUNTAINS, NEW YORK

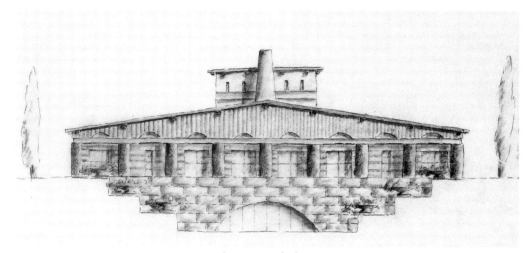

Preliminary south elevation

Site plan

This small weekend house, which was not built, was designed for a mountainous site in the Catskills. The imagery used in the design referred both to historic mountain lodges and to the natural quality of the site. Wood was proposed for the structure and the major finishes. The exterior walls would have been surfaced with log siding, while eight columns on the south facade would have consisted of large tree trunks. The interior floors, walls, and ceilings were intended to be finished in wood in a variety of textures and colors.

The house would have been entered from the north, through a small vestibule defined by the back side of a massive stone fireplace. Walking around the fireplace, one would have entered the "great room", which would have functioned as a living room, dining room, and kitchen. This room would have faced southern light and the views through large windows. A central skylight would have provided natural light and vertically opened the room.

PRIVATE RESIDENCE, CATSKILL MOUNTAINS

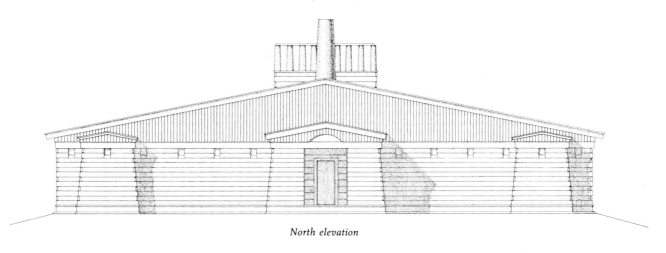

North elevation

Section looking north

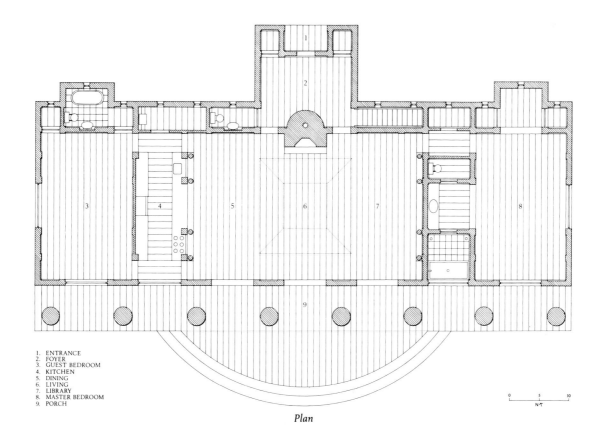

1. ENTRANCE
2. FOYER
3. GUEST BEDROOM
4. KITCHEN
5. DINING
6. LIVING
7. LIBRARY
8. MASTER BEDROOM
9. PORCH

Plan

1986

THE CROWN AMERICAN BUILDING
JOHNSTOWN, PENNSYLVANIA

View from the southeast

Vine Street facade

The Crown American corporate office building is a four-story structure of approximately 130,000 square feet organized around a central atrium which rises through the entire building, unifying the interior.

Because the building is located on a corner site, two separate entries were developed. One is primarily a pedestrian entrance for employees who park several blocks away. The other is a two-story *porte cochere* for automobiles to drop off passengers. The roof of the *porte cochere* is a steeply sloped truncated pyramid with a skylight illuminating offices and library on the third floor. The building's character responds to the diverse institutional context of the neighborhood, whose design vocabulary is reflected both in the configuration of the roofs of the Crown building and in the polychromatic values of its stone exterior. The interiors incorporate furnishings and furniture designed by Graves.

Atrium

Executive suite rotunda

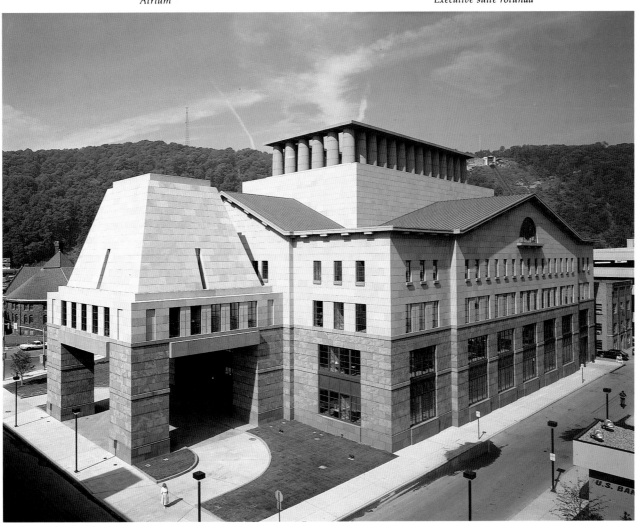

View from the northeast

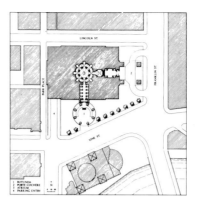

View from the southeast

Site plan

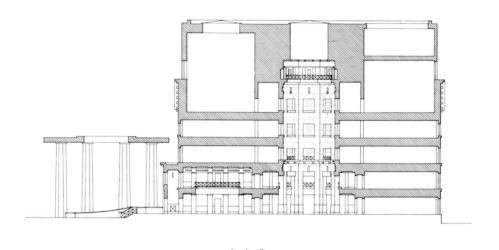

Section through entrance and atrium

Vine Street elevation study

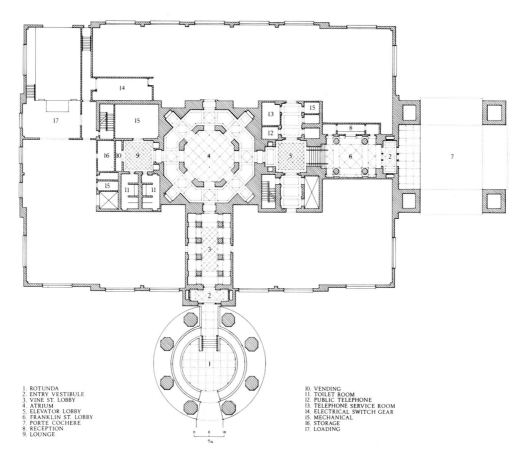

1. ROTUNDA
2. ENTRY VESTIBULE
3. VINE ST. LOBBY
4. ATRIUM
5. ELEVATOR LOBBY
6. FRANKLIN ST. LOBBY
7. PORTE COCHERE
8. RECEPTION
9. LOUNGE

10. VENDING
11. TOILET ROOM
12. PUBLIC TELEPHONE
13. TELEPHONE SERVICE ROOM
14. ELECTRICAL SWITCH GEAR
15. MECHANICAL
16. STORAGE
17. LOADING

Ground floor plan

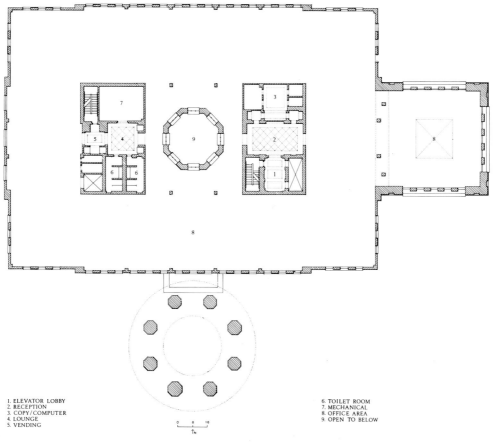

1. ELEVATOR LOBBY
2. RECEPTION
3. COPY/COMPUTER
4. LOUNGE
5. VENDING

6. TOILET ROOM
7. MECHANICAL
8. OFFICE AREA
9. OPEN TO BELOW

Third floor plan

185

East entrance lobby

Chief Executive office

Corporate Boardroom

Executive dining room

SHISEIDO HEALTH CLUB
TOKYO, JAPAN

Lower level lounge

Shiseido, an international cosmetics company headquartered in Japan and noted for its prominence in several design fields, commissioned this 14,000 square foot health club, occupying a portion of the ground floor and lower level of a new 25-story mixed use tower in central Tokyo. The program includes facilities for a total health regime for men and women. The upper level is organized hierarchically as a series of rooms for reception, counselling, exercise, dance, weight training, massage, sauna, and informal dining. The lower level includes a large swimming pool covered by a shallow vaulted ceiling.

The interior has been given the character of traditional baths through extensive use of Japanese ceramic tiles. The pool room uses the reflectivity of tile laid in an expanded checkerboard pattern to reinforce the kinetic quality of water. This lively, reflective character is repeated in several fountains which provide ambient noise as an invitation to the pool.

SHISEIDO HEALTH CLUB

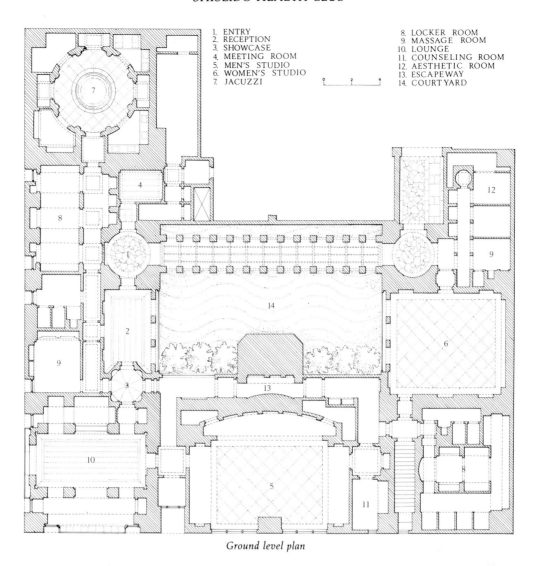

1. ENTRY
2. RECEPTION
3. SHOWCASE
4. MEETING ROOM
5. MEN'S STUDIO
6. WOMEN'S STUDIO
7. JACUZZI

8. LOCKER ROOM
9. MASSAGE ROOM
10. LOUNGE
11. COUNSELING ROOM
12. AESTHETIC ROOM
13. ESCAPEWAY
14. COURTYARD

Ground level plan

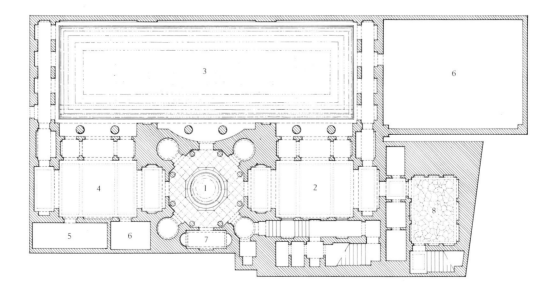

1. JACUZZI
2. LOUNGE
3. POOL
4. TANNING ROOM

5. SAUNA
6. MACHINE ROOM
7. DRESSING ROOM
8. OUTDOOR COURTYARD

Lower level plan

189

Pool loggia

Pool

Pool

THE HISTORICAL CENTER OF INDUSTRY AND LABOR
YOUNGSTOWN, OHIO

Preliminary West Wood Street elevation

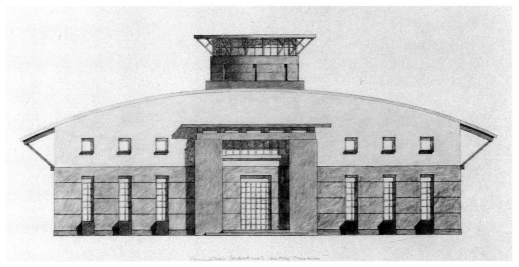

West Wood Street elevation

The Historical Center of Industry and Labor is a branch facility of the Ohio Historical Society devoted to the study and presentation of the industrial history of the Mahoning River Valley. The three-level brick and steel structure of approximately 32,000 square feet occupies a steeply sloping site located between the University and the steel mills along the Mahoning River. The site faces downtown Youngstown to the south and St. Columba Cathedral to the north. The building forms a sympathetic contextual relationship with the cathedral because of their similar polychromy and axial alignment in plan.

The center contains a museum which will have exhibitions specific to the industrial history of the area, particularly the steel industry. Also included are a research center, archives and classrooms. A George Segal sculpture of steel machinery and workers, replicas of the railroad, and various industrial artifacts are located in the garden.

The building's elements represent forms typical of the American industrial landscape. The character is derived not so much from recently built steel mills as from the extremely potent images of 19th century industrial examples. These earlier industrial compositions were based not only on the manufacturing process but also on human habitation; thus, the use of similar imagery is seen as a way of recalling both man and the machine in a museum that honors both.

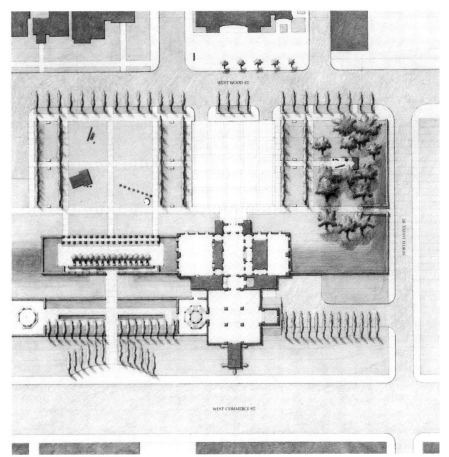

Site plan

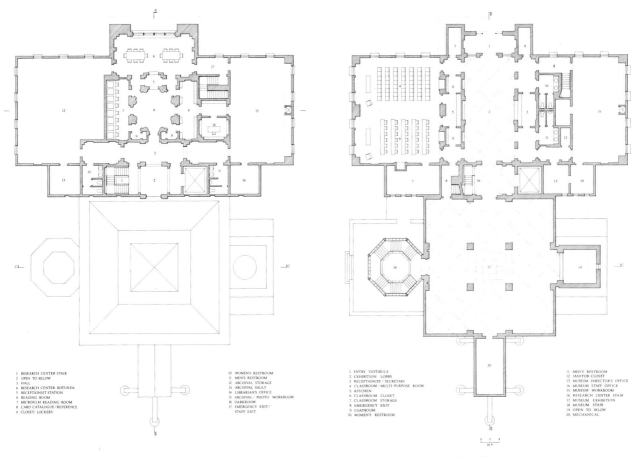

1. RESEARCH CENTER STAIR	10. WOMEN'S RESTROOM
2. OPEN TO BELOW	11. MEN'S RESTROOM
3. HALL	12. ARCHIVAL STORAGE
4. RESEARCH CENTER ROTUNDA	13. ARCHIVAL VAULT
5. RECEPTIONIST STATION	14. LIBRARIAN'S OFFICE
6. READING ROOM	15. ARCHIVAL / PHOTO WORKROOM
7. MICROFILM READING ROOM	16. DARKROOM
8. CARD CATALOGUE/REFERENCE	17. EMERGENCY EXIT/
9. CLOSET/ LOCKERS	STAFF EXIT

1. ENTRY VESTIBULE	11. MEN'S RESTROOM
2. EXHIBITION LOBBY	12. JANITOR CLOSET
3. RECEPTIONIST / SECRETARY	13. MUSEUM DIRECTOR'S OFFICE
4. CLASSROOM / MULTI-PURPOSE ROOM	14. MUSEUM STAFF OFFICE
5. KITCHEN	15. MUSEUM WORKROOM
6. CLASSROOM CLOSET	16. RESEARCH CENTER STAIR
7. CLASSROOM STORAGE	17. MUSEUM EXHIBITION
8. EMERGENCY EXIT	18. MUSEUM STAIR
9. COATROOM	19. OPEN TO BELOW
10. WOMEN'S RESTROOM	20. MECHANICAL

Second floor plan   *First floor plan*

View from southeast

View from southwest

View from West Wood Street

View from West Commerce Street

View from West Wood Street

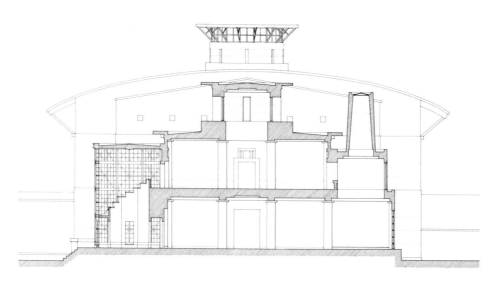

Section C

Section B

Model room facade

Octagonal museum stairs

View from southeast

1986
MARDI GRAS ARCH
GALVESTON, TEXAS

View from the Strand

Graves was one of seven architects invited to design triumphal arches for the 1986 Mardi Gras in an effort to draw national attention to Galveston and its annual Mardi Gras celebration. The arches were placed in strategic locations throughout the city to mark the parade route. Graves' arch was located on the Strand, the major commercial street in Galveston. In addition to being a traditional means of marking parade routes, the arches had particular meaning in Galveston's history, as a 19th century singing festival there was traditionally celebrated under a large arch erected for that purpose.

The Graves arch was a simple structure made of four large square columns supporting a pitched roof. Large gold stars and flags on each gabled end made reference to Texas—"The Lone Star State"—and to the Texas colors. The arch was illuminated externally to spotlight the Texas stars and internally to highlight the soffit and reflect light back to the street below.

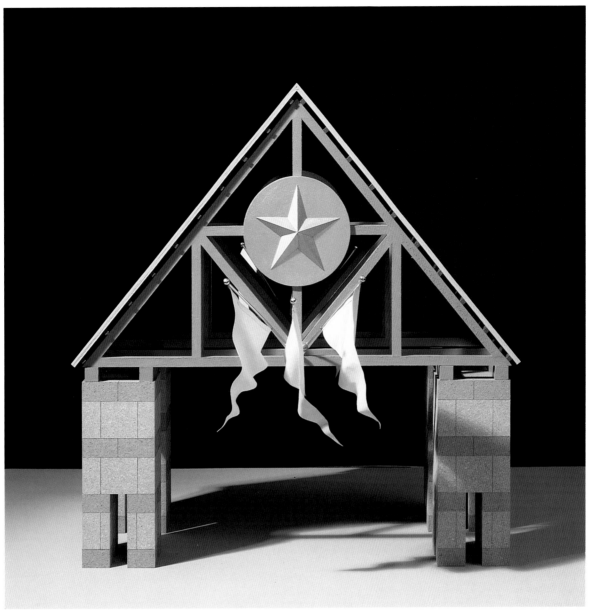

Model

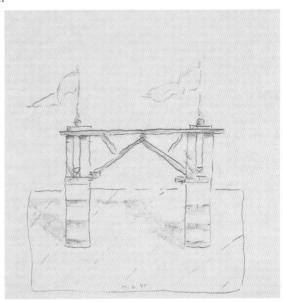

Character studies

1986

SUNAR FURNITURE SHOWROOM
LONDON, ENGLAND

Office systems display

The Sunar showroom in London is a complete renovation of the ground floor of an existing building. Similar in program to the numerous Sunar showrooms Graves has designed in the United States, the space is organized to present the collection of furniture and textiles in a variety of architectural settings. The plan creates a procession through a series of rooms differentiated by changes in ceiling height, surface finishes, color, and lighting to encourage the reading of the individual rooms. Display rooms include private offices, group work spaces for six to eight people, and a large open room for office systems.

The entry room is designed as a transitional space marking the change from public to private and outside to inside. The walls appear like the rusticated surfacing of many of the terrace houses of London. The passageway from the entry room, with ceiling coffers and articulated walls reminiscent of London's arcades, leads to the main display areas of the showroom.

A series of small rooms, acting as special "locks" or "hinges," moves visitors from the arcade to an octagonal room in which chairs and textiles are shown in surrounding niches. This room returns the visitor to the primary axis, the axis of entry from the street, and the entry to a long barrel-vaulted room for systems display. Through the articulation of the ceiling, the room has been divided into five bays. This division already existed in the structure of the large vaulted beams and in the skylights which are actually clerestory lights in the walls at the top of the room. The rhythm of the five bays reinforces the repetitive nature of the component furniture systems displayed in the room.

Entrance hall

"Hinge" room

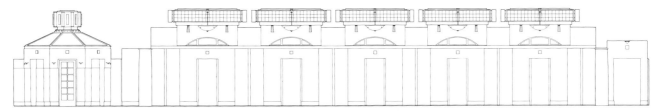

Section through office systems display

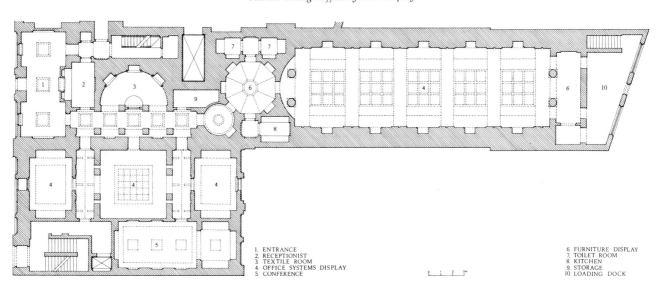

1. ENTRANCE
2. RECEPTIONIST
3. TEXTILE ROOM
4. OFFICE SYSTEMS DISPLAY
5. CONFERENCE

6. FURNITURE DISPLAY
7. TOILET ROOM
8. KITCHEN
9. STORAGE
10. LOADING DOCK

Plan

Office systems display

Furniture display

Office furniture display

Textile display

Conference room

Passage to textile display

1985

TEAKETTLE

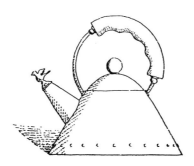

Teakettle

Sugar bowl and cream pitcher

The teakettle, manufactured by Alessi, was designed to have the character of a traditional kitchen object. It is neither overly sophisticated, nor does it play on prosaic or utilitarian kettle shapes. Its playful character is established by simple massing and decoration. The handle, knob, and whistling bird provide color and decoration for the simple shape of the pot. The conical shape allows the kettle to have a broad base, giving the greatest surface for the flame which makes the pot more efficient.

AWARDS AND MEDALS

Literary Hall of Fame award

Commemorative medal, The Humana Building

Gold medal, 1987 Pan American Games

The New Jersey Literary Hall of Fame award is given on an annual basis to commemorate significant achievements in the field of literature. The award was named after Michael Graves. The design of the bronzed plaque superimposes a traditional loving cup and scribe on an open book mounted on a reader's pedestal.

The bronze medal designed by Graves to commemorate the opening of his Humana Building in Louisville, Kentucky, depicts the Main Street elevation of the building on one side and the south elevation on the other.

The medals designed for the Pan American Games held in Indianapolis, Indiana in 1987 depict the symbolic victory torch on one side and the Roman numeral ten on the other, signifying the tenth anniversary of the event. The medals were made in gold, silver, and bronze versions.

SOUTH FLORIDA BEACH HOUSES

The magazine *South Florida Home and Garden* asked Graves to imagine the character that a series of ocean front houses in southern Florida could have. These houses all have gardens at their base, the main living levels in the center of the composition, and roof terraces which command the distant views.

1984-1986

LANDSCAPES

Composite Landscape

Archaic Landscape

The "Archaic Landscape" and "Composite Landscape" paintings merge the separate ideas of archaic and modern buildings into a continuous landscape. In the cartoon for the Plocek Residence mural entitled "Archaic Landscape," simple geometric assemblages are placed on a somewhat anonymous open landscape. These individual figurative elements might be regarded as primary forms of an architecture which are typically incorporated within a larger, simpler architectural frame.

1986

ARDLEIGH CRESCENT TOWNHOUSES
HOPEWELL, NEW JERSEY

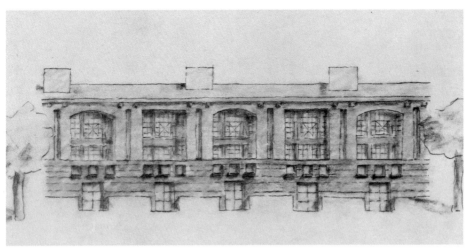

Elevation study

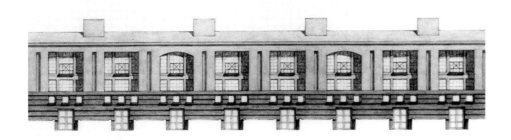

Elevation from the park

| First floor plan | Second floor plan | Third floor plan |

The master plan for Ardleigh Crescent includes fifty-two three-bedroom condominiums arranged in a long curved crescent oriented to the existing park-like setting of the site. Rather than divide the townhouses into smaller groupings scattered throughout the site in a pattern typical of many suburban developments, Graves chose to use the model of continuous terrace housing to provide unity to the composition. The crescent form also engages the landscape, enhancing and preserving its extraordinary natural characteristics.

Model view of the Crescent

Site plan

1986

SOUTH CAROLINA MARINE SCIENCE MUSEUM
CHARLESTON, SOUTH CAROLINA

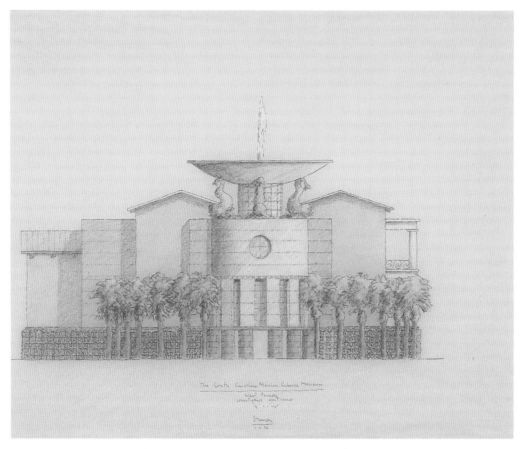

Museum, courtyard entrance elevation (west)

Graves participated in an invitational design competition for the South Carolina Marine Science Museum in Charleston. His scheme was not chosen for further development. The museum, a new institution, would have included an aquarium and exhibition halls within the main building, as well as separate buildings for a tour boat facility, restaurant, and lighthouse. In Graves' design, the visual corridor leading from the shore and the tour boat facility would have become the dominant element organizing the composition. This axis would have linked land and water, provided a garden for the museum, and unified the several different museum buildings around a common open space.

The traditional architecture of Charleston is derived from classical precedents which have been transformed into particular, local types. The design of the museum's entrance rotunda and river facade would have played on the familiar Charleston institutional version of the Greek temple. The narrow street front and south-facing piazza of this building with its attached two-story veranda would have taken its form from the city's dominant house type.

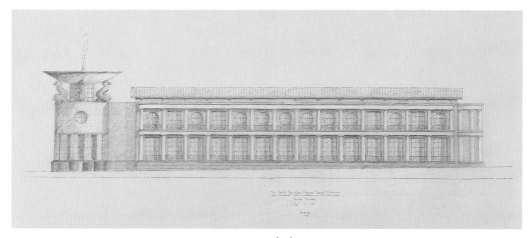

Museum, south elevation

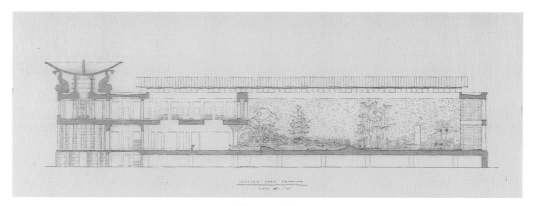

Museum section

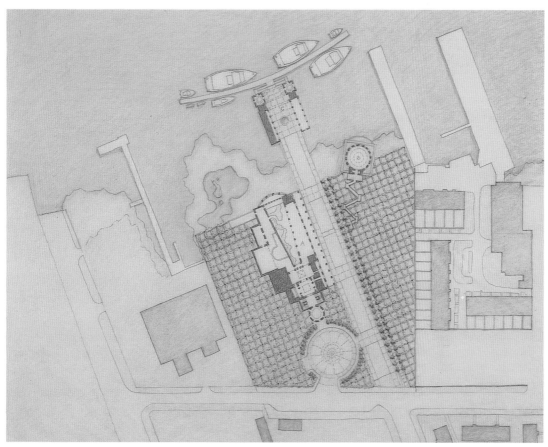

Site plan

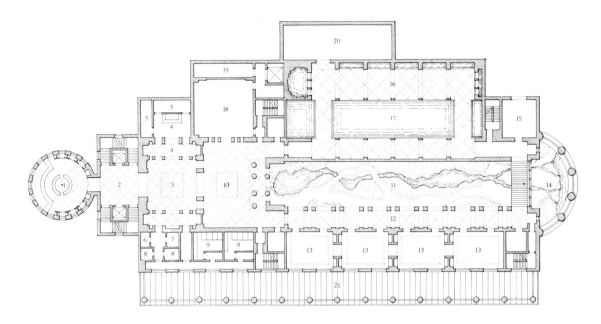

1   MUSEUM STORE
2   STAIR HALL/ENTRY
3   LOBBY
4   MUSEUM SHOP
5   SHOP STORAGE
6   COATROOM
7   STROLLER STORAGE
8   LOCKERS AND TELEPHONE
9   RESTROOMS
10 TICKETS, INFORMATION AND
    ORIENTATION

11 THE SOUTH CAROLINA HALL, EXHIBITION
12 EXHIBITION
13 EXHIBITION, PUBLIC LABORATORY DISPLAYS
14 AVIARY
15 MARSHLANDS EXHIBIT
16 MARINE EXHIBIT
17 OCEAN TANK
18 TEMPORARY EXHIBITION
19 EXHIBITION WORKSHOP
20 MECHANICAL AND EXHIBITION SUPPORT
21 VERANDA

First floor plan

Model view from the west

212

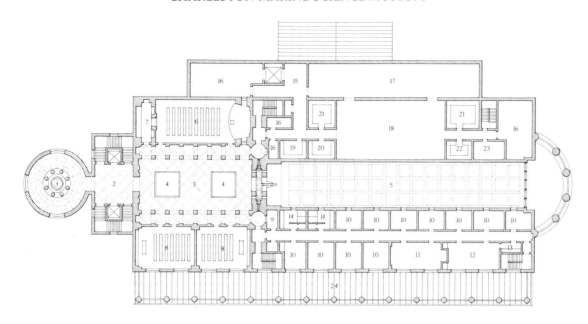

1 ROTUNDA/EXHIBITION
  "WORLD AND THE SEAS"
2 STAIRHALL
3 GALLERY
4 OPEN TO LOBBY BELOW
5 OPEN TO EXHIBITION HALL BELOW
6 AUDITORIUM
7 PROJECTION ROOM
8 CLASSROOM
9 ADMINISTRATIVE OFFICES RECEPTION
10 ADMISTRATIVE OFFICES
11 CONFERENCE ROOM
12 LOUNGE

13 STAFF KITCHEN
14 STAFF RESTROOMS
15 RECEIVING AREA
16 STORAGE
17 HOLDING ROOM/EQUIPMENT
18 ANIMAL HOLDING ROOM/WORKSHOP
19 FREEZER ROOM
20 ANIMAL KITCHEN
21 LABORATORY
22 DIVE LOCKERS
23 STAFF RESTROOM
24 VERANDA

Second floor plan

Model view from the east

Museum entrance study

Museum entrance study

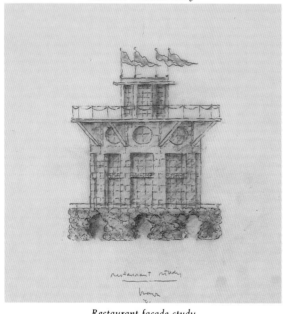

Restaurant facade study

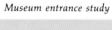

Museum entrance study

Museum, Cooper River elevation

Lighthouse study

Section through tour boat facility

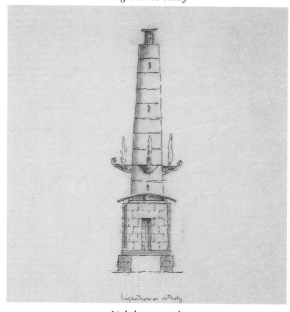

Lighthouse study

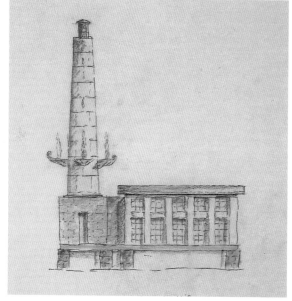

Tour boat facility study

Tour boat facility study

DISNEY OFFICE BUILDING
BURBANK, CALIFORNIA

Model view of the entrance facade

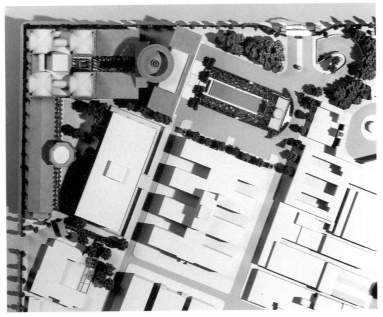

Model, overhead view

This new development reorganizes one quadrant of Disney's studio lot in Burbank, California. The program includes a 350,000 square foot office building, a 1000-car subterranean parking garage, a large pedestrian plaza with a reflecting pool, and a new entrance gate and guard house. The overall organization of the project is consistent with the existing corporate campus plan and the architectural character of the studio lot.

The new office building, divided into several major sections of 4-6 stories, wraps around the corner of Alameda Avenue and Buena Vista Street. A "tower" capped with four intersecting barrel vaults marks the corner of the intersection. The main entrance facade of the building is oriented to the pedestrian plaza. Statues representing Disney's Seven Dwarfs support the pediment of this portion of the building.

Preliminary elevation studies

Entrance elevation

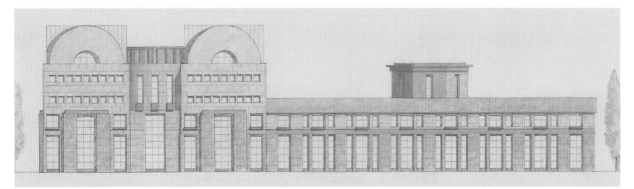

Buena Vista Street elevation

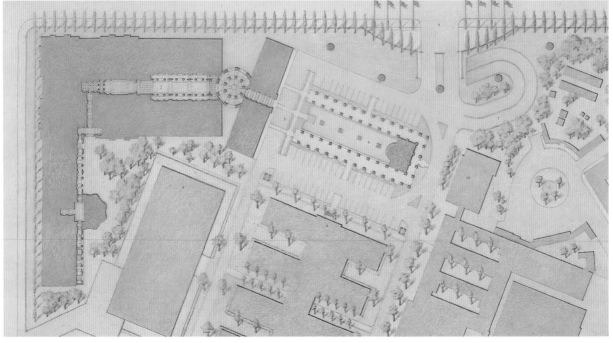

Site plan

Model view from Buena Vista Street

Model view from the east

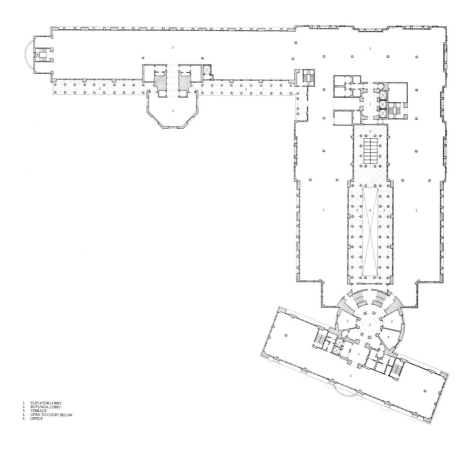

1. ELEVATOR LOBBY
2. ROTUNDA LOBBY
3. TERRACE
4. OPEN TO COURT BELOW
5. OFFICE

Typical floor plan

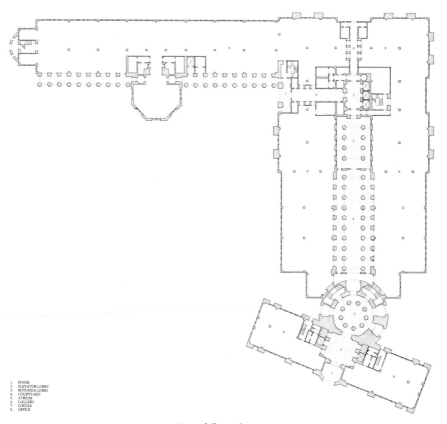

1. FOYER
2. ELEVATOR LOBBY
3. ROTUNDA LOBBY
4. COURTYARD
5. ATRIUM
6. GALLERY
7. LOGGIA
8. OFFICE

Ground floor plan

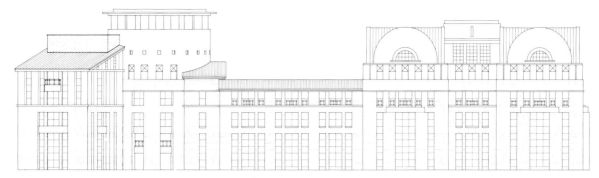

Alameda Avenue elevation

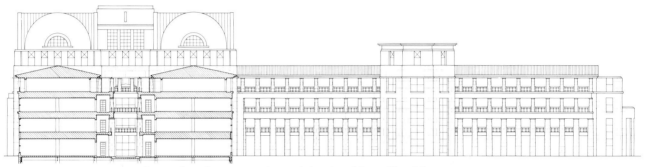

Section through corporate wings and elevation of Buena Vista Wing

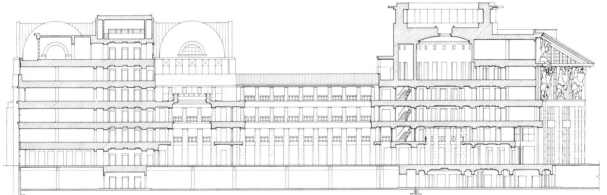

Section through entrance and courtyard

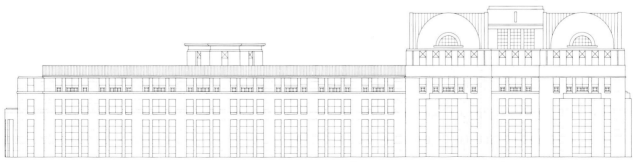

Buena Vista Street elevation

CHRISTOPHER'S WREN HOUSE

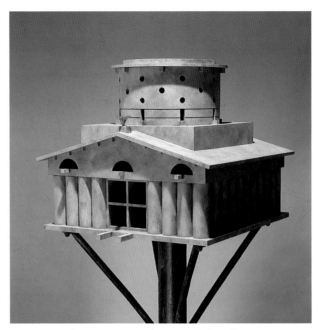

The Kay Barnett and George Clark Birdhouse

Parrish Art Museum birdhouse

The Parrish Art Museum in Southampton, Long Island, commissioned numerous architects to design birdhouses for an exhibition and benefit auction. Graves' birdhouse is called Christopher's Wren House. In addition to being a play on words, the project refers to a continual interest in traditional elements of architecture from Wren's time to the present day. The design makes no direct formal reference to Wren, but was inspired by his Sheldonian Theater at Oxford, Hampton Court, and St. Anne Soho, as well as by the potent form of the voided rondels of St. Paul's Cathedral in London. The bronze patina of the surface gives this little building a sense of weathered durability found in many garden artifacts.

VARIATION ON A THEME OF JUAN GRIS

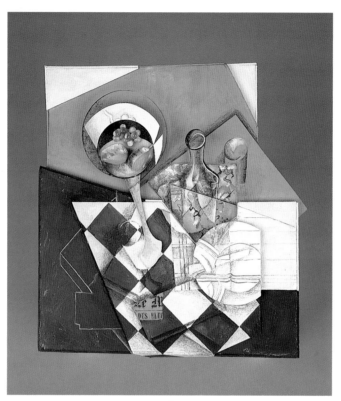

Collage

Installation

Detail of table top

To explore innovative uses for its collection of crystal, Steuben commissioned several architects and interior designers to design installations for an exhibition called "Separate Tables." Graves' design, "Variation on a Theme of Juan Gris," takes a Gris painting entitled "Still Life with Fruit Bowl and Carafe" and turns it into a three-dimensional table top incorporating a bowl, carafe, and glass pears from Steuben's crystal collection.

1987

COFFEEMAKER
SALT AND PEPPER MILL

Press filter coffee maker

Salt or pepper mill

The press filter coffee maker designed for Alessi has a glass container set into a stainless steel open mesh "basket".

The pepper mill designed for Alessi is made of stainless steel with a plastic crank handle. It can also be used for grinding salt.

1987

VASE
CHAMPAGNE COOLER

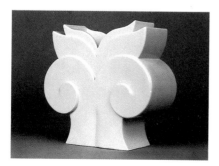

Vase prototype

Champagne cooler

The ceramic vase, suggesting floral forms, is manufactured by Swid Powell.

The champagne cooler was designed as part of a special collection of objects currently manufactured by WMF in West Germany. It is made of sterling silver with mock ivory handles. Graves also designed an accompanying floor stand.

ARCHAIC VESSELS

The Archaic Vessels, manufactured by Steuben as limited editions, were inspired by ancient Etruscan artifacts whose shapes have long been a part of Graves' lexicon. They are made of lead crystal and cradled in bronze bases.

THE BIG DRIPPER

The ceramic drip coffeemaker called The Big Dripper and its companion pieces, The Little Dripper and the matching sugar bowl and cream pitcher, were designed for Swid Powell. In its shape and decoration, the design expresses the spirit of a vessel. The cruciform base, colored dark red in reference to the heat of the stove, cradles the spherical shape of the pot itself. The green wave-like pattern wrapping the pot recalls the liquid contained within.

DINNERWARE

"Corinth" dinnerware

"Delos" dinnerware

These dinnerware sets, called "Delos" and "Corinth," were designed for Swid Powell. Both use an abstracted floral pattern on the colored band at the outer edge. The heavier edge decoration contrasts with the delicacy of the star motifs used in the center of the plates and bowls.

1986

MANTEL CLOCK

The mantel clock designed for Alessi is made of stained birds eye maple with ebonized wood columns, an enameled clock face and hands, and a gold-plated pendulum.

1987

WRISTWATCH AND JEWELRY

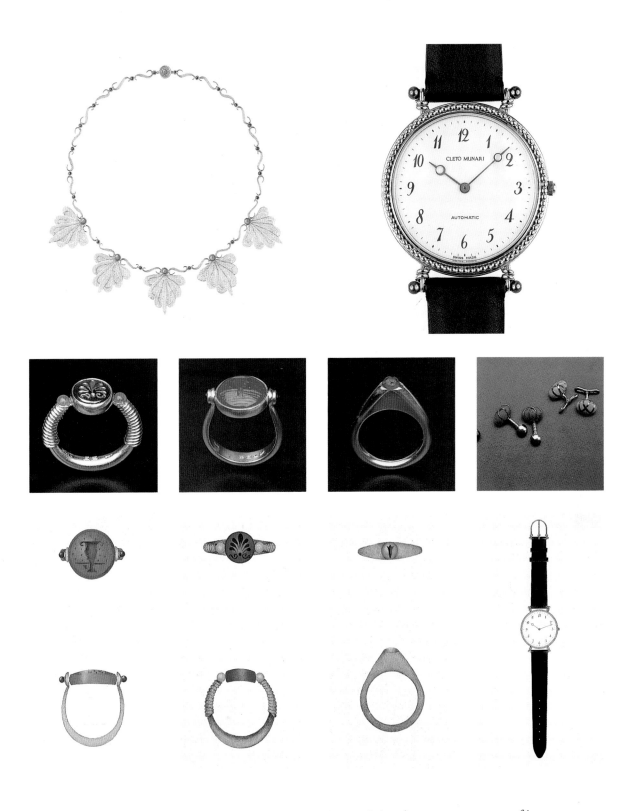

The Italian entrepreneur and collector, Cleto Munari, commissioned two separate groups of internationally known architects to design collections of wristwatches and jewelry. Graves' collection of jewelry, all handcrafted in 18K gold, includes cufflinks and tuxedo studs set with turquoise, lapis, and onyx; three rings inset with semi-precious stones; and a necklace. The wristwatch is handcrafted in Switzerland of 18K antique gold, with crowned sapphire glass, green agate balls, and a black calf-skin band.

POSTERS

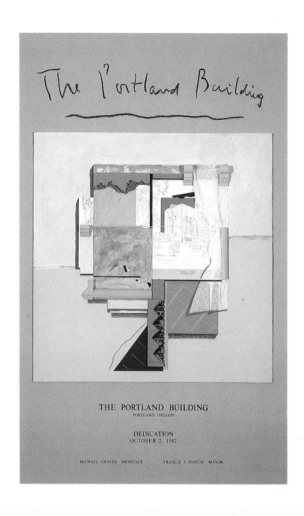

MICHAEL GRAVES
EDWARD SCHMIDT

The posters illustrated here are selected examples of graphic designs produced over several years. Each poster was commissioned to commemorate a particular event or exhibition.

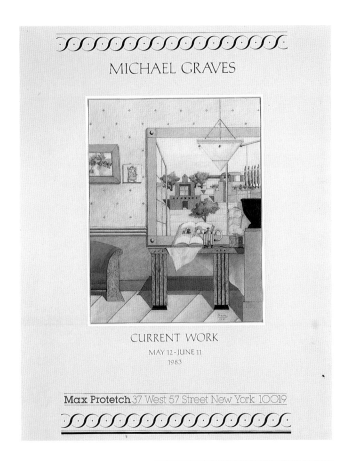

MICHAEL GRAVES

CURRENT WORK

MAY 12 - JUNE 11
1983

Max Protetch 37 West 57 Street New York 10019

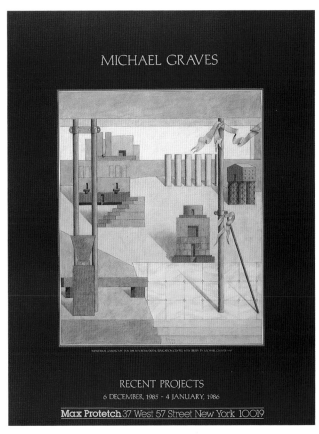

MICHAEL GRAVES

RECENT PROJECTS

6 DECEMBER, 1985 – 4 JANUARY, 1986

Max Protetch 37 West 57 Street New York 10019

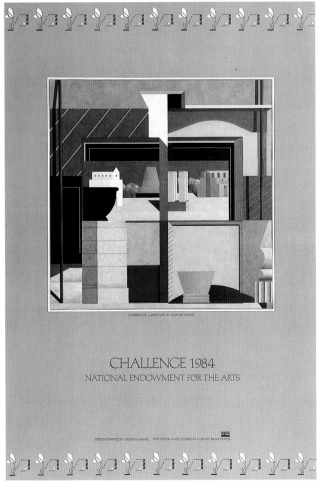

CHALLENGE 1984

NATIONAL ENDOWMENT FOR THE ARTS

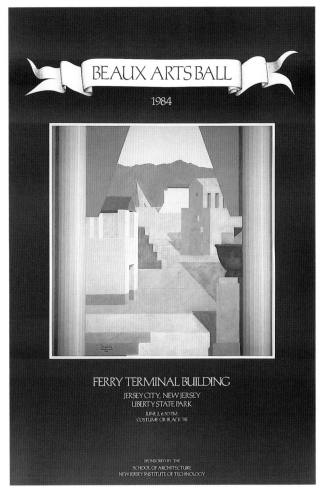

BEAUX ARTS BALL

1984

FERRY TERMINAL BUILDING

JERSEY CITY, NEW JERSEY
LIBERTY STATE PARK

JUNE 2, 6:30 P.M.
COSTUME OR BLACK TIE

SPONSORED BY THE
SCHOOL OF ARCHITECTURE
NEW JERSEY INSTITUTE OF TECHNOLOGY

1983-1986

LANDSCAPES

Tuscan Landscape

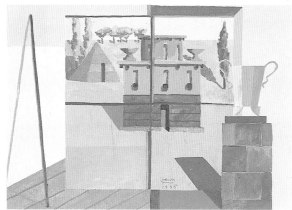

Window Landscape

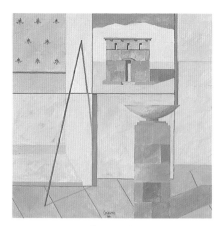

Window Landscape

The paintings illustrated here represent several different attitudes toward landscape compositions. The "Tuscan Landscapes" are remembered views of typical Tuscan buildings which attempt to capture the character of the local landscape and the architecture. The "Archaic Landscapes" place individual figurative elements within an open, anonymous field; these simple objects or buildings are seen as archetypal elements which are typically included within larger architectural compositions. The "Window Landscapes" establish the wall as an architectural datum which provides a setting for domestic objects in the foreground and frames views to the landscape beyond.

Tuscan Landscape

Archaic Landscape

Archaic Landscape

WHITNEY MUSEUM OF AMERICAN ART
NEW YORK, NEW YORK

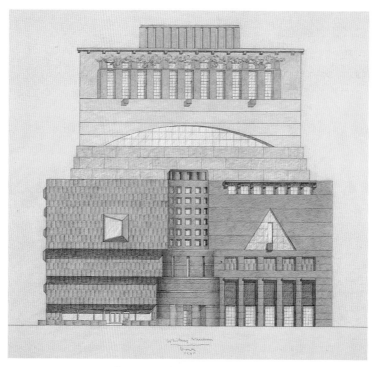

Scheme 1, Madison Avenue elevation

The Whitney Museum of American Art, located at the corner of Madison Avenue and East 75th Street, occupies a building designed by Marcel Breuer. The museum plans to expand its building south along Madison Avenue to East 74th Street. The site falls within the Upper East Side Historic District and the Special Madison Avenue Preservation District. Therefore, the building is subject to special zoning requirements and design guidelines. The two schemes illustrated here are distinguished by a change in building size, in accordance with a revised program, as well as a change in composition. Neither scheme will be realized. A third scheme, designed in 1988, is illustrated later in this volume.

Stylistically, the Breuer building is a modern monument, finished in dark gray unpolished granite, in distinct contrast to its context of smaller-scale and more elaborate facades. The particular design challenge of this project was to reconcile the apparent contradictions of the modern aesthetic with more figurative, traditional architecture. The addition needed to respond to the disparate natures of the existing building and its surrounding neighborhood. The program also required the old and new sections to be read as one museum, calling for a scheme which bound together the two halves of the building both in plan and in elevation. The first two designs would have unified the existing building and the addition by means of a central vertical cylinder, or "hinge", between them and an upper level connecting structure.

The program for the addition included: 31,600 square feet of new exhibition space for the permanent collection; a 250-seat theater for the museum's public education programs; an orientation gallery; a works on paper study center and an expanded library to make the museum's resources more available to scholars; and additional space for offices and operations. As required by zoning guidelines, the expanded museum must include commercial retail space on the ground floor along Madison Avenue. The theater would have been located at the lower levels of the addition. Exhibition space would have begun at the second floor level and continued through the sixth floor. Office space would have occupied the top two floors, and mechanical equipment would have been located in a penthouse on the roof.

For the major planes of the exterior walls, Graves chose a gray red agate granite whose tonality and veining are similar to the gray granite of the existing building. Stone of this color would have harmonized with Breuer's material and yet remain distinct, so as not to diminish either the proportions or the "object quality" of the existing building. The new color would have also harmonized with the brownstone and brick colorations of other buildings in the neighborhood. The same gray red agate would have been used throughout the facade in different cuts and finishes, allowing distinctions to be made among different elements of the composition.

Scheme 1, model looking north along Madison Avenue

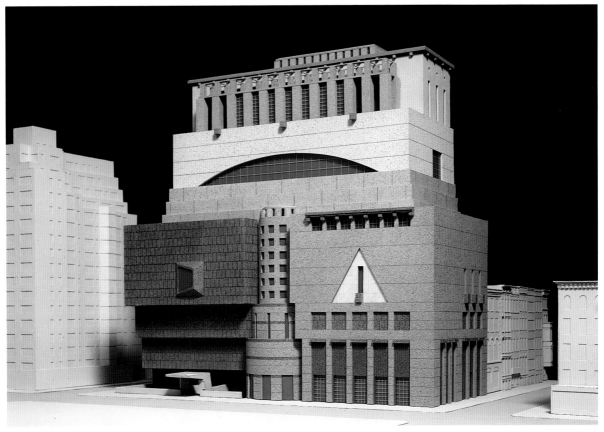

Scheme 1, model view, Madison Avenue

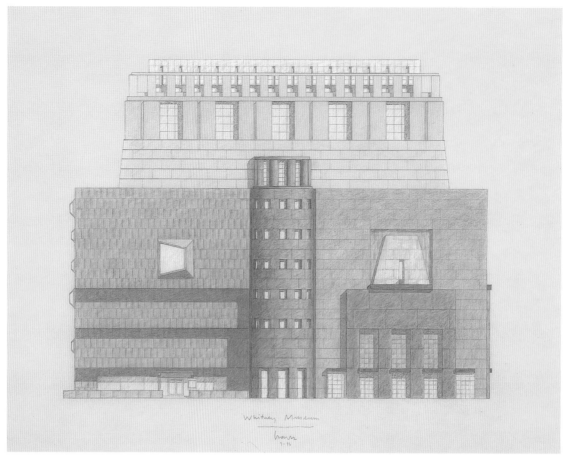

Scheme 2, Madison Avenue elevation

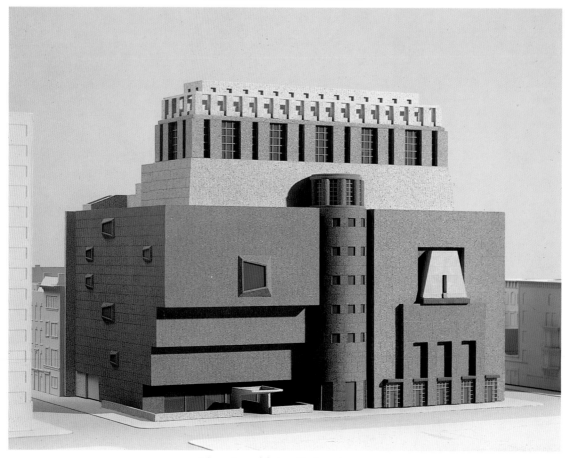

Scheme 2, model view, Madison Avenue

Scheme 2, photo collage looking south along Madison Avenue

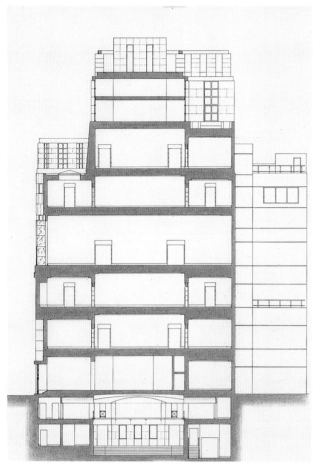

Scheme 2, east–west section

Scheme 2, East 74th Street elevation

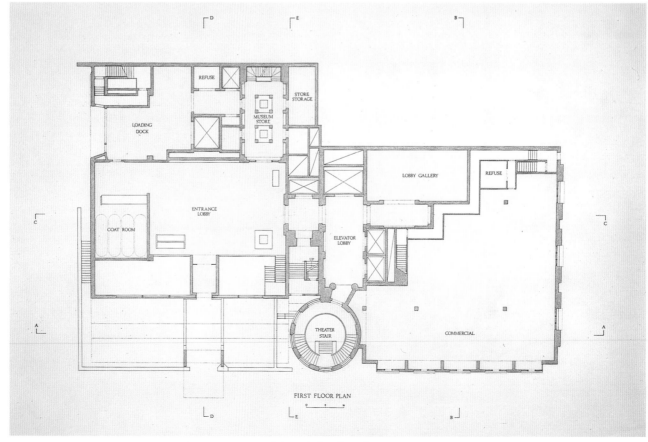

Scheme 2, first floor plan

Scheme 2, photo collage looking north along Madison Avenue

1987

ARTS AND SCIENCES BUILDING
UNIVERSITY OF VIRGINIA
CHARLOTTESVILLE, VIRGINIA

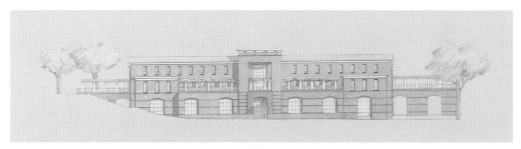

South elevation

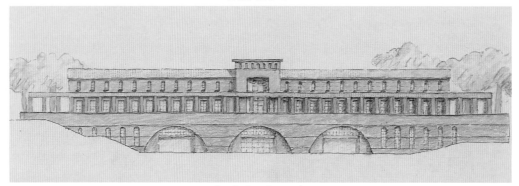

South elevation study

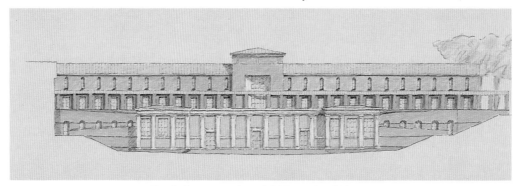

North elevation study with McIntire Amphitheater

A new 40,400 square foot classroom and office building is planned for the College of Arts and Sciences at the University of Virginia. The site is located in the South Central Grounds near the historical structures of the original "academical village" designed by Thomas Jefferson and adjacent to Fiske Kimball's McIntire Amphitheater and Stanford White's Cabell Hall. The design of the building assumes the materials, scale, and type of fenestration of the buildings within the immediate context without trying to replicate them directly. As required by the University, the building would be constructed of the same hand-formed red brick and white trim that characterize the academic and somewhat domestic scale of the Lawn and Range buildings.

The site itself is relatively flat but the topography rises sharply to the west to a terraced landform in front of Maury Hall and abuts the sheer wall supporting Cabell Hall terrace on the east. In order to improve pedestrian circulation in this section of the campus and to connect the new building to neighboring academic facilities, the project includes an elevated pedestrian walkway or bridge at the third level of the building. The bridge is designed as a relatively porous, covered peristyle or colonnade which, without imitating the buildings on the Lawn, has a similar sense of rhythm and repetition. The bridge also acts as a backdrop to the amphitheater stage building, providing a sense of enclosure to the space.

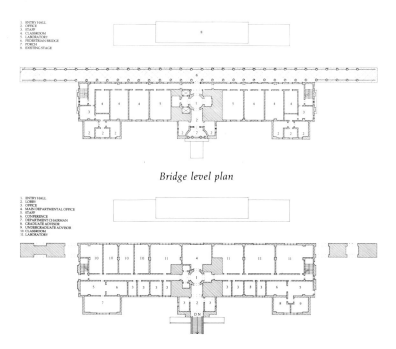

Bridge level plan

Classroom level plan

East–west section

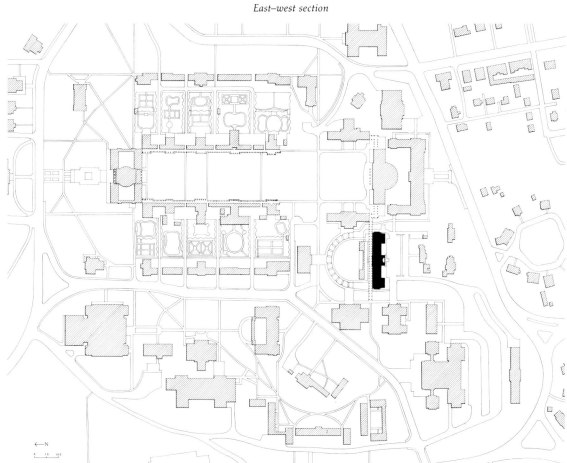

Site plan

CARNEGIE CENTER COMPETITION
PRINCETON, NEW JERSEY

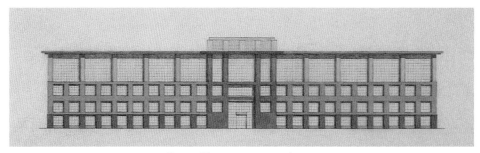

Office Building B, Greenway elevation

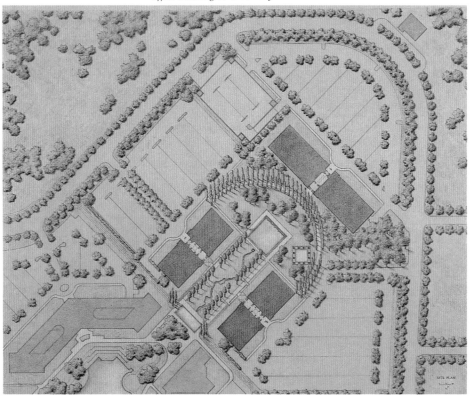

Site plan

This project was designed as an entry in a competition for three 200,000 square foot speculative office buildings which were to be built as a new phase within a larger existing development along Route One in Princeton, New Jersey. The master plan for Carnegie Center called for the continuation of a tree-lined perimeter road system, giving access to both pedestrian building entrances and associated parking structures. The developer suspended the project after the competition.

Graves organized the site as a hierarchical series of garden spaces, with the more rigorous and regular road system and building configurations providing a larger order within which more picturesque "English-type" garden elements would be located. The central garden axis, called the Greenway, would be occupied by a fountain from which a picturesque stream would flow downhill into an existing lake. The Greenway would be terminated by a large crescent of trees framing a small cafe pavilion with the character of an *orangerie*. Rather than being associated with a single building, the freestanding cafe would relate to the larger composition, allowing its visitors to occupy the landscape.

The facades of the three buildings were composed with a dark red granite base supporting two floors of repetitive offices and an ochre-toned "attic" story which would read as an open loggia. The hierarchy evident in the building's exterior would have been reflected in the spatial plan, as the pedestrian passed through the formally demarcated sequence of the parking area, to the double-height vestibule, to the elevator core, and finally through the building to the Greenway beyond.

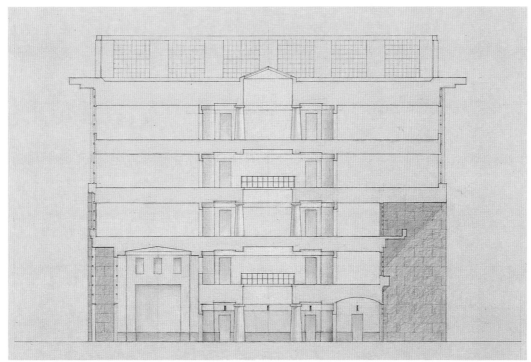

Office Building A section through lobby

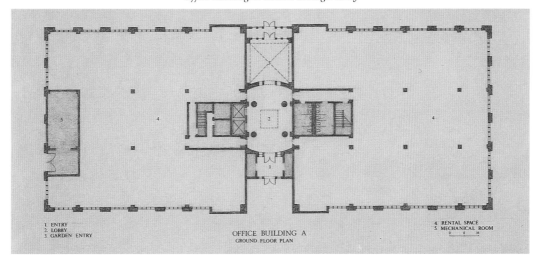

1. ENTRY
2. LOBBY
3. GARDEN ENTRY

OFFICE BUILDING A
GROUND FLOOR PLAN

4. RENTAL SPACE
5. MECHANICAL ROOM

Office Building A ground floor plan

Model view from the south

243

SANDERS DINING ROOM
PRINCETON, NEW JERSEY

Dining room

The renovation of the dining room of an existing house, located in Princeton, provides an architectural setting for furniture and artifacts designed by Graves specifically for the Sanders family. Included are a dining table of birds eye maple inlaid with ebony palmetto leaves, a matching buffet table, and upholstered dining chairs. Pendant light fixtures and wall sconces are made of onyx and bronze with a patina finish. Carpeting, table linens, dinnerware, and other artifacts were also designed for the dining room.

Wall sconce

Table top detail

Buffet table

Dining table and fireplace

Dining room

1987

BRISBANE CIVIC AND COMMUNITY CENTER
BRISBANE, CALIFORNIA

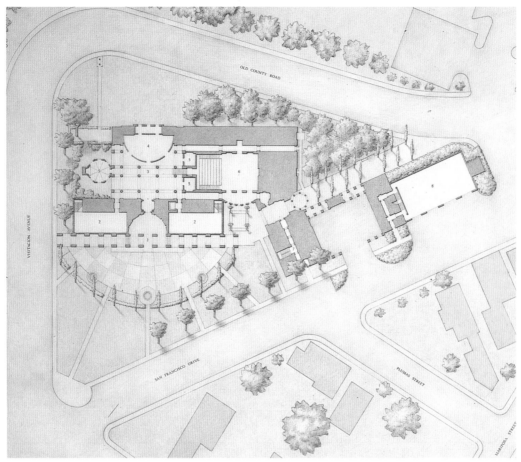

Site plan

The 32,000 square foot program for the Brisbane Civic and Community Center, never realized, would have included offices for city administration and public safety departments, City Council chambers, a community recreation center, and a free-standing firehouse. Graves prepared three preliminary schemes for local community review and comment. The schemes were intended to demonstrate different strategies for organizing the site, the buildings, and associated outdoor spaces and public entries. In all three schemes, the fire station was located at the apex of the triangular site because of the existing street pattern.

The direction of scheme A was chosen by the community for further development. Scheme A would have organized the major program components as separate wings of a single building oriented to two public pedestrian plazas. The program components would have been given their own identities through the massing of the building. Scheme B would have placed the three major program components in separate buildings within a larger open plaza, defining the edge of the plaza along San Francisco Drive by a long pedestrian arcade or pergola. In scheme C, two major program components would have been organized in one building around a central outdoor courtyard. The freestanding Recreation Center would have formed the fourth side of the courtyard, oriented to a long outdoor public space lined with trees.

In the composition of the final scheme Graves prepared before the city suspended the project, the Civic and Community Center would have been perceived as a collection of small-scale buildings or objects linked only in plan, but seen in the round. Each structure would have been given its own identity, with emphasis on the primary symbolic elements such as the main entry, the Council Chambers, and the Recreation Center. The small scale of the Center, compatible with the scale of this northern California community, would have conveyed the sense of an accessible and inviting government. The low-pitched roofs of the buildings would have been identified with the landscape of the San Bruno Mountains beyond.

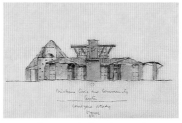

Courtyard elevation study

Old County Road elevation study

East elevation study

San Francisco Drive elevation study

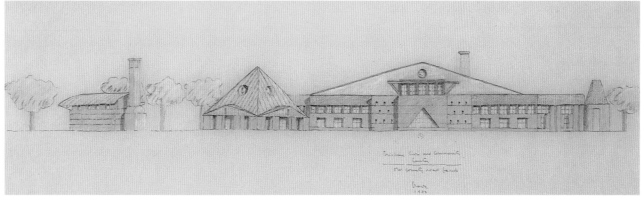

Old County Road elevation study

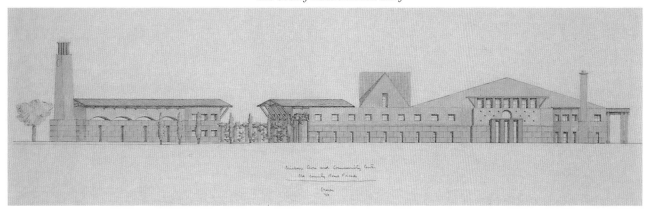

Old County Road elevation

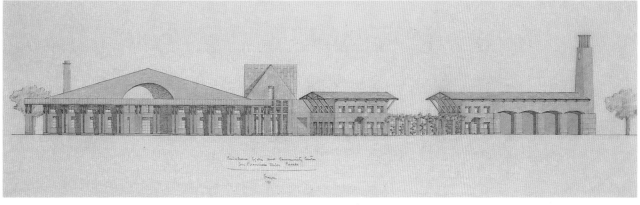

San Francisco Drive elevation

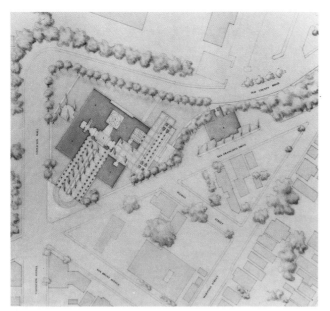

Scheme A site plan

Scheme A model view from the south

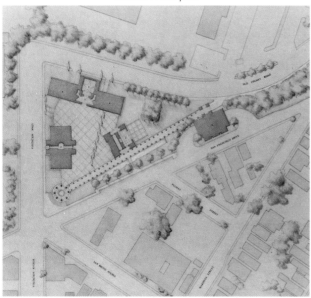

Scheme B site plan

Scheme B model view from the southwest

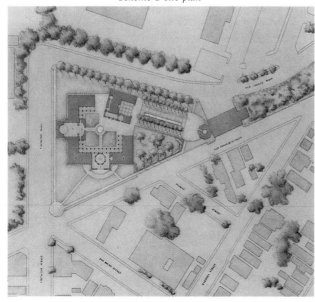

Scheme C site plan

Scheme C model view from the east

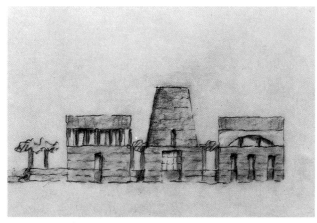

Scheme A Civic Center north elevation study

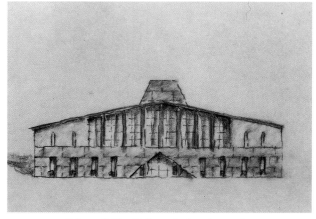

Scheme B City Hall north elevation study

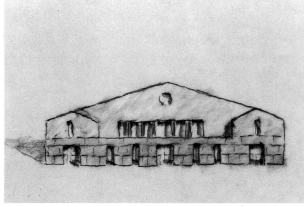

Scheme B City Hall south elevation study

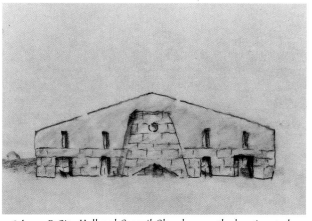

Scheme B City Hall and Council Chambers north elevation study

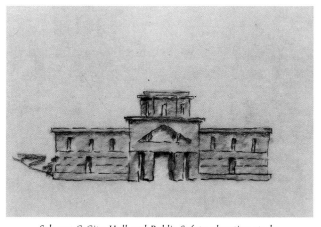

Scheme C City Hall and Public Safety elevation study

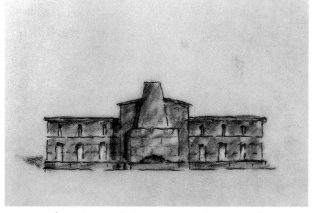

Scheme C Council Chambers street elevation study

Schemes A and B Firehouse elevation study

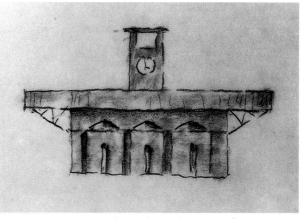

Schemes A and B Firehouse elevation study

HENRY RESIDENCE
RHINECLIFF, NEW YORK

West elevation study

South elevation study

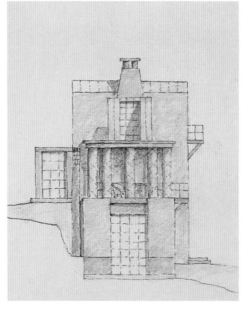

North elevation study

This small weekend house will be sited on a heavily-wooded, sloping property, facing the Hudson River. The entry will be on the main living level, which includes a large eat-in kitchen, living room, and outdoor porch. The master bedroom and bath will be located on the upper level. Bedrooms for children and guests, and a future painting studio, will be located on the lower level.

Although the primary plan arrangement of the house is compact, the several secondary building elements such as porches, stairs, and chimneys extend the main volume of the house in a picturesque manner. This strategy is characteristic of eclectic rural vacation houses in the region without being overly rustic, and suggests ways in which to add to the building in the future.

West elevation study

Model view from the southwest

Model view from the south

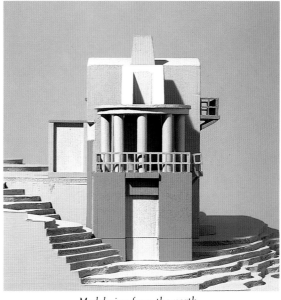

Model view from the north

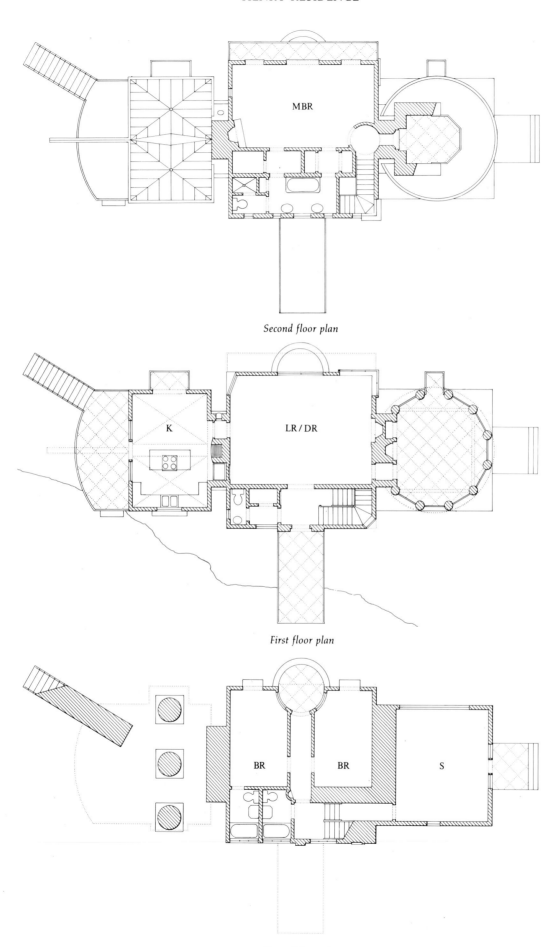

Second floor plan

First floor plan

Ground floor plan

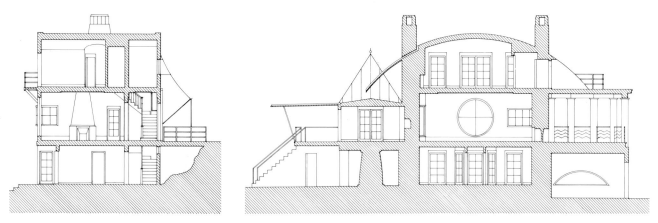

East-west section   *North-south section*

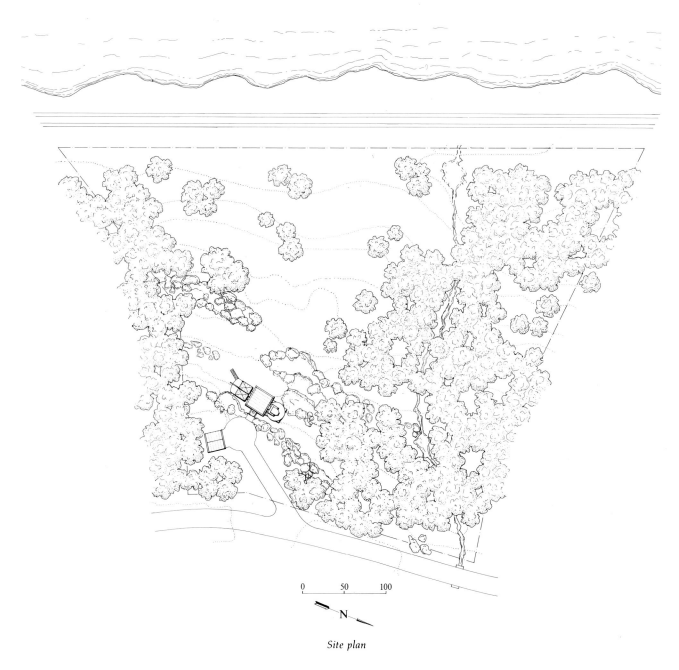

Site plan

CARPET DESIGNS

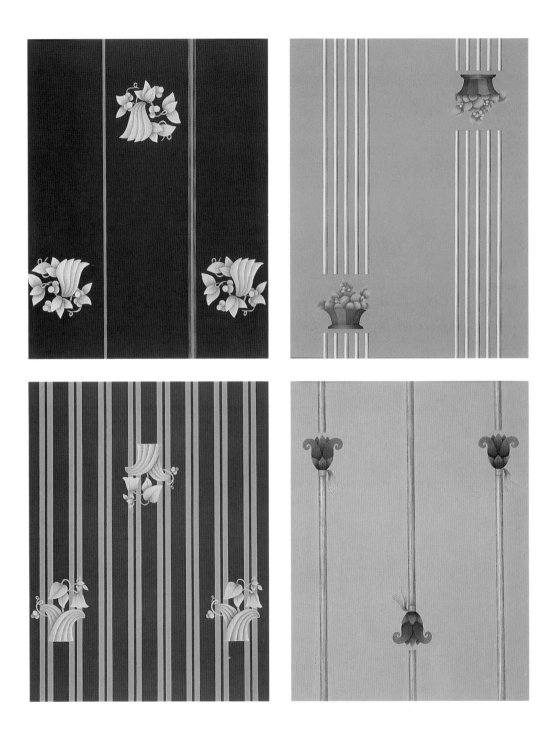

Vorwerk, a West German carpet manufacturer, commissioned a group of artists, designers, and architects to develop colors and patterns for carpets. Graves' designs incorporate floral motifs as lyrical elements within a geometric, striped field.

FLOOR TILE DESIGNS

The Tajima carpet tiles and vinyl floor tiles were designed in numerous solid colors and in floral and geometric patterns. The colors and patterns are complementary and allow a variety of commercial and domestic installations. For example, individual patterned tiles can be used as accents within a solid colored field; various colors and patterns can be combined in diagonal or orthogonal grids to create a larger floor pattern.

1987

SAMUEL C. MILLER CUP

This sterling silver chalice or loving cup was commissioned by The Newark Museum for its permanent collection in honor of the twentieth anniversary of Samuel C. Miller's directorship. It was hand-crafted by Tiffany's silversmith studio in New Jersey.

FLATWARE DESIGNS

The flatware was designed as a five-piece place setting with serving utensils. It is made of stainless steel with handles of a variety of colors.

CALIFORNIA LIFEGUARD TOWER

The lifeguard tower was designed for an exhibition at the Kirsten Kiser Gallery in Los Angeles. Though regarded as a folly, the design adheres to actual regulations of size, height, and durability. The brightly colored striped "tent" made of fiberglass, the flags, and the wave-like railings are seen as elements familiar to the local beach scene.

1987

LJ HOOKER OFFICE BUILDING
GATEWAY CENTER MASTER PLAN
ATLANTA, GEORGIA

Construction photo, view from the south

A 20-story, 300,000 square foot office tower was built to house the worldwide corporate headquarters of LJ Hooker, a real estate development firm. The tower was planned as the first phase of a larger mixed use development called Gateway Center, which was not built. The site for the office building is adjacent to an existing nine-story hotel and a rapid transit station connecting midtown Atlanta with the city's larger metropolitan region. The building includes underground parking, ground level retail and public space, 17 floors of office space, and space for a future restaurant on the top floor.

The main facade of the building faces south, aligned with a major axis through the center of Atlanta. The primary entrance to the building occurs on this facade, through a semi-enclosed loggia. A second entrance, primarily used for retail functions, is located along West Peachtree Street. The building can also be entered from a pedestrian plaza developed on the roof of the rapid transit station, allowing access to the mall level of the proposed development to the north.

The master plan for Gateway Center included office towers and parking to the south, as well as a mixed use development of approximately 6 million square feet to the north. This large block would have included three levels of underground parking, a three-level shopping mall with entertainment and food centers, additional elevated parking, and four office towers and a convention hotel to be built above the mall and parking levels. The character studies showing the general massing and configuration of the facades were preliminary attempts to establish variety and distinction among the different components of the project, while maintaining the sense of a unified ensemble.

Preliminary south elevations

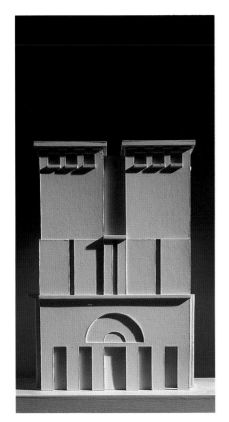
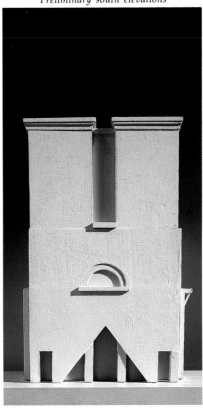
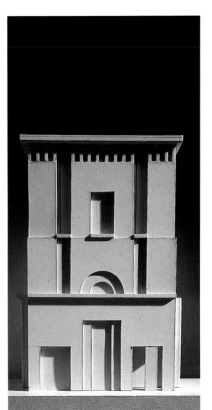

Study models, view from the south

LJ HOOKER OFFICE BUILDING

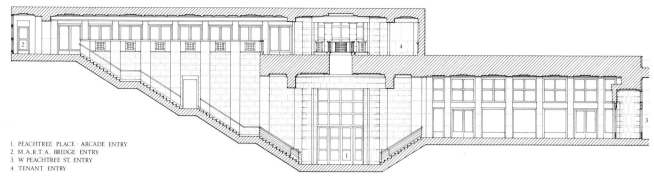

1. PEACHTREE PLACE · ARCADE ENTRY
2. M.A.R.T.A. BRIDGE ENTRY
3. W PEACHTREE ST. ENTRY
4. TENANT ENTRY

East-west base section

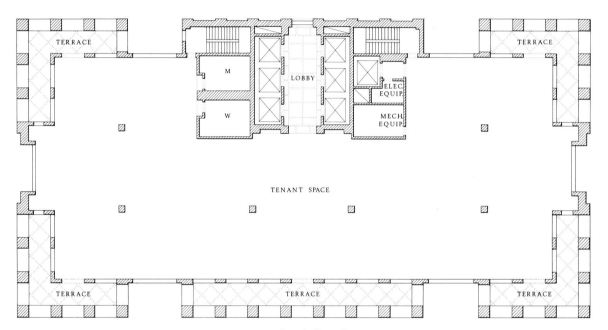

13th-16th floor plan

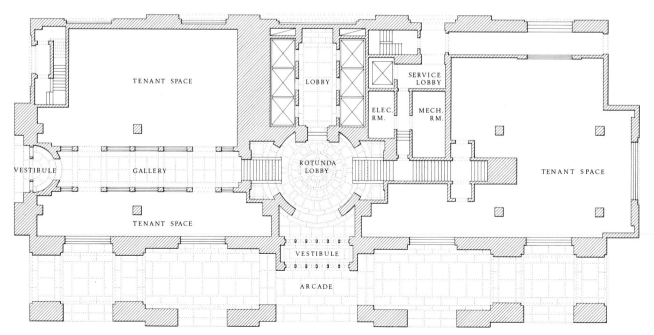

Second floor plan

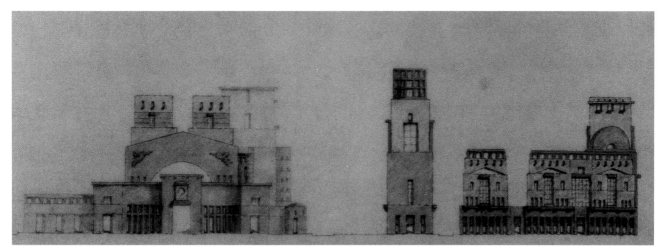

Gateway West Peachtree elevation study

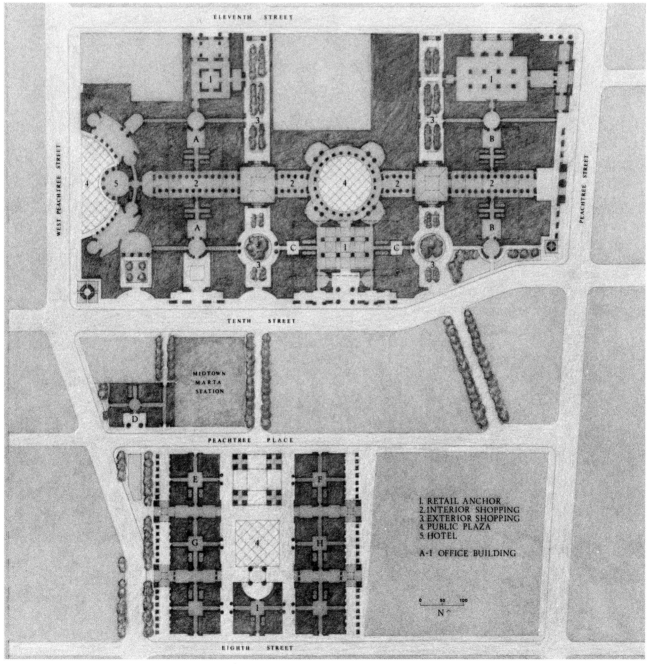

1. RETAIL ANCHOR
2. INTERIOR SHOPPING
3. EXTERIOR SHOPPING
4. PUBLIC PLAZA
5. HOTEL

A-I OFFICE BUILDING

Gateway master plan site plan

Gateway hotel elevation study

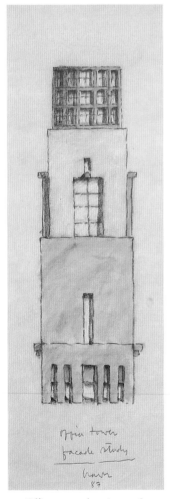

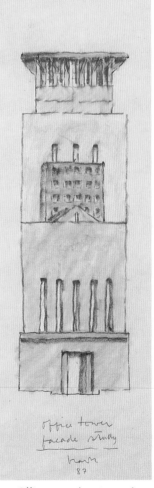

Office tower elevation study   *Gateway Tenth Street office building elevation study*   *Office tower elevation study*

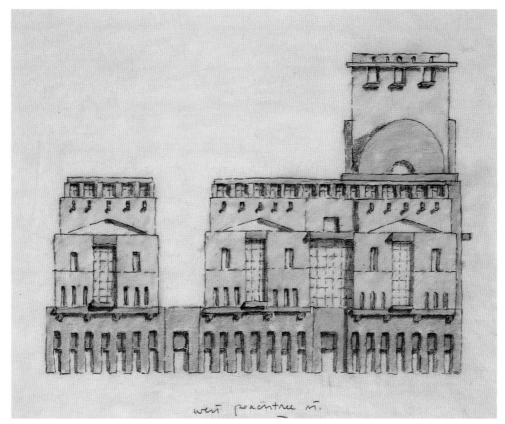

Gateway West Peachtree elevation study

Gateway Eighth Street elevation study

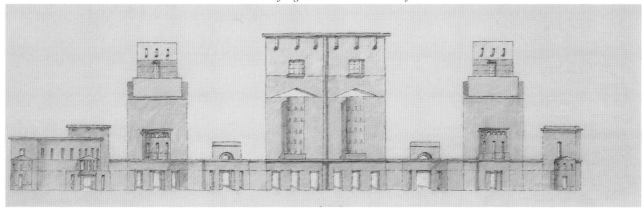

Gateway site elevation study from Tenth Street

THE SPORTING CLUB AT THE BELLEVUE
PHILADELPHIA, PENNSYLVANIA

Broad Street facade

The sporting club was built as a five-level addition on top of an existing seven-story parking garage serving the Bellevue Hotel on Broad Street in Philadelphia. The existing pedestrian entry to the garage is used as the ground level entrance to the club. The program included a swimming pool, basketball courts, squash and racquetball courts, locker rooms, sauna and steam rooms, a fitness center, exercise rooms and dance studios, a restaurant with bar, and administrative offices.

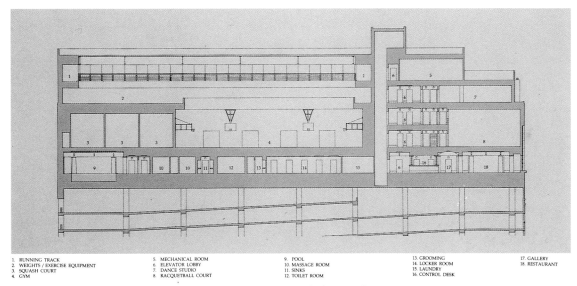

1. RUNNING TRACK	5. MECHANICAL ROOM	9. POOL	13. GROOMING	17. GALLERY
2. WEIGHTS / EXERCISE EQUIPMENT	6. ELEVATOR LOBBY	10. MASSAGE ROOM	14. LOCKER ROOM	18. RESTAURANT
3. SQUASH COURT	7. DANCE STUDIO	11. SINKS	15. LAUNDRY	
4. GYM	8. RACQUETBALL COURT	12. TOILET ROOM	16. CONTROL DESK	

Longitudinal section looking north

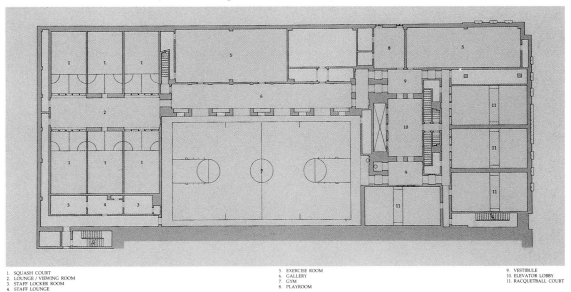

1. SQUASH COURT	5. EXERCISE ROOM	9. VESTIBULE	
2. LOUNGE / VIEWING ROOM	6. GALLERY	10. ELEVATOR LOBBY	
3. STAFF LOCKER ROOM	7. GYM	11. RACQUETBALL COURT	
4. STAFF LOUNGE	8. PLAYROOM		

Second floor plan

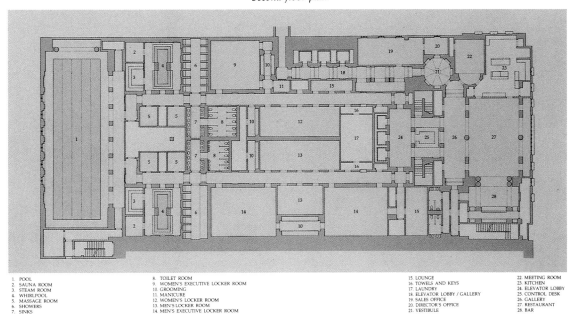

1. POOL	8. TOILET ROOM	15. LOUNGE	22. MEETING ROOM
2. SAUNA ROOM	9. WOMEN'S EXECUTIVE LOCKER ROOM	16. TOWELS AND KEYS	23. KITCHEN
3. STEAM ROOM	10. GROOMING	17. LAUNDRY	24. ELEVATOR LOBBY
4. WHIRLPOOL	11. MANICURE	18. ELEVATOR LOBBY / GALLERY	25. CONTROL DESK
5. MASSAGE ROOM	12. WOMEN'S LOCKER ROOM	19. SALES OFFICE	26. GALLERY
6. SHOWERS	13. MEN'S LOCKER ROOM	20. DIRECTOR'S OFFICE	27. RESTAURANT
7. SINKS	14. MEN'S EXECUTIVE LOCKER ROOM	21. VESTIBULE	28. BAR

First floor plan

1987

LUISENGARTEN RESTAURANT
WUPPERTAL, WEST GERMANY

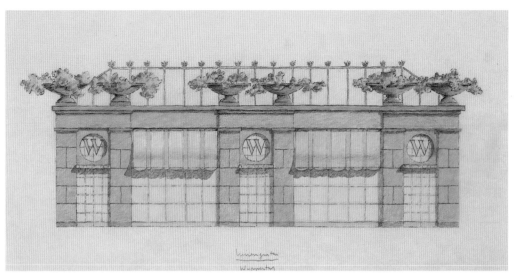

Beer garden street elevation

Model view from Luisenstrasse

As part of an international workshop sponsored by Wickuler Brewery, Graves was asked to redesign Wickuler's existing Luisengarten restaurant in Wuppertal, West Germany. The project included a complete interior renovation of the existing space and the addition of a new beer garden.

Graves' proposed interior provides for a variety of social patterns, ranging from the traditional one-on-one conversation over drinks to small groups of three or four people and larger gatherings. Tents would be used as interior decoration to impart a festive character to the restaurant and to provide a transition from the quiet, intimate dining rooms to the large beer garden open to the street.

The new beer garden would be seen as an *orangerie*, which would bring the maximum amount of light into the interior, while remaining consistent with the more traditional urban context of the street.

Fireplace elevation

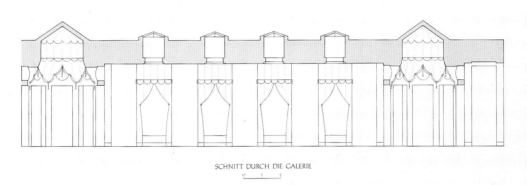

SCHNITT DURCH DIE GALERIE

Section through gallery

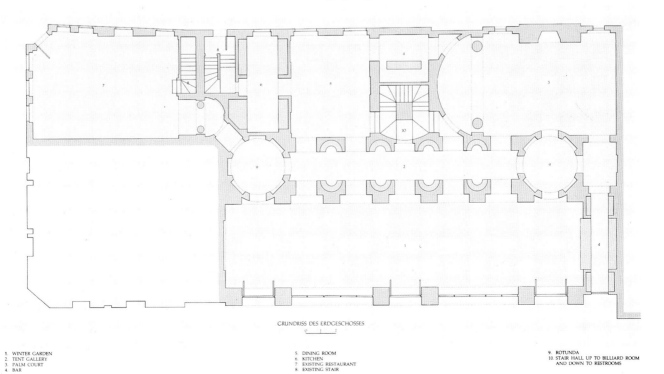

GRUNDRISS DES ERDGESCHOSSES

1. WINTER GARDEN
2. TENT GALLERY
3. PALM COURT
4. BAR

5. DINING ROOM
6. KITCHEN
7. EXISTING RESTAURANT
8. EXISTING STAIR

9. ROTUNDA
10. STAIR HALL UP TO BILLIARD ROOM AND DOWN TO RESTROOMS

Ground floor plan

BRAUKESSEL RESTAURANT
WUPPERTAL, WEST GERMANY

Model view from the pedestrian mall

The design for Wickuler Brewery's Braukessel Restaurant in Wuppertal, West Germany, involved an extensive interior renovation, the design of a new facade for the lower two stories of an existing building, and the addition of a stair tower and outdoor loggia. The loggia would allow restaurant activities to spill over into the ambience of the street. The corner stair tower, a light-filled octagonal structure crowned with a Wickuler flag, would announce the presence of the restaurant within the adjacent pedestrian mall.

Red sandstone adhered to the existing pale green stone of the facade would establish a new pattern at the base of the building, setting the lower level restaurant activities apart from the residential tower above.

The new interior for the restaurant was organized around a large two-story rotunda which would connect the two floors vertically.

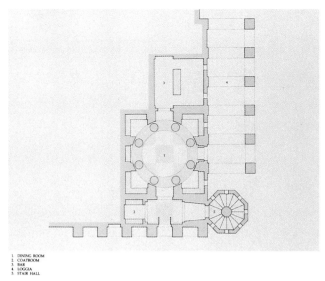

1. DINING ROOM
2. COATROOM
3. BAR
4. LOGGIA
5. STAIR HALL

Ground floor plan

3. BAR
5. STAIR HALL
6. DINING ROOM
7. GALLERY
8. KITCHEN

9. OPEN TO BELOW

First floor plan

Elevation from the pedestrian mall

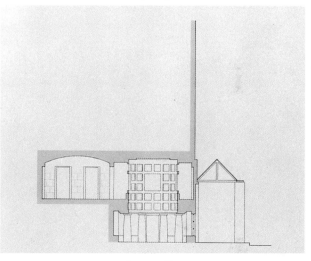

Cross section

Model view of the loggia and stair tower

1987

ST. MARKS CHURCH
CINCINNATI, OHIO

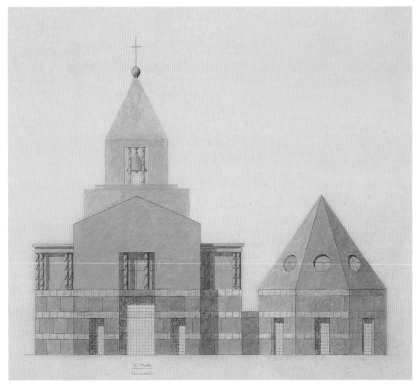

Linn Street elevation

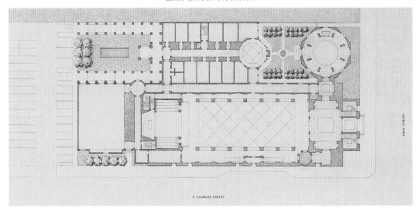

Site plan

The church designed for the St. Marks Christian Fellowship of the Church of God in Christ is located in an urban residential neighborhood in Cincinnati. The 44,000 square foot program includes a sanctuary seating 1500 people, a chapel seating 300, a fellowship hall with banquet seating for 500, offices, and a future classroom wing. The various parts of the plan are organized so that the building can be built in phases. The chapel, fellowship hall, and education wing are seen as separate elements added to the main volume of the sanctuary, thereby creating outdoor courtyards which can be used for gatherings before and after services.

The sanctuary is organized as a traditional nave subdivided into twelve bays, each with an alabaster window in the clerestory. The congregation has the option in the future of placing sculpture representing the apostles within the alabaster niches. The belltower and chapel, with their conical roofs, are intended to be viewed as familiar elements identifying the institutional character of the church within the neighborhood. The exterior materials include red sandstone with bluestone detailing, stucco, bronze columns, and alabaster windows.

View from the southeast

  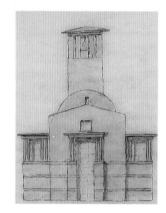

Linn Street elevation studies

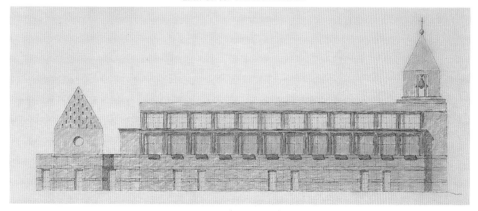

Ezzard Charles Street elevation

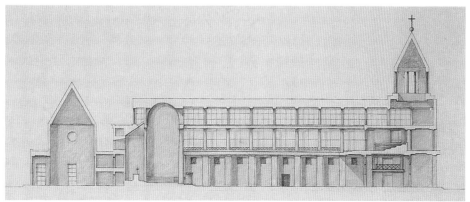

Longitudinal section

1986

WALT DISNEY WORLD RESORT HOTELS
MASTER PLAN

WALT DISNEY WORLD, FLORIDA

1,510-room hotel elevation study

Model view from the northwest

This new development at Walt Disney World in Florida connects EPCOT World Showcase with the Disney-MGM Studio Theme Park to the southwest. Graves prepared a preliminary master plan for the overall development and was subsequently asked to design two large convention hotels. Though their size, services, program, and operators are different, the two hotels were designed as an ensemble with consistent character and similar themes. The Walt Disney World Swan Hotel and the Walt Disney World Dolphin Hotel are organized around a crescent-shaped lake. The lobbies of the two hotels are connected by a landscaped pedestrian causeway that bisects the lake and serves as a dock for transportation boats to surrounding resort facilities.

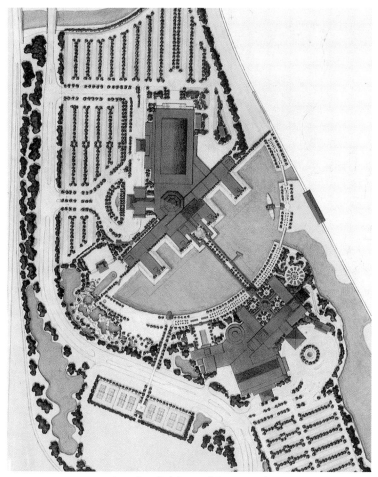

Site plan, Dolphin and Swan Hotels

Model view from the southeast

WALT DISNEY WORLD SWAN HOTEL
WALT DISNEY WORLD, FLORIDA

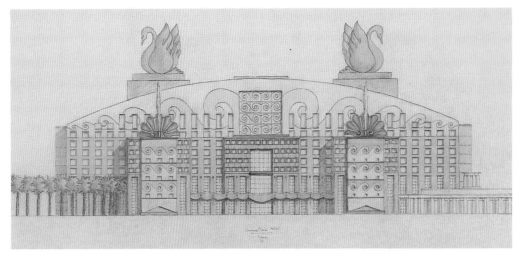

Crescent Lake elevation

Construction photo, view from the Dolphin Hotel

The Walt Disney World Swan Hotel is a 12-story, 615,000 square foot hotel and convention complex containing 758 guestrooms, a 23,000 square foot ballroom, meeting rooms, restaurants, shops, and recreational facilities. The Swan Hotel is oriented to the crescent-shaped lake shared by the Walt Disney World Dolphin Hotel, its companion hotel. The Swan is organized around a landscaped courtyard defined by two projecting wings of guestrooms. An octagonal lobby in the center of this courtyard connects the hotel, restaurants, and other facilities with the causeway that crosses the lake to the Dolphin.

The colors and decoration of the Walt Disney World Swan Hotel are consistent with the character and thematic intent of the surrounding development. Two swans, each measuring 47 feet high, rise above the roof of the hotel. The facades are painted with large abstract wave patterns, and clamshell fountains mark the ends of the two guestroom wings. Within the hotel, the entrance foyer has a tented ceiling and columns resembling bundled palm reeds. The main lobby contains a central fountain and a floral pattern on its walls and vaulted ceiling. Individual restaurants are given unique thematic identities. Guestroom corridors are decorated with wall murals depicting lake scenes and carpets resembling lily ponds. The ballroom continues the beach theme in its overscaled wall murals, which offer alternative landscapes beyond large wooden shutters.

Guestroom corridor elevation

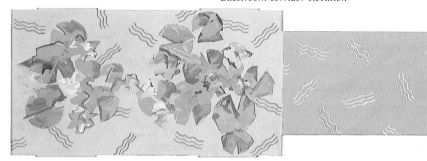

Guestroom corridor carpet

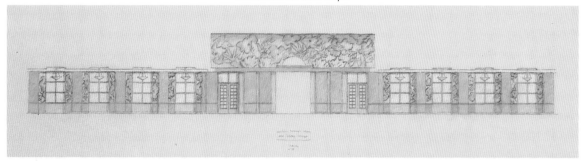

Main lobby elevation

Ballroom wall panel

SWAN HOTEL

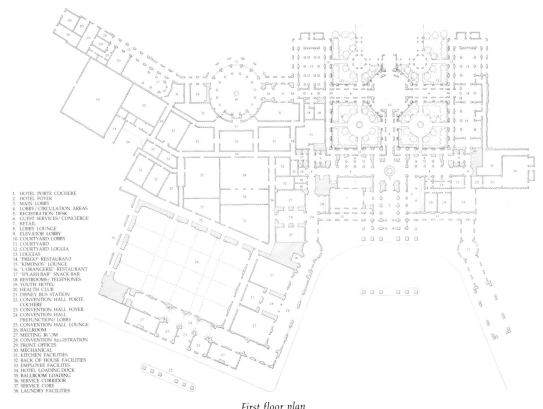

1. HOTEL PORTE COCHERE
2. HOTEL FOYER
3. MAIN LOBBY
4. LOBBY/ CIRCULATION AREAS
5. REGISTRATION DESK
6. GUEST SERVICES/ CONCIERGE
7. RETAIL
8. LOBBY LOUNGE
9. ELEVATOR LOBBY
10. COURTYARD LOBBY
11. COURTYARD
12. COURTYARD LOGGIA
13. LOGGIAS
14. "PREGO" RESTAURANT
15. "KIMONOS" LOUNGE
16. "L'ORANGERIE" RESTAURANT
17. "SPLASH BAR" SNACK BAR
18. RESTROOMS/ TELEPHONES
19. YOUTH HOTEL
20. HEALTH CLUB
21. DISNEY BUS STATION
22. CONVENTION HALL PORTE
    COCHERE
23. CONVENTION HALL FOYER
24. CONVENTION HALL
    PREFUNCTION/ LOBBY
25. CONVENTION HALL LOUNGE
26. BALLROOM
27. MEETING ROOM
28. CONVENTION REGISTRATION
29. FRONT OFFICES
30. MECHANICAL
31. KITCHEN FACILITIES
32. BACK OF HOUSE FACILITIES
33. EMPLOYEE FACILITES
34. HOTEL LOADING DOCK
35. BALLROOM LOADING
36. SERVICE CORRIDOR
37. SERVICE CORE
38. LAUNDRY FACILITIES

First floor plan

Construction photo, view from the east

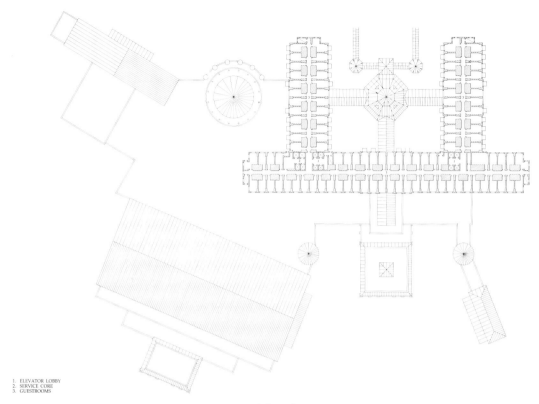

1. ELEVATOR LOBBY
2. SERVICE CORE
3. GUESTROOMS

Typical floor plan

Construction photo, view from the Crescent Lake

Ballroom prefunction

Garden Grove Cafe

Ballroom

Lobby foyer

Typical guestroom interior

Guestroom suite interior

Palio Restaurant

Kimonos lounge

Main lobby

WALT DISNEY WORLD DOLPHIN HOTEL
WALT DISNEY WORLD, FLORIDA

Construction photo, Dolphin Hotel

The new Walt Disney World Dolphin Hotel in Florida is a 1.4-million square foot convention center with approximately 1,510 rooms, a ballroom of 57,000 square feet, and an exhibit hall measuring 50,000 square feet, as well as meeting rooms, restaurants, shops, and recreational facilities. The Dolphin Hotel faces its companion building, the Walt Disney World Swan Hotel, across a large crescent-shaped lake.

The Dolphin Hotel is organized to take advantage of the waterside views. Four nine-story wings containing guestrooms project into the lake, surrounding a restaurant court with a waterfall fountain supported by dolphin statues. On the opposite side of the building, visitors enter through the *porte cochere* and lobby linking the hotel with the convention facilities contained in the northwest wing of the building. The large vaulted entrance foyer, flanked by grottos with running water, leads to a tented octagonal lobby with a central fountain. From this lobby, visitors gain access to the convention facilities, the hotel check-in, guestroom elevator lobbies, public restaurants, lounges, and retail shops.

The color and decoration of the hotel and its surroundings suggest the character of Florida resorts and provide a thematic context consistent with Disney's program for "entertainment architecture." The lakeside facade of the Dolphin Hotel is decorated with murals depicting large banana leaves resting on a trellis base. Wave patterns and dolphin murals adorn the long convention hall facade. Two gigantic dolphin statues mark both ends of the hotel roof, making the theme of the hotel visible from a distance. Roofs visible from guestrooms above are shaped and striped to appear like tents, reinforcing the hotel's festive resort themes.

In the hotel, the guestroom corridors are lined with thematic beach scenes. Doors are reminiscent of striped cabanas, and carpets depict boardwalks and beach towels scattered along a sandy shore. The restaurants are each given a thematic character consistent with the overall design. In the convention center, the structural columns in the large prefunction spaces are decorated to look like stylized palm trees. The ballroom walls are decorated with large-scale abstract floral patterns; the carpet contains a wave and starfish motif. These oversized elements attempt to give the ballroom and prefunction spaces a life and energy not typical of convention facilities.

Convention hall and hotel entry elevation

Crescent Lake elevation study

Crescent Lake elevation

Construction photo, view from the Swan Hotel

Ballroom wall panel study

Ballroom carpet study

Ballroom prefunction elevation

Lobby foyer elevation

Guestroom corridor elevation

Guestroom corridor carpet

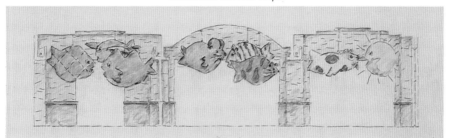

Coral Cafe elevation

Copa Banana Lounge elevation

Rotunda lobby elevation

DOLPHIN HOTEL

1. HOTEL PORTE COCHERE
2. HOTEL FOYER
3. GROTTO
4. ROTUNDA LOBBY AND FOUNTAIN
5. GUEST REGISTRATION
6. GUEST SERVICES/ CONCIERGE
7. RETAIL
8. RETAIL STORAGE
9. LUGGAGE
10. FRONT OFFICES
11. LOBBY AREAS
12. ELEVATOR LOBBY
13. LOBBY LOUNGE
14. OPEN TO RESTAURANT BELOW
15. TERRACE
16. OPEN TO LOBBY BELOW
17. TELEPHONES/ STORAGE
18. RESTROOMS
19. SERVICE CORE
20. RESTAURANT ENTRY
21. "SAFARI GRILLE" RESTAURANT
22. "COCONUTS" LOUNGE
23. COCKTAIL LOUNGE
24. KITCHEN/ PANTRY
25. GUESTROOMS
26. COVERED WALKWAY
27. DISNEY BUS STATION

28. GUESTROOMS
29. ADMINISTRATION OFFICES
30. CONVENTION HALL PORTE COCHERE
31. CONVENTION HALL FOYER
32. CONVENTION HALL PREFUNCTION/ LOBBY
33. CONVENTION REGISTRATION
34. MEETING ROOMS
35. CONVENTION SERVICE CORE
36. SERVICE CORRIDOR
37. BOARDROOM
38. OPEN TO EXHIBITION HALL BELOW

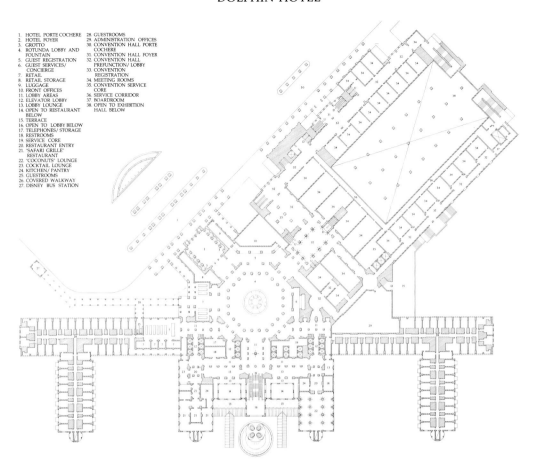

Third floor plan

1. STAIR HALL
2. LOBBY/ CIRCULATION
3. "DOLPHIN FOUNTAIN" CAFE
4. "CORAL CAFE" RESTAURANT
5. "MARCO POLO" RESTAURANT
6. "SUM CHOWS" RESTAURANT
7. "CHECKERS" RESTAURANT
8. ELEVATOR LOBBY
9. TELEPHONES/ RESTROOMS
10. GAME ROOM
11. BEAUTY SALON
12. NURSERY
13. HEALTH CLUB
14. GUESTROOMS
15. MECHANICAL
16. KITCHEN FACILITIES
17. SERVICE CORE
18. SERVICE CORRIDOR
19. LAUNDRY
20. BACK OF HOUSE FACILITIES
21. EMPLOYEE FACILITIES
22. HOTEL LOADING DOCK
23. STORAGE
24. EXHIBITION HALL LOBBY
25. EXHIBITION HALL
26. EXHIBITION HALL LOAD- ING
27. FOUNTAIN COURTYARD

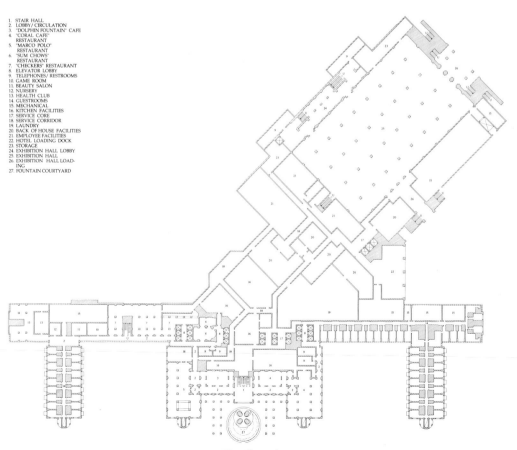

First floor plan

284

1. ELEVATOR LOBBY
2. SERVICE CORE
3. GUESTROOMS
4. SUITES

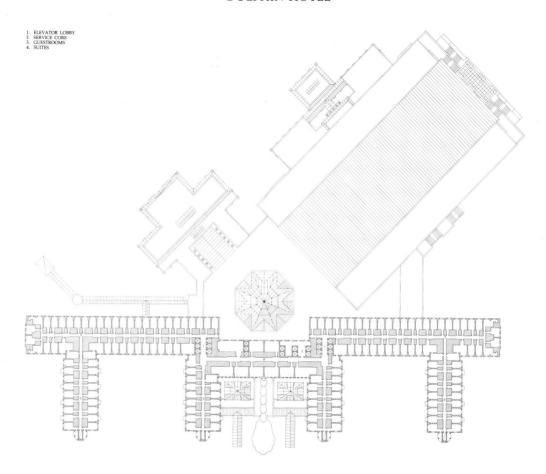

Seventh floor plan

1. ELEVATOR LOBBY
2. SERVICE CORE
3. GUESTROOMS
4. MECHANICAL
5. OPEN TO BELOW
6. BALLROOM PREFUNCTION
7. BALLROOM LOBBY
8. BALLROOM
9. TELEPHONES/ RESTROOMS
10. SEMINAR ROOM
11. SERVICE CORRIDOR
12. SERVICE CORE
13. PANTRY
14. BALLROOM BACK OF
    HOUSE
15. TERRACE AND STAIRS

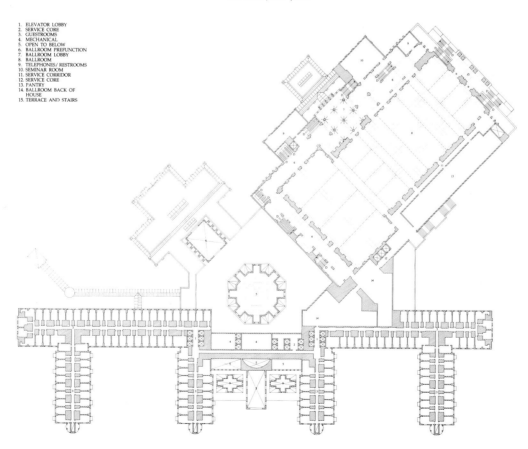

Fifth floor plan

FURNITURE AND FURNISHINGS
WALT DISNEY WORLD DOLPHIN HOTEL
WALT DISNEY WORLD SWAN HOTEL

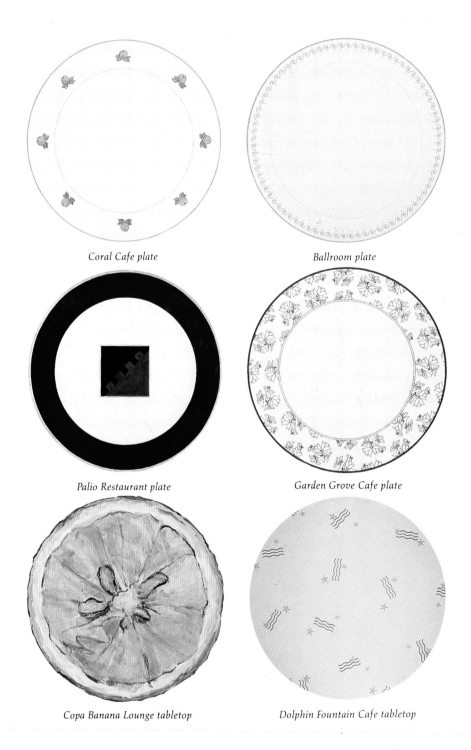

Coral Cafe plate   *Ballroom plate*

Palio Restaurant plate   *Garden Grove Cafe plate*

Copa Banana Lounge tabletop   *Dolphin Fountain Cafe tabletop*

Graves was commissioned to design and/or select the furniture and furnishings for the guestrooms, restaurants, and public spaces within the Walt Disney World Swan Hotel and the Walt Disney World Dolphin Hotel. The designs utilize the whimsical resort themes of the hotel. For example, the tabletops in the Copa Banana Lounge depict sections of oranges, lemons, and limes, complementing the stand-up cocktail bars rendered as overscaled slices of fruit. The brightly-colored guestroom furniture is stenciled with abstract patterns of waves, fruit, and flowers.

 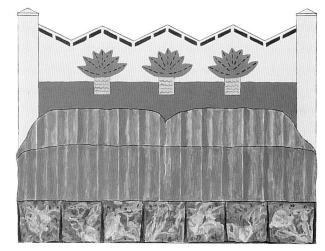

Bed and headboard studies

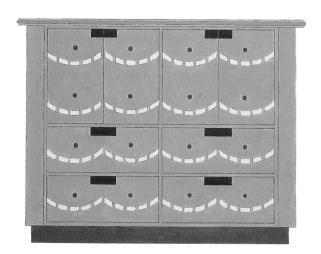 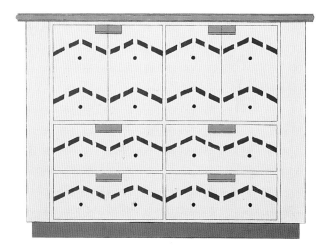

Dresser studies

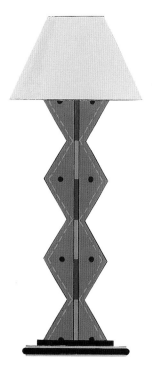

Desk lamp studies

Floor lamp study

Desk chair study

Floor lamp study

1988

PORTSIDE APARTMENT TOWER
MINATO MIRAI 21
YOKOHAMA, JAPAN

Portside elevation

This 27-story, 235,000 square foot apartment tower is being planned in Yokohama's new Portside District D, an area called Minato Mirai 21, "Waterfront for the 21st Century." The district is a landfill which will contain mixed use facilities, the most significant of which are this apartment tower and an adjacent office building of a similar scale.

The building is organized as a tripartite composition where the base, middle, and top can be seen as discrete elements identifiable by both visitors and occupants. The base of the building, intended primarily for public use, contains shops, galleries, and a school for culinary and fashion arts. The tower above is subdivided into two major sections whose distinctive fenestration and balconies allow the residents a choice of apartment types. Continuous balconies are required on all levels of the building to meet local fire exit codes. Special apartments such as artists' studios occupy the top of the building and, together with the activities planned at the base, offer the sense of a building where the arts might flourish.

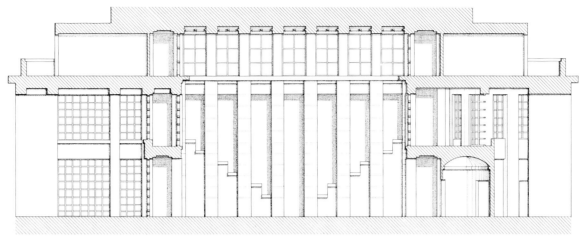

Atrium section looking east

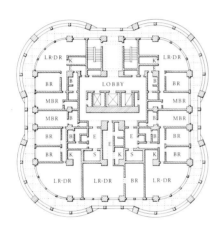

Apartment plans 4-16

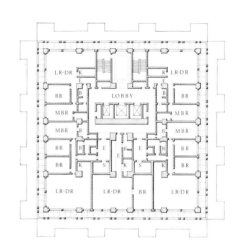

Apartment plans 17-26

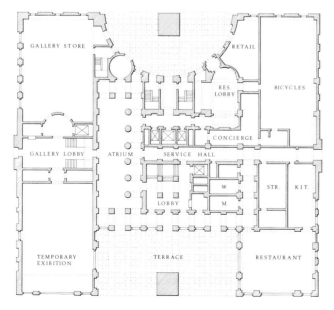

Ground floor plan

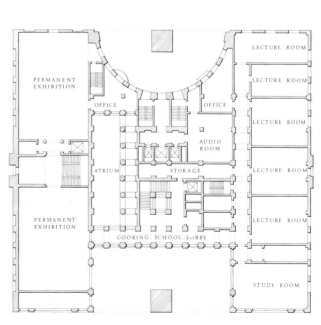

Second floor plan

1988

IZUMISANO CENTER
IZUMISANO, JAPAN

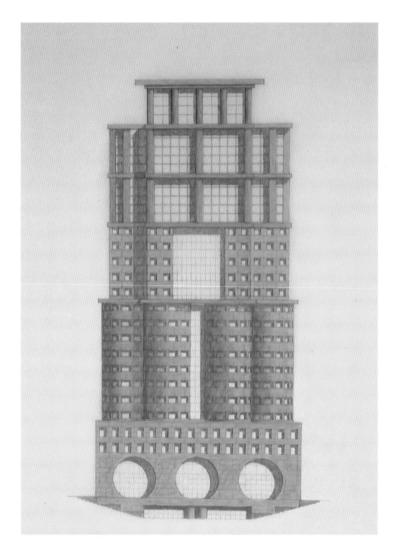

East elevation

This new office building was designed as part of an international competition. If it had been built, it would have been one of the first major developments in the formerly agrarian town of Izumisano, a suburb of Osaka, Japan. Because of the large scale of the project (315,000 square feet) it was crucial to give the building a humanistic or personal character. The tripartite division of the building into base, middle, and top would have helped mediate its large scale by making these sections of the building more identifiable and accessible to the observer.

The ground level of the building would have been used for retail shops. A large central atrium would have helped orient visitors and daily users within the building. People could have gained access to the lower terrace through two gently sloping flights of stairs, flanked by garden *parterres* which would also have been used as places to congregate. The stairs and public areas within the plaza would have focused on a stage, where a variety of performances could enliven this area during the day and evening. The abstract wave patterns, textures, and colors throughout the project referred to the building's orientation to the nearby ocean.

Within the building's facades, hierarchies of windows and other openings would have allowed the articulation of a variety of private offices and collective spaces, such as conference rooms and boardrooms. The top of the building would have contained restaurants with commanding views of the city and the water beyond. The building was proposed to be clad in red sandstone and cast stone, which would have blended effectively with the traditional structures of the surrounding city.

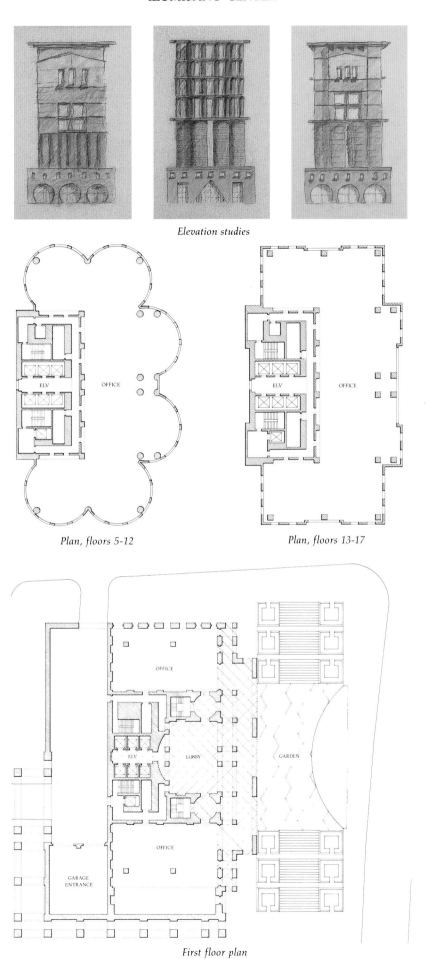

Elevation studies

Plan, floors 5-12

Plan, floors 13-17

First floor plan

NAIMAN RESIDENCE
LA JOLLA, CALIFORNIA

Model view from the east

The Naiman Residence is located on a steeply sloping site facing the Pacific Ocean in La Jolla, California. The main level, entered from an automobile court, includes a two-story living room and porch overlooking the ocean, a study, and a dining room and kitchen. A master bedroom suite with an exercise room is located on the second floor. Additional bedrooms are located on the lower level, which is at grade at the rear of the lot.

The character of the building is appropriate for its beachfront site. While not intended as a weekend or vacation house, it has an aspect of a folly in that the idiosyncratic elements of the design reflect a casual attitude about living on the beach.

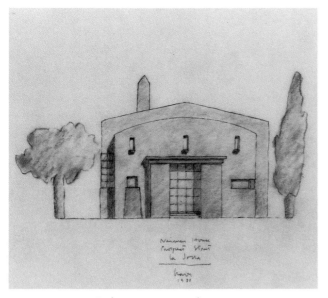

Preliminary entrance elevation

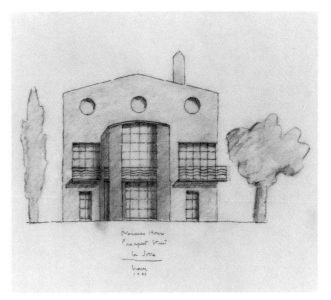

Preliminary oceanfront elevation

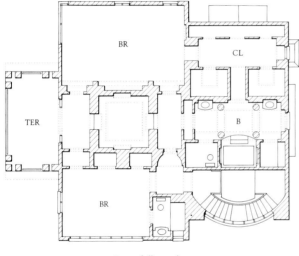

Second floor plan

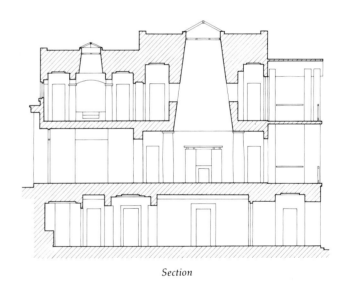

Section

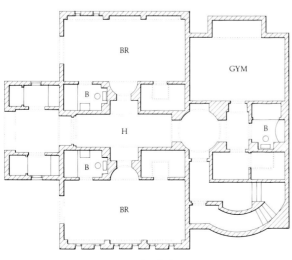

Lower level plan

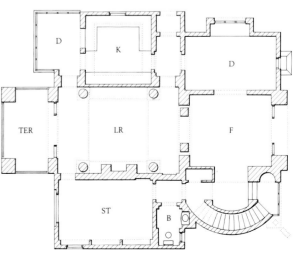

First floor plan

LENOX IDENTITY PROGRAM

Lenox packaging

The Lenox china company commissioned Graves to design a new corporate identity program, packaging for its china, glassware, and giftware, and several retail stores and boutiques. Included in the identity program and packaging are a new logotype, development of a color palette to be used in a variety of ways, and graphic design of corporate stationery and related items.

The logotype designed by Graves incorporates the wreath and traditional style of lettering which have been associated with Lenox for many years. The packaging is given a uniform look through the new green color and the cream-colored logotype. Small terra cotta stripes at the center points of each side of the boxes and bags are seen as abstracted ribbons.

1988

LENOX STORE AT THE GARDENS
PALM BEACH GARDENS, FLORIDA

Entrance rotunda

Bridal registry tent

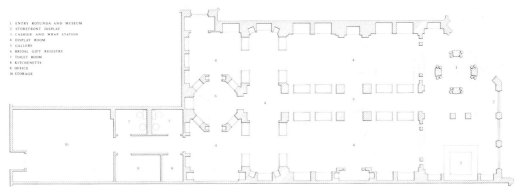

Plan

The new Lenox retail store at the Gardens shopping mall in Palm Beach Gardens, Florida displays the entire line of china, glassware, and gifts produced by Lenox. At the entrance to the store, historical examples of Lenox products, including the numerous place settings designed for The White House over the years, are exhibited within a freestanding rotunda. The plan of the store is organized along a central passage. Room-like spaces to either side of this axis include a fireplace and a niche for a Christmas tree, conveying the sense of the domestic settings where Lenox products are typically used. At the end of the axis, a striped tent is used for bridal gift registry. The new green color and logotype designed by Graves as part of a corporate identity program are used throughout the store.

China gallery

Giftware gallery

Storefront

LENOX BOUTIQUE AT BLOOMINGDALE'S
NEW YORK, NEW YORK

The new Lenox boutique at Bloomingdale's department store in New York is located at one of the entrances to the china department on the sixth floor. Each manufacturer's boutique on this floor is given its own identity, though specific design guidelines for layout, lighting, materials, color, and signage create an overall appearance of unity.

Lenox china and glassware is displayed in cabinets around the perimeter of the space, in freestanding vitrines, on tables, and on a central pavilion which is the focal point of the selling area. The front faces of the perimeter cabinets are made of cherry wood with ebonized wood columns resembling bundled reeds held together by bronze straps. The circular pavilion is made of ebonized wood columns surrounding a cherry wood pedestal base; a small tempietto-like folly on top acts as a backdrop for changing displays of the Lenox merchandise.

DAIEI OFFICE BUILDING
YOKOHAMA, JAPAN

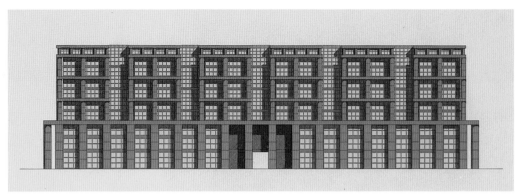

Grand Mall elevation

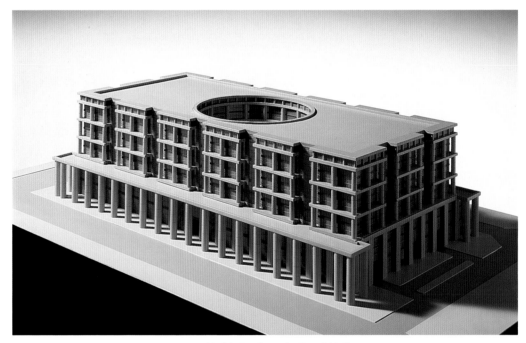

Model view from the Grand Mall

The site for Daiei's new building occupies two full city blocks along the Grand Mall in Yokohama, adjacent to the Yokohama City Museum of Arts. The program includes a new commercial art museum, located on the east side of the first three floors facing the city museum; retail space on the west side of the first three floors and on the basement level; approximately 100 parking spaces at the sub-basement level; and rental offices on upper floors.

The building is organized around a central circular courtyard which is seen as a large outdoor room to be used as a public park or garden. The different facilities within the building are accessible from the courtyard as well as from the street. The north and south entrances to the courtyard are located along an urban axis established by the City's master plan.

The building's exterior has been articulated as a series of smaller parts to offset the large scale of this development. Horizontal divisions establish a base, middle, and top to the composition. The three-story base, where the major public spaces are located, is treated as a pedestrian arcade along the Grand Mall. Six vertical elements which act like towers or pavilions, rest on the base on the north and south sides of the building, and help break up the scale of these very long facades. The glass is continuous behind the columns of the facade, allowing generous views from all spaces within the building. An ochre-colored semi-glazed ceramic tile is proposed as the main exterior material.

METROPOLITAN HOME SHOWHOUSE
NEW YORK, NEW YORK

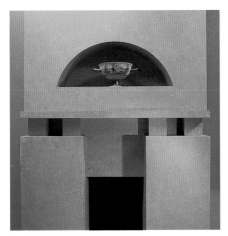

Wall cabinet detail

Powder room vanity

Foyer

Graves was one of several architects and designers invited by the magazine, *Metropolitan Home*, to redesign a townhouse in the Upper East Side of Manhattan. The townhouse was open to the public to raise money for and public awareness of DIFFA, the Design Industries Foundation for AIDS. Graves was given the task of redesigning the entry sequence to the house beginning with a festive banner and sidewalk awning announcing the event outside and including the foyer and powder room. A new fireplace and banks of arched vitrines were used to display objects within the foyer and to introduce an imaginary family that might have lived there.

MOMOCHI DISTRICT APARTMENT BUILDING
FUKUOKA, JAPAN

Model view from the southeast

The city of Fukuoka, on the island of Kyushu, at the southwestern tip of Japan, embarked on a project to reclaim 193 acres of its waterfront on which to build a model city for the Asian-Pacific Exposition in 1989. Several sites for five-story apartment buildings were assigned to different pairs of architects. Graves was assigned the corner site at the main highway entrance to the exposition. The placement of the building was determined by strict requirements for setbacks and massing. The ground level was to be linked by retail space and restaurants to a companion apartment building designed by the Chicago architect, Stanley Tigerman.

The program for the apartment building, now completed, includes ground level retail shops and four upper stories containing ten apartments with a mix of one to four bedrooms. An octagonal corner tower provided outdoor porches for the retail shops at the ground level and living rooms in the upper level apartments. Continuous balconies on the southern and eastern sides of the building enhanced the quality of light and life in each apartment.

Construction photo, view from the south

Construction photo, view from the southeast

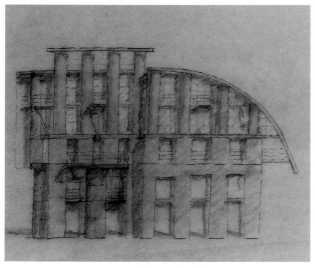

East elevation study

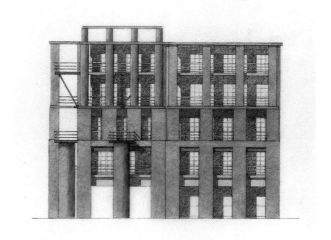

East elevation

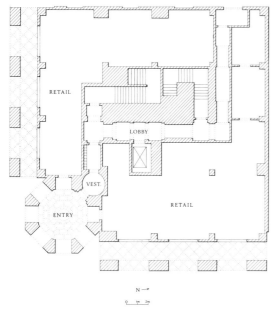

First floor plan

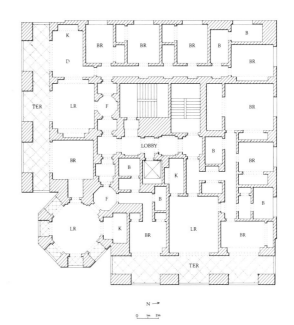

Third floor plan

301

MIDOUSUJI MINAMI OFFICE BUILDING
OSAKA, JAPAN

Midousuji Minami elevation

This 10-story, 60,000 square foot speculative office building, is located on a corner site on Midousuji Minami, the main commercial street in downtown Osaka, Japan. A major retail clothing store is located on the first floor of the building, restaurants are located on the lower levels, and rental office space is provided above.

The facades are subdivided into several sections with a variety of window treatments. This compositional strategy allows the building's several functions to be identified and also refers to the small-scale elements of the more traditional surrounding buildings.

Elevation studies

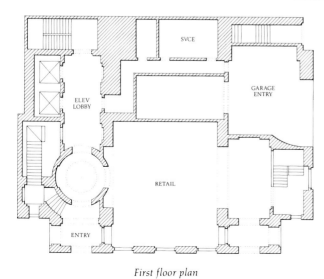
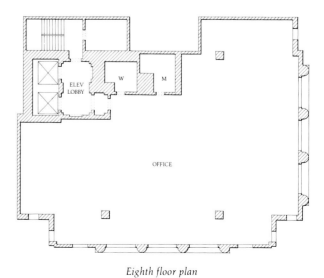

First floor plan

Eighth floor plan

SPORTS CENTER
SARAH LAWRENCE COLLEGE
BRONXVILLE, NEW YORK

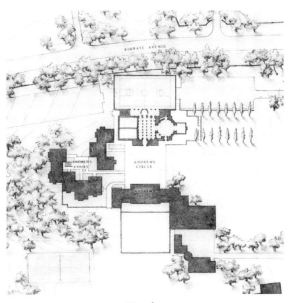

Site plan

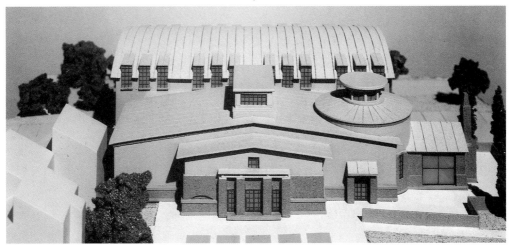

Model view from Andrews Circle

The new Sports Center at Sarah Lawrence College includes a gymnasium, swimming pool, squash and racquetball courts, exercise rooms, locker rooms, student lounges and administrative offices. The two large volumes of the gymnasium and pool are stacked above each other on the downhill side of the sloping site along Kimball Avenue. A smaller volume containing the remaining facilities is appended to the building on the campus side, facing an existing courtyard and a building of similar massing. The Sports Center is entered from this upper courtyard; the main entrance leads to the sports facilities and a separate, smaller entrance is used for the student lounges.

The appearance of the large scale of the building has been diminished by expressing each of the several functional components in the massing of the building and by articulating the facades with smaller scale elements such as dormer windows. Within the building, the individual rooms each have their own characters, distinguished in part by the treatment of natural light. Large orangerie windows admit plentiful daylight into the swimming pool; side light enters through dormer windows in the large roof over the gymnasium; and clerestory light emanating from a large roof lantern illuminates the octagonal student lounge.

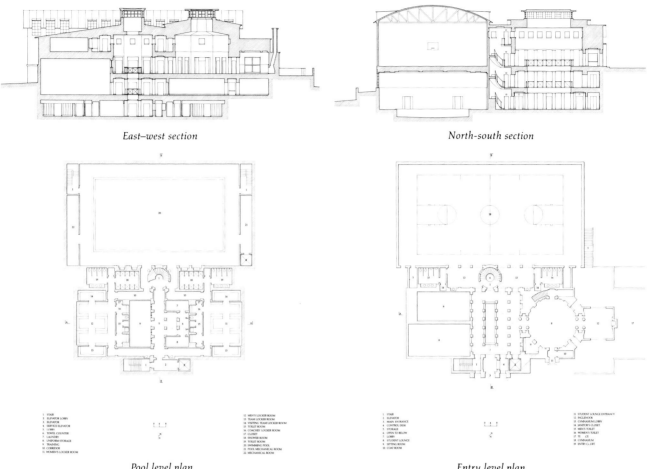

East–west section

North-south section

Pool level plan

Entry level plan

Entrance courtyard elevation

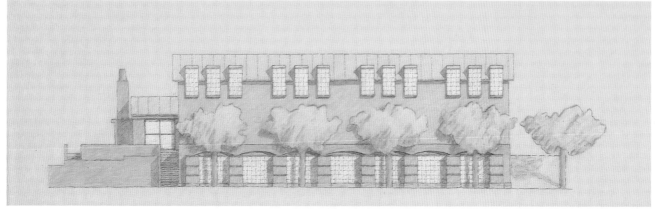

Kimball Avenue elevation

PARC DE PASSY
PARIS, FRANCE

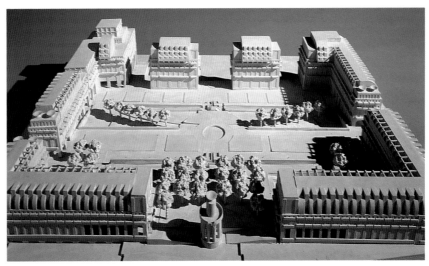

Model view from Quai du President Kennedy

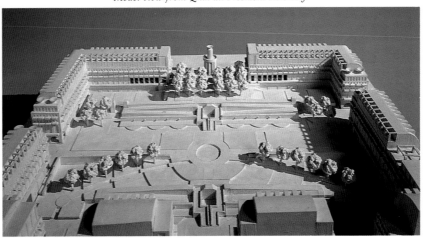

Model view from Rue Marcel Proust

The city of Paris sponsored a developers' competition for the design of a new residential project and public park near the banks of the Seine. The development team was not chosen for the project. The project would have included five stories of apartments and underground parking for 780 cars, as well as a gymnasium, a library, and other facilities for the use of neighborhood residents. The buildings, which were designed in accordance with height and setback limitations, were conceived as a porous wall defining the street edge and enclosing the garden. The design attempted to re-establish the character of traditional Parisian residences. The exterior materials of limestone and sandstone would have reinforced the relationship of this new project with its surrounding urban context. The three levels of the buildings were differentiated on their facades by changes in materials and in the sizes of openings in the building's skin. The loggia at the base, with its large, rusticated arches, related to the ground or garden. The central floors were characterized by traditional balconies. At the top of the buildings, large dormer windows were set into the two-story vaulted copper roofs.

Access to the park would have been provided on all four sides of the complex. However, since most visitors would descend from the Heights of Passy above the site, Graves established a pedestrian bridge connecting the Rue Raynouard with a circular tower at the uppermost entrance to the garden. The bridge, in the form of an aqueduct, was intended to symbolize the site's historical connection with water. The mineral springs discovered here in the 19th century were also recalled by a fountain to be set in a grotto just below the Rue Raynouard. The fountain would have become a prelude to the garden, establishing its theme. The garden itself was designed as three wide terraces descending with the natural slope of the land toward the river. The uppermost terrace included an orchard built on top of the gymnasium. Ramps provided access to the second terrace, which would have offered ample space for unstructured play and general recreation. Fountains set into the rubble base of the ramps evoked the original mineral springs of the site. The lowest terrace was to have included colorful *parterres* planted with annual flowers.

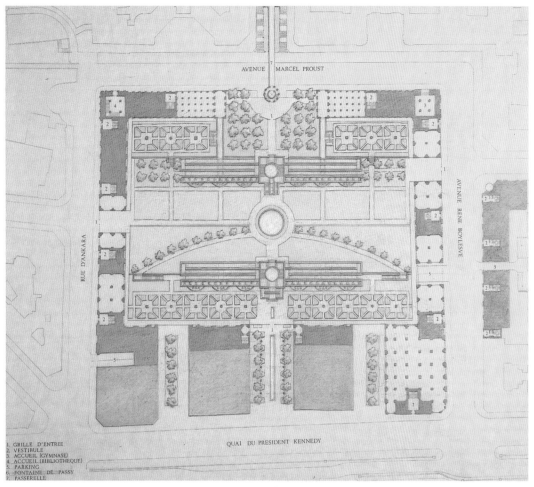

1. GRILLE D'ENTREE
2. VESTIBULE
3. ACCUEIL (GYMNASE)
4. ACCUEIL (BIBLIOTHEQUE)
5. PARKING
6. FONTAINE DE PASSY
7. PASSERELLE

Site plan

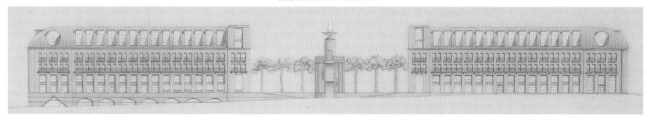

Rue d'Ankara elevation

Rue Marcel Proust elevation

Northwest elevation of the garden

1988

METROPOLIS MASTER PLAN
LOS ANGELES, CALIFORNIA

Preliminary master plan elevation

Preliminary master plan model

The site for the proposed 2,700,000 square foot Metropolis Master Plan occupies a pivotal position in a rapidly growing section of Los Angeles. The project will contain rental offices, a hotel, retail space, and structured parking. The preliminary master plan by Graves, which won an international design competition, is organized into two pairs of similar towers that flank a central rotunda. The office tower in the northeast quadrant will be built in the first phase.

As one approaches the city from the west along Harbor Freeway, the proposed pair of towers becomes a portal or gate framing the view of downtown Los Angeles to the east. This site strategy will allow a simple legibility of the various components of the development as well as identification of the site from a distance. A continuous rusticated base will unify the composition of the master plan. The base will include pedestrian and vehicular entrances to the buildings as well as major public components of the program.

Master plan model, view from the east

Master plan model, view from the southeast

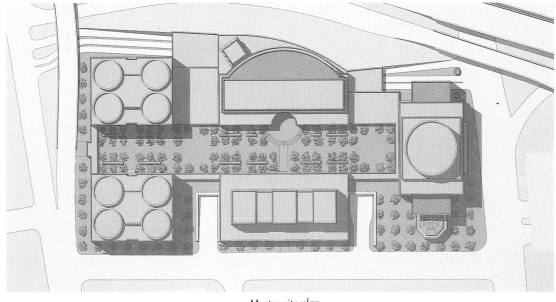

Master site plan

1988

METROPOLIS PHASE ONE OFFICE BUILDING
LOS ANGELES, CALIFORNIA

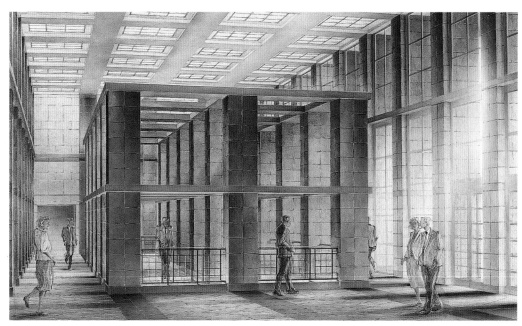

Entrance lobby and stairhall

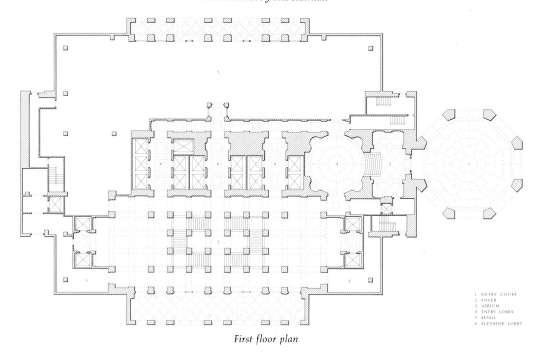

1 ENTRY COURT
2 FOYER
3 ATRIUM
4 ENTRY LOBBY
5 RETAIL
6 ELEVATOR LOBBY

First floor plan

The first phase of the Metropolis Master Plan is being developed as an office building located on the east side of the site along Eighth Street. The building will include approximately 630,000 square feet of office space on 31 floors; 360,000 square feet of underground parking; and 10,000 square feet of retail space on the ground floor. The building will be entered from the corner of Eighth Street and Francisco Street, through a nine-story octagonal structure serving as an open porch. A dining club is planned for the third floor of the octagon, while offices will occupy the five floors above. A variety of windows will be provided within the body of the building, offering diverse types of offices. The top of the building will offer two special tenant floors contained in a rotunda. The exterior of the building will be clad in panels of colored ceramic tile.

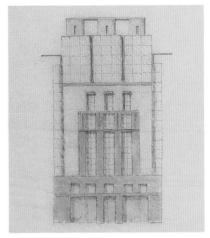

Elevation studies

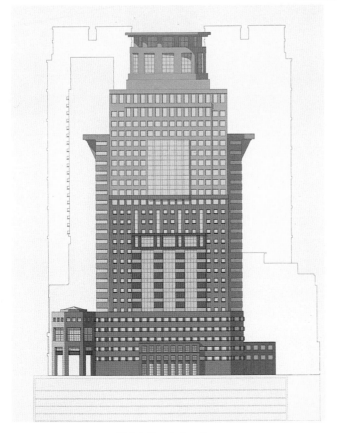

Eighth Street elevation

Model view from the south

TAJIMA OFFICE BUILDING
TOKYO, JAPAN

Kanda River elevation

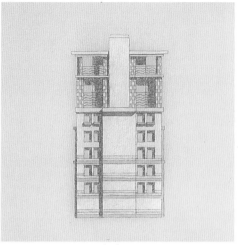

Park elevation

Elevation study

Elevation study

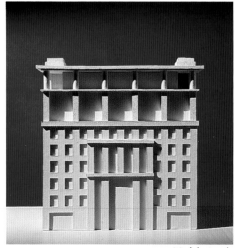

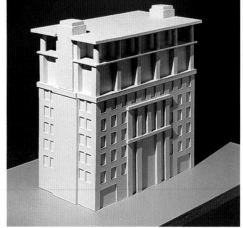

Model view from the Kanda River

This nine-story corporate office building for Tajima, a Japanese tile manufacturing company, is located along the Kanda River in Tokyo. The building's tile exterior is colored and decorated to incorporate imagery evocative of its waterfront location.

1988

2101 PENNSYLVANIA AVENUE
WASHINGTON, D.C.

Photo collage view from Washington Circle

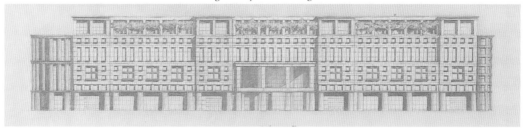

Pennsylvania Avenue elevation

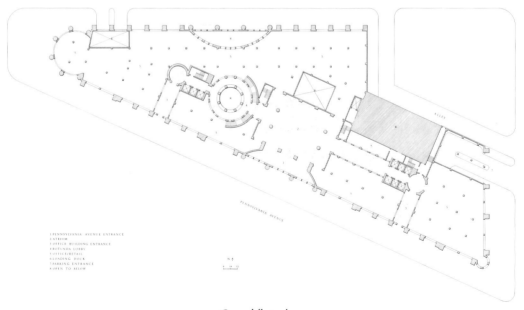

Ground floor plan

The site for this 10-story mixed use building is bounded by Pennsylvania Avenue, K Street, 21st Street, and Washington Circle. The two major entrances, located along Pennsylvania Avenue and K Street, lead to an atrium lobby overlooking a multi-use community theater at the basement level. The first two floors of the building are designed for retail use; rental offices are provided above.

Following the cornice height typical of the surrounding blocks, the major facades are subdivided and articulated with a variety of window types to offer relief along their 600-foot length. A cylindrical belvedere turns the corner at Washington Cicle, allowing views in all directions. Proposed materials include agate granite and Kasota stone.

NEW UMEDA CITY MASTER PLAN
OSAKA, JAPAN

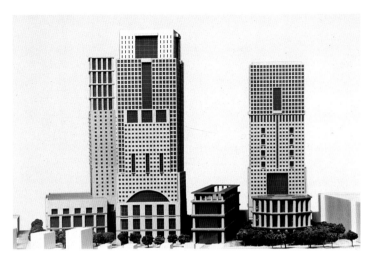

Model view from the west

Model view from the east

The master plan for New Umeda City was a phased mixed use development for the Umeda Kita district of Osaka. The first phase included a 39-story Osaka Westin Hotel and a 46-story rental office building. The second phase was a linear, 6-story building with restaurants on the first floor, a sports center on the second floor, and design showrooms called the "Living Gallery" on the upper floors. The third phase included a 41-story office building and a 3-story retail pavilion on the north side of the site. The project was designed as part of an international competition; Graves' scheme will not be built.

The locations of the buildings respected the irregular property lines of several parcels of land under different ownership and would have conveyed an informal, or picturesque, site organization. Two existing parks to the east and west would have been extended into the site by the placement of new landscaped gardens within the master plan. In the first phase, the Oyodo-Naka Park would have been acknowledged by a corresponding garden with an octagonal water fountain, located at the rear of the hotel. In the third phase, an axis of movement would have led from the first garden through the center of the linear Phase 2 building, into a second public garden facing the existing Nakatsu-Minami Park. The Phase 3 retail center would have stood within this second garden as a pavilion. Consistent with the surrounding urban area, retail space and other public activities would have been provided at the base of each building, enlivening the pedestrian space.

The architectural character of the project would have allowed both the individual expression of each building and a sense of commonality in the ensemble. The height and coloration of the bases of the three tall buildings would have provided continuity at the ground level and reflected the height of existing buildings adjacent to the site.

Office building elevation

Hotel elevation

Office building elevation

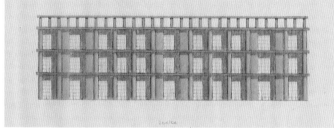

Retail pavilion elevation

Sports Center and Living Gallery elevation

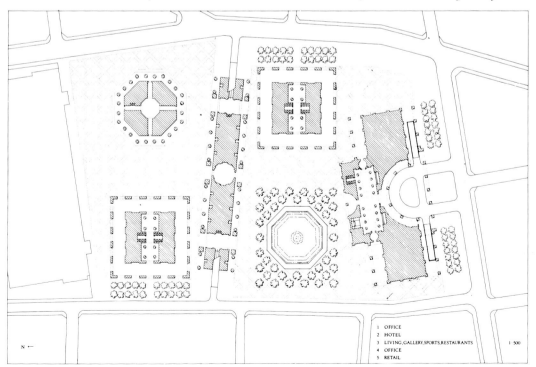

1	OFFICE
2	HOTEL
3	LIVING, GALLERY, SPORTS, RESTAURANTS
4	OFFICE
5	RETAIL

1 500

N ←

Site plan

1988

WHITNEY MUSEUM OF AMERICAN ART
NEW YORK, NEW YORK

Scheme 3, East 74th Street elevation

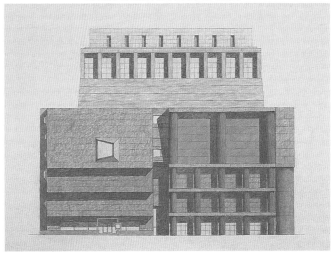

Scheme 3, Madison Avenue elevation

The 1988 revisions to the design of the addition to the Whitney Museum (seen earlier in this monograph) attempt to preserve the visual integrity of the 1966 Marcel Breuer building as a modernist object within the city. The cylindrical "hinge" which stood at the center of the former compositions has been removed, revealing the recess between the existing granite facade and the remainder of the block and setting the museum apart from its urban context, as Breuer intended.

As a composition, the revised scheme is less figurative and more abstract than the previous schemes. It is therefore closer to the existing building in character and spirit. The Madison Avenue facade superimposes a series of colonnades whose levels match the heights of Breuer's setbacks. The lower groups of columns also reflect the scale and coloration of the low-rise brownstones in the neighborhood. The revised design visually turns the corner at East 74th Street by means of a dramatic column. The Breuer building similarly places special emphasis on the northern corner and thus the two ends frame the new composition. The addition will be built of gray-green slate, red-gray granite, and the same gray granite used in the present museum. These colors and materials are intended to be sympathetic with both the existing building and the surrounding urban context.

Scheme 3, photo collage views along Madison Avenue

Scheme 3, model, Madison Avenue

1988-89

COLUMBUS CONVENTION CENTER
COLUMBUS, OHIO

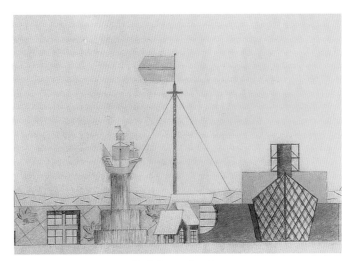

High Street elevation

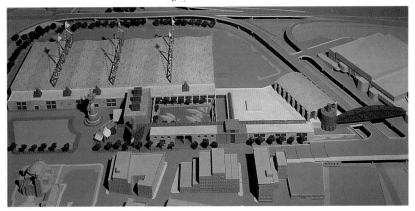

Model view from High Street

Graves' entry in the design competition for the Columbus Convention Center attempted to create a unique architectural image that would capture the spirit of the city. It was thought that the building should be a popular monument, engaging the city's residents and visitors in a lighthearted spirit of discovery. The narrative themes of the architecture relate specifically to Ohio's state symbol, a cluster of leaves and nuts from the buckeye tree, and to the city's namesake, Christopher Columbus, whose 500-year anniversary will coincide with the opening of the building.

The organization and design of the Convention Center are specific to its site and sensitive to the surrounding neighborhoods. The site is characterized by different edge conditions and different contextual influences. The High Street frontage should encourage continuity between downtown Columbus and the retail neighborhood to the north. Thus, located along High Street are the facilities most public in nature and most compatible in scale with the adjacent neighborhood, including the main entrance and concourse, restaurants, a large public garden, and a future hotel. Each building element is given its own identity while also being seen as part of a larger composition.

The largest component of the Convention Center program, the exhibition hall, is located on the northeast side of the site. It is seen in relation to the surrounding highways, whose scale is more compatible with this large volume than the pedestrian scale of High Street. The ballroom, the second largest component, is articulated as its own pavilion, facing the Ohio Center located to the south of the site. Beyond the obvious programmatic link with this neighboring facility, the ballroom acts as a scalar bridge between the large mass of the Ohio Center and the lower height and smaller scale of the Convention Center.

Graves' scheme, developed in conjunction with Acock Schlegel Architects of Columbus, was not chosen for further development.

View from High Street

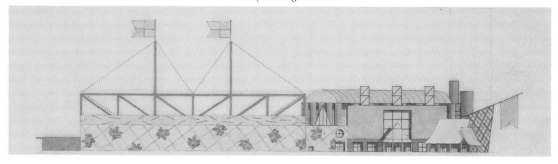

North elevation

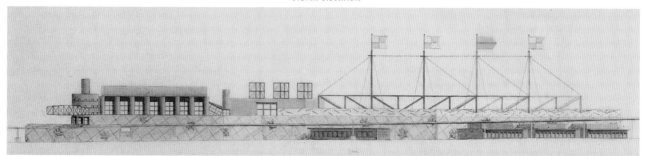

South elevation

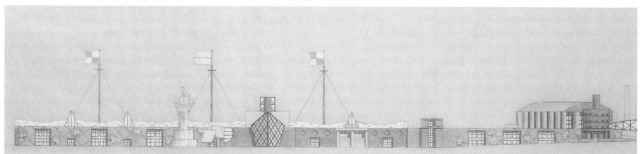

West elevation

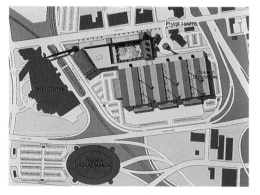

Master plan

Arena elevation study

HOTEL NEW YORK
EURO DISNEYLAND, FRANCE

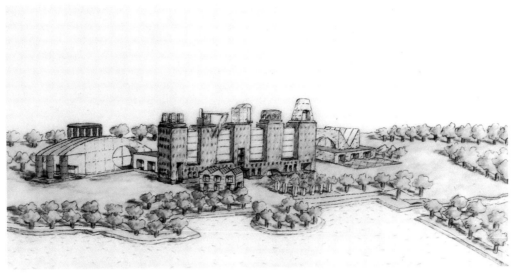

Character study

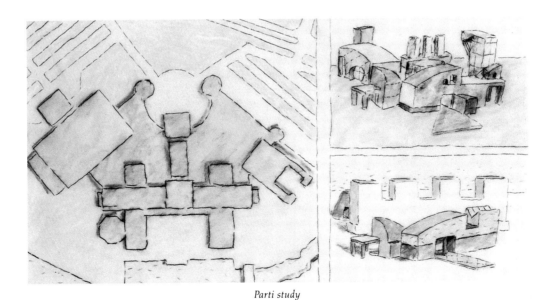

Parti study

The Hotel New York is located at the edge of the lake within the Euro Disneyland resort complex outside Paris. It contains 575 guestrooms, meeting facilities, restaurants, and a health club. The composition represents diverse building types, places, scales, and experiences to convey the richness and character of New York City. The tallest portion of the building, centered on the axis of the lake, is an eight-story slab seen as a series of five midtown towers. To the west, the four-story Gramercy Park wing represents a small-scaled residential neighborhood surrounding a landscaped garden. To the east, the Brownstones wing is angled to take advantage of the views to Central Park and the lake. The hotel is entered from the northern end of the site through a grand curved arcade which also gives access to the convention center and health club buildings.

Model view from the southwest

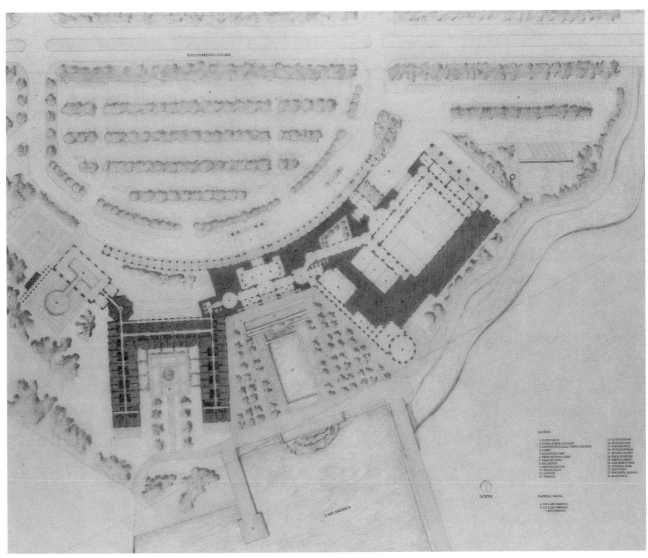

Site plan

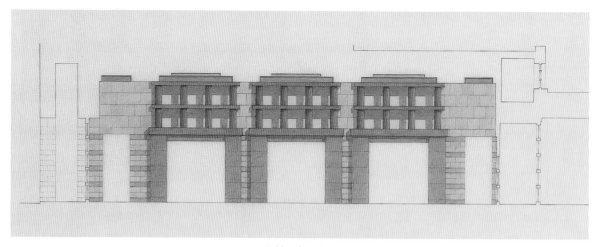

Lobby elevation

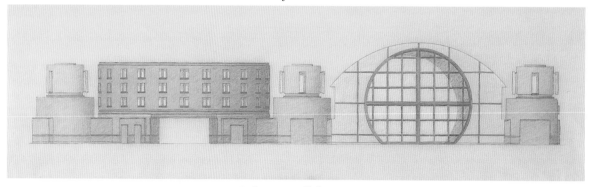

Prefunction Hall elevation

Ballroom partial elevation

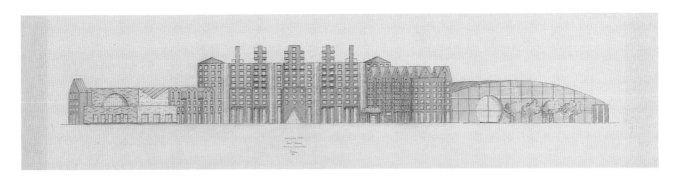

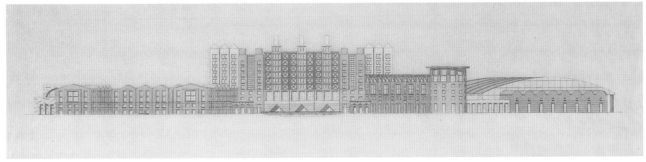

Lake elevation studies

Model view from the south

1989

FINESTRA AND OCULUS CHAIRS
ATELIER INTERNATIONAL

The Finestra and Oculus Chairs are manufactured by Atelier International. They are available in a variety of finishes including cherry, mahogany, and matte black ebonized wood.

1989

AVENTINE LOUNGE CHAIR

The upholstered lounge chair was originally designed for the Hyatt Hotel at the Aventine Mixed Use Development in La Jolla, California.

THE KYOTO COLLECTION
ARKITEKTURA

Table and chairs

Floor lamps

Bureau and table lamp

Desk, chair, table lamp

Armoire

The Kyoto Collection designed for the furniture company Arkitektura explores the rather ambiguous relationship between the abstract and the archaic. Graves intended the furniture to be without decoration, deriving its interest instead from simple forms and proportions—a notion that the Japanese have perfected over the centuries. The 23-piece furniture collection is available in a variety of colors. The furniture was originally installed in a model apartment in the Momochi District Apartment Building in Fukuoka, Japan, illustrated here.

THE FEDERAL TRIANGLE DEVELOPMENT SITE
WASHINGTON, D.C.

Photo collage looking west

The Pennsylvania Avenue Development Corporation sponsored a developers' competition for a mixed use complex to be located on the only major building site remaining on Pennsylvania Avenue between the White House and the Capital. The 3.1 million square foot program included: federal office space; the Woodrow Wilson Memorial and International Center for Scholars; and exhibit space, performing arts theaters, restaurants, retail, and service activities comprising the new International Cultural and Trade Center. Graves participated in the competition as the design architect for Triangle Partners; the team was not chosen for the project.

Graves' design called for the creation of two freestanding buildings linked at several levels. The buildings would take advantage of the frontage on Pennsylvania Avenue and 14th Street as the symbolic images of the complex. The Pennsylvania Avenue Building was to contain the Performing Arts Center and the Woodrow Wilson Center. The cylindrical form of the Woodrow Wilson Memorial would help guide visitors to the major public open space in the hemicycle facing the Ariel Rios Building. The 14th Street Building was proposed as the primary location for the ICTC exhibitions and retail space, at grade and one level below. Skylit public concourses along the east-west and north-south axes converged on the World Link Theater, a multi-media presentation which would become the symbolic and physical center of the building.

The mixed use nature of the project and the need for public accessibility called for a spirited architecture that would become a vital part of its context. As required by the competition guidelines, the nine-story buildings were designed to be sympathetic to the surrounding context. The limestone facades were to have a horizontal tripartite division of a rusticated base, middle section with window patterns similar in scale to the surrounding structures, and a top consisting of a large cornice and red clay tile gable roof.

Photo collage view of the ICTC Performing Arts Center

Photo collage view of 14th Street from Pershing Park

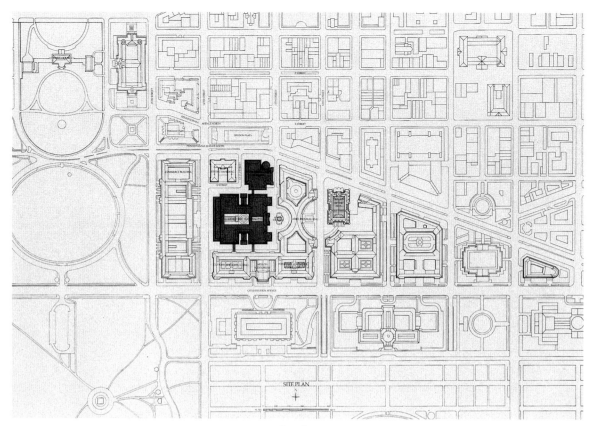

Site plan

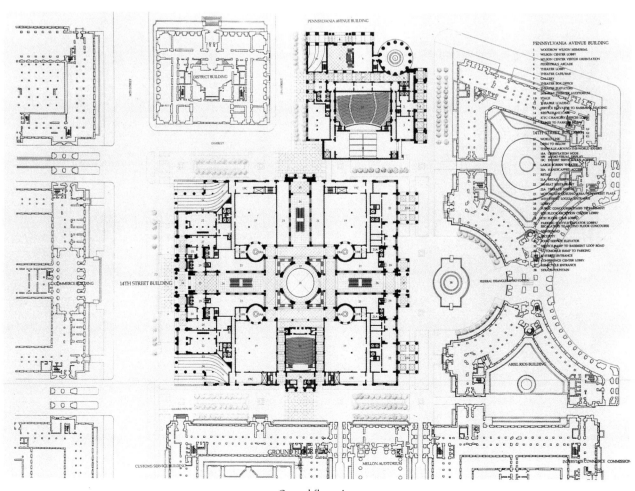

Ground floor plan

328

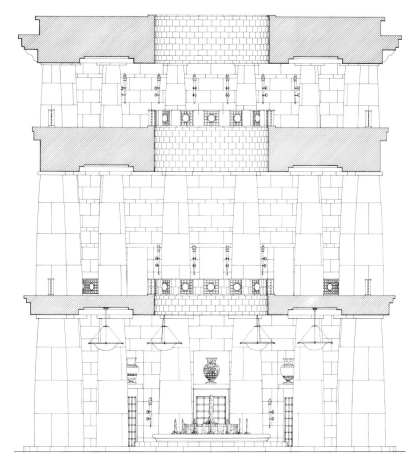

Woodrow Wilson Memorial section

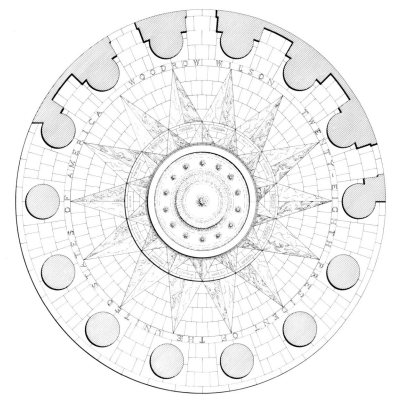

Woodrow Wilson Memorial plan

Main concourse study

World Link Theater study

Theater marquee

2400-seat theater

Outdoor cafes study

Club and Reception Center dining terrace

14th Street entrance model detail

Photo collage view along 13th Street

Photo collage Pennsylvania Avenue view of Wilson Memorial

Hanselmann Residence
Fort Wayne, Indiana, 1967

Snyderman Residence
Fort Wayne, Indiana, 1972

Plocek Residence
Warren, New Jersey, 1977

THE INDIVIDUAL FEELING
FOR COLLECTIVE BEAUTY

by Robert Maxwell

In reality, thousands of reasons and thousands of analyses will never suffice to explain the final choice of a form for there always comes a moment when the requirements of technique open before the imagination to achieve form. In this moment, which lies beyond technique, in the individual feeling for collective beauty, architecture releases all its valencies, it becomes complex and ineffable because instantaneously and unwaveringly the will has made a choice, reducing the range of possibilities to one solution, the most appropriate.

Massimo Scolari [1]

Michael Graves' first retrospective volume[2] covered a comparatively long period—1966 to 1981—during which many things happened in the larger world. The energy crisis of 1973 was probably the most important of these, as much for cultural as for practical reasons, since it initiated a new ecological point of view that stressed continuity and context and promoted conservation. At about the same time, the failure of public housing, dramatized in the demolition of the Pruitt-Igoe estate in St. Louis, seemed to express disillusion with the rationalist procedures of modern design. It was not surprising that Charles Jencks seized upon that event as suitably symbolizing the death of modernism and anticipating the birth of postmodernism.

Quite independently from the business of inventing stylistic labels, a certain change in the public perception of architecture did occur in the mid-seventies. The "failure" of public housing is only one aspect of this, but a crucial one, since it pointed to the deficiencies of a purely rational approach and led to the emergence of a professional attitude bent on seducing rather than instructing the users of buildings. Public man, it now appears, is no more susceptible to brusque rational treatment than anyone else: he too has aspirations, likes old things as well as new, and wants to have everything nice. He is no longer a cipher, he has become a client. As the professional assurance of the sixties encountered the uncertainties of the seventies, a period of adjustment set in. This had little to do with the moral attributes of the various styles and a great deal to do with economic survival. The "post-modernist" architect was able to take over the functionalist credo intact, continuing to justify everything by reference to the program with the difference that the program was no longer reductive but now included anything that could be deemed to affect the satisfaction of the user. This change from didactic to opportunistic motiva-

tion in the professionals is in itself a confirmation of the shift in public opinion.

The shorter period 1982 to 1988, on the other hand, does not appear to coincide with a fundamental shift in public awareness. Superficially, at least, it seems to involve a continuation of those influences that were already in play. During this period the world retrenched. A hunger for the enjoyment of life, or at least for increased consumption, has become a universal aspiration and has led to the adoption of revisionist policies, even within former enclaves of dogmatic socialism. In architecture, the exploitation of images in the postmodern manner for the "satisfaction" of the client has become the new orthodoxy of commercial architecture. The steady exploitation of a settled repertoire of images is the perfect reflection of the bull market in shares and will probably continue as long as confidence in laissez-faire economics prevails.

Looking at Michael Graves' work over these two periods, one might be tempted to see it as sensitively reflecting events. First, in volume I, the adoption of a new style at a psychological moment when change was in the air; then in volume II, the exploitation of an established line, along with the profession as a whole. That view would be totally simplistic.

What we see, rather, is the consolidation of a remarkable talent, not of adaptation, but of origination.

It is true that the change that occurred in the mid-seventies in the public view of architecture coincided with a change of emphasis within Graves' work. That was not confined to him; it was very general. Isozaki's work shows a similar transformation, more dramatic in its completeness. There we see the exchange of an out-and-out brutalist mode, in which architecture sculpturally mimics its program, for a representative style full of allusions, taking as much from European as from Japanese tradition. The change that occurred in Graves' work is a move in the same direction, but what strikes us in his case is less the discontinuity than the continuity. There is an exchange of a Corbusian language for a Ledouvian one, to be sure, a substitution of wall for frame. The effect of this is no more than that framed structures (Benacerraf, Snyderman, Alexander) that celebrate the frame by rupturing it are exchanged for walled structures (Crooks, Plocek) that celebrate the wall by rupturing it. The fascination with rupture and juxtaposition remains. Along with his color, his use of figural metaphor, his sense of frontality, runs the constant preoccupation with juxtaposition and rupture as a substitution for composition and closure, to the point where we are beginning to accept composition and closure as the result of his method.

There is a theme that unifies all these projects, the early ones and the recent ones equally: the search for an architectural language that is consistent and complete, that can be taught, that is bound by rules. And what is the purpose of these rules? Not, evidently, to bring an end to growth and change, but to allow the additional pleasure, in the very condition of the rules having been established, of breaking them.

This assertion may appear to hearken back to the theme of Colin Rowe's 1950 essay, "Mannerism and Modern Architecture," and indeed I believe that this theme is one powerful influence to be reckoned with. But with Graves this is not in any sense a derivative exercise or the cultivation of erudition for its own sake. It stems rather from his response to a chronic condition of our times, the ideological imperative that forbids both rules and the sense of closure and insists on the artist reflecting a reality which is hypostatized as being in a state of constant evolution and change. Works that are open are preferred to works that are closed. The creative posture favored in our times has been that prescribed in Tatlin's tower for the Third International: a leaning forward in the direction of change, an identification with the future. The future is privileged, since it wipes out the uncertainties of the present. And though an architect's discoveries are due to be superceded, if they can be categorized as leading on to a later state of the art, they will be vindicated as "progressive."

This posture encourages creative art, certainly, since it encourages any gesture that looks with some degree of confidence to its completion in the future. In these times an *artist* is someone who has the necessary degree of confidence, and *art* is what such a person produces. Since there are few social constraints, fragmentation and ellipsis are the most evident consequences, as is a certain freedom of action. It is very difficult for critics to reject a work as "bad" if it conforms to no clear rule other than the single rule of being incomplete, which makes it part of a future condition that evades judgement.

With art now enjoying a hitherto unknown status as the key to a better life, both material and spiritual, it is in a situation that reproduces the conditions of a sellers' market. The artists have the fortitude of knowing that if the future should judge them more harshly, at least it cannot demand any back taxes. Not all the arts are equal in the degree to which they are embedded in immediacy. With certain arts a summary judgement is executed at once: if a show doesn't make it with the critics on Broadway, it closes; some Broadway successes are revivals of plays that were once summarily rejected by the critics of their time. Architects are comparatively fortunate, in that they don't have to depend on critics' approval in any one case; even designs disapproved by the critics are not totally rejected once built, provided they work in a practical sense. And even at that level, when they work in a practical sense, there is still an opportunity for the architect as artist to communicate rebellion or disaffection through the fragmentation of the formal vocabulary. Against the implied wholeness of the building's social acceptability, formal fragmentation can be read as an ironic comment on the social necessity which forces a conditional closure.[3]

These remarks are prompted by the prospect that Michael Graves proposes, of considering architecture as an art in spite of the fact that it is also a utility. Considered as a dancer, architecture has always been handicapped by its big feet. Aristotle, we remember, consigned it to the second class, the useful arts, because it was unable through myth or poetry to recite and reflect upon the history of man and convey the story of his heroic aspirations and tragic destiny. Modern investigations in the psychology of art and the potency of symbolic forms have suggested, however, that even the mute forms of architecture are capable of "speaking" when considered as a hermeneutic tradition. It is no accident that Graves' experiments with architecture refer so strongly to that moment in the Enlightenment when, with Ledoux, architecture was presented as an expressive system, the system of "architecture parlante." There is no question that Graves is concerned to redefine the conditions under which architecture can again be considered as an art in its own right. If it is to be an autonomous discipline, it will not be enough for it to put into play the "easy" open-ended dialectic between transitory social purpose and fragmented forms: the speaking system must be able to produce a more demanding dialectic from within its own resources, whatever its dependence on the social program that gave rise to its formation.[4]

This is no easy quest. The spirit of our times is an all-pervading influence, and it brings an inhibition against any kind of closure. It is not just a question of going along with a social system that is ideologically fixed on the idea of "free" competition and an ever-expanding market (that framework no doubt took decisive shape with the Spencerian modification of Darwin's theory of evolution) but, in a general sense, it is dependent on a more powerful, eschatological influence: our belief in a perfectible future and the power of technology to achieve it. The dominant model for our thinking is the experimental method of science, which teaches us that every discovery, however important, is due to be superceded by another discovery yet to come. The piecemeal, step by step nature of scientific advance denies closure and perfectly reflects the contingent nature of all our schemes. Science, accompanied by technology, leans like an impressive structure into the future and so questions the status of every statement that is rounded and attempts closure.

Graves' dilemma is a tough one: in a time when all resolutions are considered to be provisional, he has to fight as hard to establish the rule system that will permit closure as he must fight to put the rules into question by transgressing them, thus experiencing for us the joy of freedom. There is no joy in breaking flimsy rules. Equally, the rules must not appear as arbitrary or out-moded. This is why the mutually dependent concepts of juxtaposition and rupture, composition and closure, are so important in Graves' work and why his principal method, the use of "collage," is at once problematic and essential for his purpose. Like all artists, he must ride a narrow ridge between order and disorder, but unlike most, he must invent the difficulties in his path as well as the means of overcoming them. This view of Graves may seem rather melodramatic in a world where constant adjustment to changes of program is expected and where the client is almost always right. No doubt the Graves office has its share of crises, sudden changes in program, all-night charettes. Impossible to succeed in the practical sense without the will to engage in that primary struggle. What we are talking about here is another kind of struggle which is born of the sense of the building as a potential work of art. Few professional offices today give any indication of the existence of that inner struggle. The normal attitude is that all the elements in a design should be perfectly free to respond to whatever pressures are put upon them, whether these arise from changes in the market or from the whims of the client. Indeed, in responding to those pressures most architects allow themselves to feel virtuous, since the inherited dogma of modernism demands that form follow function and justifies the primacy of empirical data. The impact of abstraction in the early years of the twentieth century greatly extended the scope of this doctrine, since abstract forms were in principle *sui generis* and free from any representational duty; they could be given free rein according to the secret subjectivity of the architect—a condition which is now again exerting its appeal. If in Graves' case there is an inner struggle, it is a struggle of his own choosing, and one, moreover, which he has the strength to undertake.

If architecture's only purpose is to reflect function, to become visible and have form only to the degree that it transparently reveals the program, composition becomes impossible. But it can be recuperated if some space can be inserted between form and function. This has been done. Primarily through the use of abstract forms, a secret program can be put in place and subjective values added on top of the empirical data. This was the unannounced discovery of the masters who practiced in the name of the Modern Movement. A masterpiece such as the Villa Savoye responds in rational mode to the functional program to which it answers—itself a radical statement—but it adds another layer of meaning that in large measure contradicts the rational story by extending it into a realm of ideal form.

When Graves, as a member of the "New York Five,"[5] took his departure from the rational language of the Villa Savoye, this space between form and function became the space of his exploration. With his painterly eye, which had absorbed certain resonances from the work of Juan Gris, he was able to give the semi-abstract forms of his Corbusian vocabulary a power to interact with each other freely and even to take on certain representational duties by being symbolically keyed to concepts derived from Italian Renaissance painting: ground and sky, air and water, interior and exterior. But this added depth of meaning still encountered a barrier to communication. The abstract aspect of the chosen forms allowed them to be deformed at will, so that they offered insufficient resistance to the sense of rule. To this critic at least, the change that occurred around 1975 with the introduction of frankly representational forms that derived, more or less freely, yet definitively, from the classical tradition changed this decisively and introduced a new intensity into his work. From this time on, one can speak about a real effort of exploration. The aim of this exploration is, I believe, to recover a sense of the substance of architecture. For this purpose, the more or less classical aura is probably indispensible as an element of continuity with the past and the built present. It guarantees in the beholder a certain basic willingness to suspend disbelief, to acknowledge a widely held attitude that defines the common ground from which to approach the basic idea: that this building is not only a utility but wants to measure up to the notion of the building as an inherited asset; it asks to be compared to the common stereotypes.

The classical aura is not exactly the same as the classical language of architecture, which to be reproduced in our time requires an unnatural rigidity of adherence to the rules. But neither is it the mere semblance of a classical architecture, a more or less superficial additive that allows the environment to be patchworked together with a measure of decorum. Somewhere in between that loose permissiveness and the narrow-mindedness of replication, Graves has opened up a fertile zone of discovery. The extent and richness of this zone are best realized from a perusal of his sketch drawings, exploratory speculations that precede the production of particular designs and that accompany all his practical achievements. The architecture defined in these sketches is both an examination of typologies and a review of all the possibilities of assemblage.

It has a further quality: because the medium is a wavy line, in some degree developed from Le Corbusier's wavy line, it allows a peculiar balance of vagueness and precision. The volumetric relationships adumbrated are primary and do not depend on the exact definition of edges or the creation of surface tension or the sense of composition within a tight frame—all the attributes of cubist collage. In some essential aspect the assemblages that result are generated outward from the volumetric entities and are free from the caesuras imposed by the act of collage. No doubt the translation of these ideas into definitive compositions will re-introduce the notion of collage, but that operation is given a separate identity, a subsequent task of improvisation and of adjustment. The sketches seem to provide the basic material from which solutions are generated, but they do not themselves have the nature of solutions, nor appear to bow to any necessity, but are produced freely and with joy. They are the source of Graves' power when he proceeds finally to engage in the game of composition.

The mastery with which a limited array of elements and figures is combined and re-combined should not deceive us into seeing this architecture as facile: it is experimental. The choice of elements no doubt reflects the author's taste, with allusions to his preferred gallery of masters—Ledoux, Gilly, Schinkel, and so on—but the interest does not arise from any allusions as such but from the coherence of the formal relations that are established within that taste. In that respect also there is a parallel with the sketches of Le Corbusier, which projected a kind of mental material, infinitely adaptable and manipulable, like a sort of intellectual cheese: the

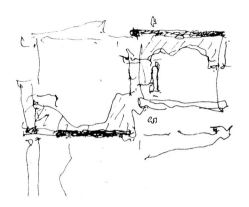
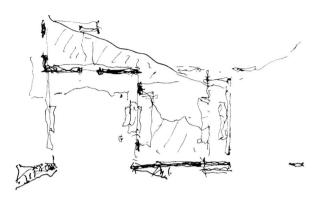

Crooks Residence
Fort Wayne, Indiana, 1976

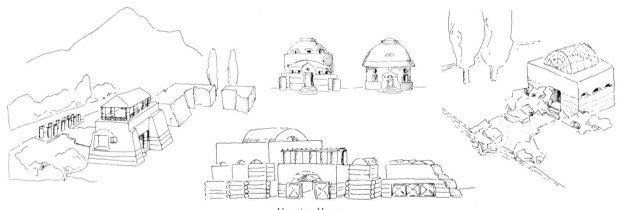

Crooks Residence
Fort Wayne, Indiana, 1976

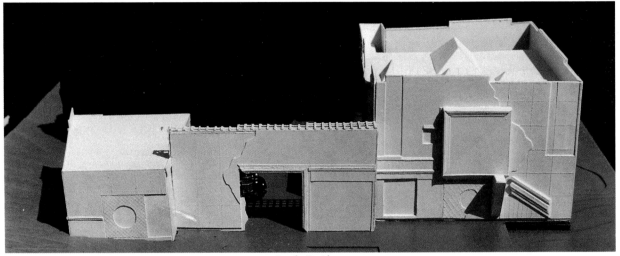

Vacation House
Aspen, Colorado, 1978

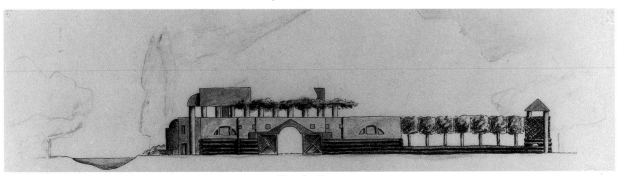

Vacation House
Aspen, Colorado, 1978

form, I would claim, of a substance of architecture. With Corbu, the forms were more abstract but never entirely devoid of representational significance. With Graves, they are more representational but never entirely free from abstraction. To that degree they are subject to his free rein, but insofar as they are also mythic material they are resistant to complete manipulation, they are never entirely subjective. This is what gives them their potency.

Are they nostalgic? Do they merely recall a past era as a perfume? If that were the case they would have a limited viability, somewhat in the manner of the indefinite nostalgia evoked by the multifarious designs of Ralph Lauren, a language of clothes and accessories intended to communicate, which generalizes the past in order to render it consumable.[6] It hardly seems that Michael Graves has any comparable project to get rich from marketing his architectural motifs. I do not think that they are intended for consumption, but they are certainly intended to be legible, and to that extent they are accessible, learnable even. I find it of interest, though, that although his students exercise themselves with the repertoire that he provides and follow the principles of composition that he enunciates (and as a result create Graves-like projects), there is no industry grown up in his wake. Compare his influence with that of Aldo Rossi. Rossi's image of the basic cabin or portico—the rectangle surmounted by a triangle—has been fully exploited by the architecture industry; it is the dominant motive used for accent in thousands of designs by commercial architects for shopping malls and condominiums. It *is* an archetypal form, yes, but its generality has made it widely adaptable. In contrast, Graves' forms seem to lose their power when they are lifted out of their context in his composed ensembles. His "hallmark," the Ledouvian arch or eyebrow, is a case in point. It cannot be re-used without recalling his style, his manner. He has made it his own through the intensity with which he has infused it with a total aesthetic, an aesthetic that derives not alone from the choice of elements, but from the ways in which those elements are combined.

There is little doubt that by restricting the range of his system and intensifying his search for varied combinations within the system, Graves has created an architecture—his architecture. But can one speak without hyperbole of the rediscovery of a *substance* of architecture? If the Gravesian effect can only be imitated by imitating it wholesale, this might speak for the degree to which it is self-integrated and condensed, but it does not necessarily mean that it has attained that level of independence that would open it to all comers as a source of meaning, a level attained by the Corbusian language of 1927.

If there is some hesitation at this point, it appears to emanate from two aspects of his work: first, doubts about the general validity today of a neo-classical language; second, the question of the residual use of collage as a method of reviving the elements and putting them in play within a non-classical system.

The use of the classical repertoire, however restricted it may be, can only be justified in social terms if it helps to give meaning to the works. There can be little doubt that it does so at a basic level, certainly far beyond the capability of pure abstract forms.[7] We have already noticed that the forms Graves uses are more abstracted than the inherited forms of classical architecture as promulgated by Alberti or Palladio or whoever. The revivalist architect must choose precisely where he wants to attach to the classical tradition and to what degree he may attempt to extend it into modern times. That is a legitimate project, and there are a few who follow it, with varying degrees of success. Such architecture may indeed claim to be the only legitimate successor to classical architecture and the only serious attempt to revive the substance of architecture; but the narrowness of the system may make it incapable of dealing with modern subjects, and at that point it would risk appearing as precious and irrelevant. Clearly this is not Graves' project. By opening the classical repertoire to include archaic and primitive elements as well as a range of specific references from within architecture and a directed range of expressive gestures more or less abstract and symbolic, he is asserting the right to be eclectic at will, not in the matter of making a choice of style to suit the situation (as with Schinkel or the Edwardians) but in the right to cull his motifs freely from an inherited body of architecture. Exercising this right need not vitiate the quality of the work, as Picasso demonstrated.

He is clearly aiming at a wide public and an international capability. Yet it seems to me that he does not simply join the international business set who will offer to go anywhere and build with "sensitivity" in any local tradition. In this respect the intensity of his personal taste becomes important as the guarantor of the integrity of his language. The versatility of his formal explorations and the complexity of character that he produces from them are essential as the antithesis to the relative simplicity of the classical elements in themselves.

More troubling, perhaps, is the issue of collage. In a sense, the very use of collage throws into question the integrity of the pre-ordained language.

It has been suggested that the emotion engendered by the use of collage is melancholy.[8] If this would not apply to the earliest uses of collage made by the cubists, it does seem to apply to the types of collage practiced by the surrealists. There the disjunctions produced by collage are not decorative and compositional in intent, but are meant to induce disquiet and recall the mysterious elisions experienced in dreams. If one thinks of the way in which Max Ernst used engravings of mythical entities to offset his own painted figures, it is clear that the fragments are rendered impotent by their submission to the new system, with very different rules of composition. At the same time, those fragments are disruptive of the new as much as they are disrupted by it, since they are undigested fragments that interrupt the organic wholeness of the work. In such works collage seems to put into question both sides of the equation. The old engraving is rendered impotent by its excision from a total system; it becomes a fragment and speaks of loss of belief. At the same time its presence here introduces a *deus ex machina* power, the power of modern technology to reproduce and multiply images without sweat or tears, to disrupt or extend the organic processes of the artist with a device. The

Private Residence
Catskill Mountains, New York, 1986

Graves Residence
Princeton, New Jersey, 1986

ambiguity of this confrontation can go beyond a sense of melancholy to convey irony or despair. The lack of organic wholeness is given a symbolic weight, expressing the impossibility of encompassing modern life in a complete synthesis and reflecting equally the disillusion with systems of belief that once allowed such a synthesis and with the rational extension of man into machines, which risks reducing him to a monster. It is this aspect of collage which has been seized upon by neo-expressionist artists in more recent times to act as a badge of sincerity. In the age of holocaust, recent or imminent, its use exonerates the artist from charges of hedonism or frivolity.[9]

This metaphysical interpretation, however, may seem excessive in relation to the huge mass of salon or board-room art produced today, much of which uses collage as a matter of course. We are bound to suspect that its adoption in so many cases is less a matter of acknowledging the human plight as of being in the swim. In this sense, the message of collage as originally practiced by Ernst and others has been dimmed by use. Even in the case of Eisenman's shifted grid, the effect is increasingly aesthetic rather than metaphysical.

"Metaphysical" certainly seems too portentous a word to describe the first uses of collage made by the synthetic cubists in Paris, which consisted of adding metallic candy wrapping or fragments of newspaper (LE JOURN. .) to small still life paintings. The effect of that use of collage was to reduce the project of cubism from its metaphysical preoccupations with the analysis of perception and the search for the fourth dimension towards an aesthetic celebration of life and the acceptance of the flat plane of the canvas. Painting became plainly decorative, and Le Corbusier and Ozenfant were moved to invent their *Purisme* in protest.

My impression is that collage in Graves work is more a question of decorative richness than of metaphysical doubt. It stems from the work of the synthetic cubists, not from the surrealists. Just as latterday American architects have appropriated the forms of twenties modernism in Europe without intending to reproduce the social content of that decade, so one senses in Graves' use of collage a nonchalance that hardly presages disaster. The seamless transition that is evident between his early cubist murals, the uses made of such murals in his Sunar showrooms, and the predominantly classical layout of those showrooms suggest that the aim is limited to richness of effect, that collage is accepted as a

modern device for creating accent and movement. Collage also seems to constitute a decorative element in the work of other architects: Venturi, Isozaki, Gehry, and Stirling all come to mind in this connection.[10]

If its use is now widespread, collage must have the status of convention, rather than the opposite. It means that the disruptive power of collage has been reduced, that it no longer has to be interpreted as irony or despair, and that the juxtaposing of pieces of different provenance is a simple reflection of the eclectic nature of art in a world now composed of many specializations, where local tradition has been broken or put in doubt. It may seem odd to speak of the classical tradition as a local one, but that conclusion is forced on us by the ever-growing evidence that the world is headed towards a cultural homogeneity based on the universal belief in science as the agent of human betterment. One may bemoan the loss of other beliefs or regional identities, one may bury one's head in a local tradition, but the positive work that can still be undertaken is one of transformation, with the aim of bringing ancient wisdom into modern knowhow. In this view the new animates the old, but the old validates the new. The relationship is reciprocal, and constitutes an indefinite dialectic, without end.

Such a realistic point of view would detect the play of illusion in all human formulations, in ancient wisdom as well as in modern knowhow. In science all formulations are *pro tem*, and in art all formulations are of their time. The loss of belief, which abolishes wholeness, is potentially a blessing if it liberates from prejudice. The acknowledgement of the limits of our power to assert any kind of final truth is an essential part of science, and it seems impossible that that skepticism would not extend to all matters of cultural judgement, at the risk of inducing the same unification of culture as is evidenced in the unity of science. If art is to offer resistance to the homogenization of culture (and I hope that it can and will) it will not be through an emotional reflex that returns us to a former state of innocence, but by opening new prospects of re-integrating apparently opposed forces in new syntheses. This seems very much to be Graves' project. The classical aura serves as a *point de repere*, a multiple reference that ensures the engagement of the beholder. But the result is never negative towards modern life. The fitted kitchens in Graves' houses do not appear as anachronisms.

To savor the blend of old and new we can do no better than

338

Clos Pegase Winery
Calistoga, California, 1984

to study the design for a Rustic House of 1985, designed for a mountainous site in the Catskills near Woodstock, New York. The house looks south through a belt of trees into a clearing in the woods; it can be glimpsed through the trees as we approach it, but one circles round behind to enter through the rear wall back towards the view. The spread of the front is emphasized by the shape of the roof, which doubles as a pedimental cap to the range of rustic columns fashioned from tree-trunks, each three feet in diameter. The synthesis of opportunistic present and mythic past is plain. We have re-invented the doric in an American situation, we have re-activated Ledoux's architecture parlante without abolishing the telephone.

The plan of this house achieves a delicate balance between classical symmetry and modern convenience. The large central living room is tied to the peak of the roof and the masonic chimney and is defined on each side by a set of columns set in front of pilasters. At one end this colonnade is pierced to reveal the fitted kitchen. At the other end, the symmetrically disposed small bay corresponding to the kitchen is closed off and becomes the bathroom to the master bedroom. Back to the other end, the guest bedroom has to find its bathroom from the rear space of the house, space which at the master bedroom end is used to amplify the owner's domain. These asymmetries precisely answer to the program without in any way impugning the classical format. This house seems to be perfectly classical, without any strain. The artifice is all open to be read, in the conceit of combining rustic, American, modern with doric, European, mythic.

The same elegance in the combination of functional sequence and formal order is supremely present in the spaces of Michael Graves' own house, the Warehouse, in Princeton. The strong frontality which in the Rustic House forms up behind the row of eight doric columns is repeated in front of the pairs of *in ante* doric columns which are placed against the back wall of the Warehouse. The house can be enjoyed simultaneously as a grand statement and as a place of detente and relaxation. The columns are archaic, partly abstracted but plainly doric. They have the appearance of trophies and are at the same time a sort of badge of commitment. The sequence of rooms is perfectly practical but can be understood as a formal movement laterally through the living room towards the library, a two-story high loggia fronting the east end towards the morning sun. In the high space, the level of the upper floor is marked by a small set-back so that

the additional height can be seen to be added without disrupting the classical order. In an abstract modern design, this marking of the floor level would appear as an unnecessary hesitation. Yet it does not prevent the enjoyment of the double-height space as an element of *modern* tradition. The spaces articulated in this house have the harmonic resonance of a Palladian plan: the space flows, but its parts are delimited. It defines a quality that is neither classical nor modern, but both.

These relatively simple designs are best for the purpose of revealing the peculiar enjoyment that this architecture brings. In the larger works, there is more struggle, the responsibilities are greater, the interpretations more involved. The same dialectic can be found, though. Modernity is not rejected, but welcomed as a necessary condition; however, it is not accorded a primary place in opposition to formal values but is as far as possible treated as a source of additional strength. The projecting lattice bracket on the front of the Humana Building is not an assertion of the power of steel, but a symbolic gesture by which the building reaches out to the river and its lattice bridges.

The work that Graves is doing is a work of reconciliation and synthesis. In his designs he is free to make use of the power of abstraction: the shape of a gesture, the color of a shape, can evoke a complex of feelings and meanings from within the wider sphere of expression. By putting these gestures into a more specific framework, which seeks to reconstitute the body of architecture, he can call on an additional realm of architectural feelings and meanings. The combination of the two fields is what gives his work such an enormous range and such expressive power.

By contrast, the adherence to a world of abstract purity is compromised as soon as it attempts to transform the living environment. Richard Serra's *Tilted Arc* is a case in point: its interpretation as a work of fine art is diametrically opposed to its absorbance into every-day life. On the other hand, the Vietnam Memorial in Washington succeeds, not only because the space it invades is itself more mythic, but also because the names with which it is inscribed span the gap between the mundane and the mythic. The hovering rectangles of Malevich or El Lissitzky work as graphic gestures with a freedom that will be compromised as soon as they are rendered as built substance: the Proun rooms are thus a hair's-breadth from bathos. All abstract forms have to be

framed, so that their fugitive meaning is not destroyed by the bathos of their connections to actuality. It seems to me that Graves takes on this duty, along with the duty towards the difficult whole, as part of the total entity that he creates.

Not only does he synthesize the functional with the formal, but within the formal he also synthesizes the abstract and the representational. The row of columns that extends across the back of the Warehouse or the front of the Rustic House is doing a double job: it is declaring the zone of formal relations and establishing their domain as well as acting to recall the history and theory of architecture.

Attitudes towards Graves' work vary and will change. There are three ways of dismissing his work that should be discounted: that it is easy and self-indulgent; that it is reactionary and irrelevant; that it is pernicious and immoral. All of these attitudes stem from ideological prejudice and the

inability to examine the work and reflect upon its meaning. If we can think of Graves' inner struggle as directed towards the recuperation of a substance of architecture, it is not in terms of reinvigorating a local tradition alone but of bringing that tradition into modern 'culture. If we speak of the rediscovery of a substance of architecture, this is not to be thought of as an unchanging substance, like gold, but of an essence secreted by living culture and uniting the mythic dimension with the renewed will to live. Viewed in this way, the work of Michael Graves takes on the character of play (as with any artist), a continual experimenting with his preferred materials and the opportunities that come to hand. That is not to deny its underlying seriousness. But it does enable us to assert its experimental nature and, in this sense, to recognize that he is as much entitled to his space as any other artist, of whatever ideological color. And perhaps to recognize also that he is doing useful work for the rest of us.

1. Massimo Scolari, "Architecture in Extremis," in Rational Architecture (Brussels: Archives d'Architecture Moderne, 1978).

2. Michael Graves Building and Projects 1966–1981, eds. Karen Vogel Wheeler, Peter Arnell, and Ted Bickford (New York: Rizzoli International, 1982).

3. The very successful neighborhood center at Columbus, Ohio, by Robert Mangurian and Craig Hodgetts, is one such project. The improvisatory nature of the forms conveys simultaneously the transitory status of the social purpose and the lost virtues of classical architecture.

4. The idea of a more demanding dialectic may be compared with Robert Venturi's striking phrase: "the duty towards the difficult whole." In a recent private conversation with me, Graves referred to collage as being "just too easy."

5. Five Architects: Eisenman, Graves, Gwathmey, Hejduk, Meier (New York: Oxford University Press, 1975).

6. See Witold Rybczynski, Home: A Short History of an Idea, (Viking Penguin, 1987), Chapter I: Nostalgia.

7. An interesting case of the ambiguities of abstract form may be seen in the case of Richard Serra's Tilted Arc erected in a plaza in New York City. The meanings ascribed to this form by the local inhabitants of the area, by the artist, and by the learned critics were entirely at variance with each other.

8. See the discussion of Benjamin's concept of allegory in Peter Burger, Theory of the Avant-garde (Minnesota, 1984), 68–73.

9. See Peter Burger, Theory of the Avant-garde. For Burger, the meaning of surrealist disjunction is primarily political, and derives from Duchamp's attempt to wrest art from the bourgeois. The strength of bourgeois assimilation, however, is such that disjunction in art is now accepted as a mark of the "sincerity" of the artist. In this framework even surrealist disjunction becomes part of the decorative attributes of art.

10. In a not unrelated episode, James Stirling in a broadcast videotape stated very frankly that he relied on the use of collage to animate classical forms which otherwise might be rejected as dead or irrelevant. He was referring specifically to the steel constructions collaged to the facades of the Staatsgalerie in Stuttgart, which have in themselves largely accounted for the popularity of the building with the younger generation.

AWARDS

AMERICAN INSTITUTE OF
ARCHITECTS
NATIONAL HONOR AWARDS

Hanselmann House, 1975
Gunwyn Ventures Investment Office, 1979
Schulman House, 1982
The Portland Building, 1983
San Juan Capistrano Library, 1985
The Humana Building, 1987
Emory University Museum, 1987

NEW JERSEY SOCIETY OF
ARCHITECTS
DESIGN AWARDS

Oyster Bay Town Plan, 1967
Hanselmann House, 1973
Union County Nature and Science Museum, 1974
Alexander House, 1975
E.N.T. Medical Offices, 1975
Snyderman House, 1976
Crooks House, 1976
Graves Warehouse Conversion, 1977
House in Aspen, Colorado, 1978
Schulman House, 1978
Abrahams Dance Studio, 1978
Fargo-Moorhead Cultural Center Bridge, 1978
Sunar Furniture Showroom, New York, 1980
Sunar Furniture Showroom, Houston, 1980
New Jersey Railroad Station, 1980
Environmental Education Center, 1980
San Juan Capistrano Library, 1981
Sunar Furniture Showroom, New York, 1981
Sunar Furniture Showroom, Dallas, 1982
San Juan Capistrano Library, 1983
Environmental Education Center, 1983
Riverbend Music Center, 1983
Stamford Mixed Use Development, 1984
Humana Building, 1985
Clos Pegase Winery and Residence, 1985
Clos Pegase Winery, 1987
Shiseido Health Club, 1987
Sunar London Showroom, 1987
Sotheby's Tower, 1987
Henry Residence, 1987
U.Va. Arts & Sciences Building, 1987
Walt Disney World Dolphin Hotel and
Walt Disney World Swan Hotel, 1988
Emory University Museum, 1989
Sarah Lawrence College Sports Center, 1989

INTERNATIONAL DESIGN
AWARDS

Consumer Products; Alessi Peppermill, 1989
Furniture, Honorable Mention; Vorwerk Carpet, 1989

AIA MID-FLORIDA CHAPTER
DESIGN AWARD 1988

Walt Disney World Dolphin Hotel and
Walt Disney World Swan Hotel

INTERIORS MAGAZINE
AWARDS

Designer of the Year, 1980
Sunar Furniture Showroom, New York, 1981
The Humana Building, 1986
Emory University Museum, 1986

NEW JERSEY SOCIETY OF
ARCHITECTS

Honor Award, 1982

PROGRESSIVE ARCHITECTURE
DESIGN AWARDS

Rockefeller House, 1970
Snyderman House, 1976
Crooks House, 1977
Chem-Fleur Factory Addition, 1978
Graves Warehouse Conversion, 1978
Fargo-Moorhead Cultural Center Bridge, 1979
Plocek House, 1980
Kalko House, 1980
Beach House, 1980
Environmental Education Center, 1983
Historical Center of Industry and Labor, 1988
Henry House, 1989
Walt Disney World Dolphin Hotel and
Walt Disney World Swan Hotel, 1989

PROGRESSIVE ARCHITECTURE
FURNITURE DESIGN AWARDS

Sunar Arm Chair, 1982
Sunar Side Chair, 1983

RESOURCES COUNCIL
COMMENDATIONS

Rug #1, 1980
Sunar Table, 1982

INSTITUTE OF BUSINESS
DESIGNERS

Sunar Casement Fabric, 1982
Sunar Lounge Chair, 1982

HENRY HERING MEMORIAL
MEDAL, 1986

honoring collaboration between architect/
artist/owner for distinguished use of
sculpture on a building, The Portland Building

ARNOLD W. BRUNNER
MEMORIAL
PRIZE IN ARCHITECTURE

American Academy and Institute of Arts and Letters,
1980

INDIANA ARTS AWARD, 1983

EUSTER AWARD, 1983

Miami, Florida

SILVER SPOON AWARD, 1984

Boston University

GOLD PLATE AWARD, 1986

American Academy of Achievement

HONORARY DOCTORATES

University of Cincinnati, 1982
Boston University, 1984
Savannah College of Art and Design, 1986

SELECTED WRITINGS ON MICHAEL GRAVES

1966

Stern, Robert A.M. "The Jersey Corridor Project." *40 Under 40.* New York: Architectural League, 1966.

1967

The New City: Architecture and Urban Renewal. New York: Museum of Modern Art, 1967.

1968

"The Newark Museum." *Architecture of Museums.* New York: Museum of Modern Art, 1968.

"Union County Nature and Science Museum." *Architecture of Museums.* New York: Museum of Modern Art, 1968.

1970

"14th Annual Design Awards: Private Residence, Pocantico Hills, New York." *Progressive Architecture* (January 1970).

1972

Five Architects: Eisenman, Graves, Gwathmey, Hejduk, Meier. New York: Wittenborn, 1972; New York: Oxford University Press, 1975.

Gandelsonas, Mario. "On Reading Architecture." *Progressive Architecture* (March 1972).

1973

Bonfanti, E., Bonicalzi, R., Rossi, A., Scolari, M., and Vitale, D., eds. "Projects at the XV Triennale." *Architettura Razionale.* Milan: Angeli Editore, 1973.

Carl, Peter. "Towards a Pluralist Architecture." *Progressive Architecture* (February 1973).

Giurgola, Romaldo. "The Discreet Charm of the Bourgeoisie"; Greenberg, Allen. "The Lurking American Legacy"; Moore, Charles. "In Similar State of Undress"; Robertson, Jaquelin. "Machines in the Garden"; Stern, Robert A.M. "Five on Five." *The Architectural Forum* (May 1973).

"Esposizione Internazionale delle Arti Decorative e Industriali Moderne e dell' Architettura Moderna." *XV Triennale di Milano* (November 1973).

Papademetriou, Peter. "Architecture." *Architectural Design* (November 1973).

Goldberger, Paul. "Architecture's Big Five Elevate Form." *The New York Times* (November 26, 1973).

1974

"Benacerraf House"; "Hanselmann House"; "Alexander House." *Global Interiors 6: Houses in U.S.A..* Tokyo: A.D.A. Edita, 1974.

Goldberger, Paul. "Should Anyone Care about the 'New York Five'?" *Architectural Record* (February 1974).

Tafuri, Manfredo. "L'architecture dans le Boudoir." *Oppositions 3* (May 1974).

Smith, C. Ray. "Painterly Illusion and Architectural Reality." *Interiors* (September 1974).

1975

Frampton, Kenneth. "Five Architects." *Lotus International* (February 1975).

Stephens, Suzanne. "Semantic Distinctions." *Progressive Architecture* (April 1975).

"Honor Awards: Hanselmann Residence." *AIA Journal* (May 1975).

McKean, John Maule. "The Architect as Intellectual Artist." *Building Design* (October 10, 1975).

1976

Sky, Alison and Stone, Michele. *Unbuilt America.* New York: McGraw Hill, 1976.

Tafuri, Manfredo. *Five Architects New York.* Rome: Officina Edizioni, 1976.

Colquhoun, Alan. "New York Five, an English Reply"; Dean, Yvonne. "The Famous Five, a Literary Exploration." *Art Net* (no. 2, 1976).

"23rd Annual Design Awards: Snyderman House." *Progressive Architecture* (January 1976).

Tafuri, Manfredo. "American Graffiti: Five × Five = Twenty-Five." *Oppositions 5* (Summer 1976).

Smith, C. Ray. "Layers of Space and Symbol." *The New York Times Magazine: The Home* (September 26, 1976).

1977

Jencks, Charles. *The Language of Post-Modern Architecture.* London: Academy Editions, 1977.

Stern, Robert A.M. and Nevins, Deborah. *200 Years of American Architectural Drawing.* New York: Watson-Guptill, 1977.

Stern, Robert A.M. *New Directions in American Architecture.* New York: George Braziller, 1977.

"Crooks House." *Progressive Architecture* (January 1977).

1978

"Claghorn House Addition." *Global Architecture Houses 5.* Tokyo: A.D.A. EDITA, 1978.

"Chem-Fleur Factory Addition and Renovation"; "Warehouse Conversion: Private Residence." *Progressive Architecture* (January 1978).

"Michael Graves: Benacerraf House." *Architectural Design* (January 1978).

Stephens, Suzanne. "Living in a Work of Art." *Progressive Architecture* (March 1978).

Pommer, Richard. "Architecture: Structures for the Imagination." *Art in America* (March/April 1978).

Russell, Beverly. "Color from the Outside In." *House & Garden* (September 1978).

Jencks, Charles. "Late Modernism and Post-Modernism." *Architectural Design* (December 1978).

1979

Colquhoun, Alan. "From Bricolage to Myth: or How to Put Humpty Dumpty Together Again"; Eisenman, Peter. "The Graves of Modernism." *Oppositions 12* (Spring 1978, published 1979).

Drexler, Arthur. *Transformations in Modern Architecture.* New York: Museum of Modern Art, 1979.

Dunster, David, ed. *Michael Graves.* London: Academy Editions, 1979.

"Fargo-Moorhead Cultural Center Bridge." *Progressive Architecture* (January 1979).

Marlin, William. "Prairie Cultural Causeway a Dream Bridge." *The Christian Science Monitor* (April 27, 1979).

Goldberger, Paul. "Architecture: Works of Michael Graves." *The New York Times* (May 11, 1979).

Osman, M.E. "1979 AIA Honor Awards: Creating a New and Colorful Interior Work." *AIA Journal* (Mid-May 1979).

Huxtable, Ada Louise. "A Unified New Language of Design." *The New York Times* (May 27, 1979).

Bletter, Rosemarie Haag. "About Graves." *Skyline* (Summer 1979).

Filler, Martin. "Grand Allusions." *Progressive Architecture* (June 1979).

———. "Better and Better." *Progressive Architecture* (September 1979).

"The Power of Color." *The New York Times Magazine, Home Design* (September 30, 1979).

Scully, Vincent. "On the Michael Graves Monograph." *Architectural Design* (October/November 1979).

Smith, Philip. "Graves' New World." *Gentlemen's Quarterly* (November 1979).

Cohen, Edie. "Sunar, Chicago." *Interior Design* (December 1979).

1980

Jencks, Charles. *Late Modern Architecture.* New York: Rizzoli International, 1980.

"Snyderman House." *Global Architecture Document Special Issue, 1970–1980.* Tokyo: A.D.A. EDITA, 1980.

"27th Annual Design Awards: Kalko House, Green Brook, New Jersey; Plocek House, Warren, New Jersey; Beach House, Loveladies, New Jersey." *Progressive Architecture* (January 1980).

Horn, Richard. "Connecting with Color." *Residential Interiors* (January 1980).

Viladas, Pilar. "Cutting up the Rug." *Interiors* (January 1980).

Filler, Martin. "The Man Who's Rewriting the Language of Color." *House & Garden* (March 1980).

Jencks, Charles. "Post Modern Classicism: Introduction"; "Sunar Showroom, Plocek House, Portland Building." *Architectural Design* (May/June 1980).

Gandee, Charles K. "Sunar Houston: The Allusive Language of Michael Graves." *Architectural Record* (June 1980).

Constantine, Eleni. "The Case for Michael Graves' Design for Portland." *Architectural Record* (August 1980).

Filler, Martin. "Michael Graves: Before and After." *Art in America* (September 1980).

Davis, Douglas. "Building with Symbols." *Newsweek* (September 1, 1980).

Huxtable, Ada Louise. "The Boom in Bigness Goes On." *The New York Times* (December 28, 1980).

1981

Turner, Judith. *Five Architects: Photographs by Judith Turner.* New York: Rizzoli International, 1981.

Wolfe, Tom. *From Bauhaus to Our House.* New York: Farrar Straus Giroux, 1981.

"Architecture and Vegetal Inclusions." *Lotus International* (Number 31, 1981).

Viladas, Pilar. "Michael Graves: Designer of the Year." *Interiors* (January 1981).

Huxtable, Ada Louise. "Architecture at the Crossroads." *Dialogue* (March 1981).

Saltzman, Cynthia. "Architect Michael Graves: Changing the Horizon." *The Wall Street Journal* (May 1, 1981).

Miller, Nory. "Full Circle." *Progressive Architecture* (August 1981).

Anson, Robert Sam. "Michael Graves: The Rise of the Architect-Poet." *Metropolitan Home* (November 1981).

1982

Arnell, Peter and Bickford, Ted, eds. *A Tower for Louisville: The Humana Competition.* New York: Rizzoli International, 1982.

Jensen, Robert and Conway, Patricia. *Ornamentalism.* New York: C.N. Potter, 1982.

Davidson, Peter. "The Wildlife Center: Revealing the Artifice of Representation." *International Architect* (Issue 7, 1982).

"Showroom Design Winner." *Interiors* (January 1982).

Jencks, Charles. "Free Style Classicism"; "San Juan Capistrano Public Library." *Architectural Design* (January/February 1982).

Andrus, Lisa Fellows. "Taking its Architectural Place on the Portland Skyline." *Northwest Magazine* (February 14, 1982).

Mitz, Rick. "Michael Graves: THE Architect." *TWA Ambassador* (March 1982).

Wiseman, Carter. "Why is Everyone Talking About Michael Graves?" *Saturday Review* (March 1982).

Betsky, Aaron. "Matters of Small Gravity." *Crit 2* (Spring 1982).

Durbin, Kathie. "The Shape of Things to Come." *Passages* (Northwest Airlines, May 1982).

"The Schulman Residence." *AIA Journal* (Mid-May 1982).

"New Vistas." *House & Garden* (June 1982).

Goldberger, Paul. "Architecture of a Different Color." *The New York Times Magazine* (October 10, 1982).

Brenner, Douglas. "Portland." *Architectural Record* (November 1982).

Knobel, Lance. "The Portland Building: Graves Deco." *The Architectural Review* (November 1982).

Davis, Douglas. "The Sky's the Limit." *Newsweek* (November 8, 1982).

1983

Wheeler, Karen Vogel, Arnell, Peter, and Bickford, Ted, eds. *Michael Graves: Buildings and Projects 1966–1981*. New York: Rizzoli International, 1983.

Jencks, Charles. "Abstract Representation." *Architectural Design* (Vol. 53, Issue 7/8, 1983).

"Architectural Design Citation: Environmental Education Center." *Progressive Architecture* (January 1983).

"Portland Building Issue." *Skyline* (January 1983).

"Graves Tries His Hand." *Progressive Architecture* (February 1983).

"Sunar Showroom Chicago." *Architectural Review* (March 1983).

"Sunar: Post-Modern Tectonics." *Visual Merchandising and Store Design* (April 1983).

Campbell, Robert. "Graves Has the Courage." *The Boston Globe* (April 12, 1983).

Pastier, John. "First Monument of a Loosely Defined Style." *AIA Journal* (May 1983).

Amery, Colin. "The Poetry and Prose of Michael Graves: Graves' Elegy." *The Architects' Journal* (May 1983).

Furniture Design Award. *Progressive Architecture* (May 1983).

Wilson, Richard Guy. "Michael Graves at Mid Career." *Architecture* (July 1983).

Doubilet, Susan. "Pliny's Villa: Environmental Education Center." *Progressive Architecture* (August 1983).

Guenther, Robert. "Newer Than New? In Architects' Circles, Post-Modern Design is a Bone of Contention." *The Wall Street Journal* (August 1, 1983).

Jordy, William H. "Aedicular Modern: The Architecture of Michael Graves." *The New Criterion* (October 1983).

"Fairy Tale Library to Open in California." *American Libraries* (October 1983).

"Follies." *Domus* (November 1983).

1984

Arnell, Peter and Bickford, Ted, eds. *A Center for the Visual Arts.* New York: Rizzoli, 1984.

Jencks, Charles. *Kings of Infinite Space: Michael Graves and Frank Lloyd Wright*. London: Academy Editions, 1984.

Page, Clint and Cuff, Penelope. *The Public Sector Designs.* Washington, D.C.: Partners for Livable Places, 1984.

Filler, Martin. "Romance Comes Back to Capistrano." *House & Garden* (March 1984).

"The Newark Museum." *Architectural Design* (March/April 1984).

Posner, Ellen. "A Post-Modernist in His Pre-Modernist Office." *The Wall Street Journal* (April 10, 1984).

Kay, Jane Holtz. "A Way Station for Environmental Education." *The Christian Science Monitor* (April 17, 1984).

Pastier, John. "Mission Imagery, Introverted Spaces." *Architecture* (May 1984).

"Fitting the Style." *Domus* (May 1984).

"Cincinnati Symphony Summer Pavilion;" "St. James Townhouses;" "The Republic Building;" "The Humana Building;" "Art History Department;" "Public Library;" "Environmental Education Center;" "The Portland Building." *Global Architecture Document 10*. Tokyo: A.D.A. EDITA, May 1984.

Giovannini, Joseph. "Museums Make Way for the Art of Architecture." *The New York Times* (May 20, 1984).

Viladas, Pilar. "Ex Libris: San Juan Capistrano Library." *Progressive eArchitecture* (June 1984).

Goldberger, Paul. "Romantic Modernism is Now at the Cutting Edge of Design." *The New York Times* (July 8, 1984).

Pastier, John. "Missionary Graves." *The Architectural Review* (October 1984).

Hine, Thomas. "An Architect with a Very Personal Approach to Design." *The Philadelphia Inquirer* (October 21, 1984).

Williams, Sarah. "Galleries for Tomorrow's Art." *Art News* (November 1984).

Campbell, Robert. "Graves Triumphs with Capistrano Library." *The Boston Globe* (November 27, 1984).

"Diane Von Furstenberg: Couture in a New Shop." *The New York Times* (December 7, 1984).

Goldberger, Paul. "Design Consciousness Reached a New High." *The New York Times* (December 30, 1984).

1985

Gilbert, David L. "The Portland Building." *The Critical Edge*. Ed. by Todd A. Marder. New Brunswick: Rutgers University Press, 1985.

Michael Graves/Henry Hornbostel: Emory University Museum of Art and Archaeology. Exhibition catalog. Atlanta: Emory University, 1985.

Hine, Thomas. "Shall we build just for today or build for immortality?" *Philadelphia Inquirer* (January 6, 1985).

Giovannini, Joseph. "Humana's Bet on Innovation." *The New York Times* (January 20, 1985).

Sachner, Paul. "Design Awards Competitions: Domaine Clos Pegase." *Architectural Record* (February 1985).

Martin, Richard. "Michael Graves." *ARTS* (February 1985).

Filler, Martin. "Vintage Graves." *House & Garden* (February 1985).

Bethany, Marilyn. "Let There be Luxe." *New York Magazine* (February 11, 1985).

"Diane Von Furstenberg Boutique." *Art & Design* (March 1985).

Portoghesi, Paolo. "Michael Graves." *Eupalino* (March 1985).

Davis, Douglas. "The Decorative Touch." *Newsweek* (March 11, 1985).

White, Dan. "Will This be the Best Tall Building in America?" *The Philadelphia Inquirer* (March 24, 1985).

"Athenian Graves." *Domus* (April 1985).

"Profile: Michael Graves." *Metropolitan Home* (April 1985).

Biemiller, Lawrence. "The Fanciful Imagings of Postmodern Brought to Venerable Building at Emory University." *The Chronicle of Higher Education* (April 10, 1985).

"Fifth Annual International Furniture Competition." *Progressive Architecture* (May 1985).

Goldberger, Paul. "A Daring and Sensitive Design." *The New York Times* (May 22, 1985).

"Michael Graves." *Connaissance des Arts* (June 1985).

Kamm, Dorothy. "The Making of a Temple." *Visual Merchandising and Store Design* (June 1985).

Goldberger, Paul. "The Humana Building in Louisville: Compelling Work by Michael Graves." *The New York Times* (June 10, 1985).

Dixon, John Morris. "Graves' Humana Tower: Built for Eternity." *Progressive Architecture* (July 1985).

Gandee, Charles K. "Humana." *Architectural Record* (August 1985).

Filler, Martin. "The Sum of Its Arts." *House & Garden* (August 1985).

Scully, Vincent. "Buildings Without Souls." *The New York Times Magazine* (September 8, 1985).

Stein, Karen D. "A Fitting Shrine." *Architectural Record* (Mid-September 1985).

Pastier, John. "Strong, Quirky, Abstract, Monumental." *Architecture* (November 1985).

Norberg-Schulz, Christian. "On the Way to a More Figurative Architecture." *Global Architecture Document 14*. Tokyo: A.D.A. EDITA, December 1985.

"The Humana Building;" "Michael C. Carlos Hall: Museum of Art and Archaeology." *Global Architecture Document 14*. Tokyo: A.D.A. EDITA, December 1985.

1986

Stephens, Suzanne, ed. *Building the New Museum*. New York: Princeton Architectural Press, 1986.

From The Ground Up. Donna Lawrence Productions, 1986.

Wheeler, Karen Vogel, Arnell, Peter, and Bickford, Ted, eds. *Michael Graves: Obras Y Projectos 1966–1985*. Barcelona: Editorial Gustavo Gili, 1986.

Maxwell, Robert. "In Search of Civic Space: Michael Graves' Recent Projects." *Lotus International* (No. 50, 1986).

Leifer, Loring. "Landmark in Louisville"; "In Support of the Arts." *Interiors* (January 1986).

Stephens, Suzanne. "Corporate Culture." *Manhattan, Inc.* (January 1986).

Anderson, Kurt. "Breaking Out of the Box." *TIME* (January 6, 1986).

"The Art World: Modern vs. Postmodern." *The New Yorker* (February 17, 1986).

Anderson, Kurt. "Form Follows Fantasy." *TIME* (February 17, 1986).

Phillips, Patricia C. "Figure in Architecture." *Artforum* (March 1986).

Dorian, Donna. "The Biedemeier Factor." *Art & Antiques* (September 1986).

Allies, Bob. "Walls Within Walls: Sunar's London Showroom." *Designer's Journal* (September 1986).

"Critique: Two Environmental Centers." *Architecture New Jersey* (October 1986).

Stein, Karen D. "On the Waterfront." *Architectural Record* (October 1986).

Lavin, Sylvia. "Interiors Platform." *Interiors* (November 1986).

1987

Merkel, Jayne. *Michael Graves and the Riverbend Music Center*. Cincinnati: Contemporary Arts Center, 1987.

Orendahl, Nora. "The New Newark Museum." *Architecture New Jersey* (Issue 1, 1987).

Norberg-Schulz, Christian. "On the Way to Figurative Architecture." *Places* (vol. 4, No. 1, 1987).

Gaskie, Margaret. "Homecoming." *Architectural Record* (March 1987).

Goldberger, Paul. "Adding a Little Less to the Whitney." *The New York Times* (March 15, 1987).

"Aventine University Center." *Global Architecture Document 18*. Tokyo: A.D.A. EDITA, April 1987.

"The Post Modern Object." *Architectural Design Special Edition* (April 1987).

Jencks, Charles. "The Plocek Residence." *Architectural Digest* (May 1987).

"AIA Honor Awards 1987: The Humana Building"; "Emory University Museum." *Architecture* (May 1987).

Goldberger, Paul. "Museum Piece." *Artforum* (May 1987).

Filler, Martin. "A Shrine to Wine." *House & Garden* (September 1987).

"In the Living Room of Michael Graves." Photography by Langdon Clay. *Esquire* (November 1987).

Andrews, Colman. "The New Face of Napa." *Metropolitan Home* (November 1987).

1988

Staebler, Wendy W. *Architectural Detailing in Contract Interiors*. New York: Whitney Library of Design, 1988.

Wilkes, Joseph A., ed. *Encyclopedia of Architecture: Design, Engineering and Construction*. New York: John Wiley & Sons, Inc. Publishers, 1988.

"Clos Pegase Winery." *Global Architecture Document 19*. Tokyo: A.D.A. Edita, January 1988.

"Design Citation: Historical Center of Industry and Labor." *Progressive Architecture* (January 1988).

Giovannini, Joseph. "At Disney, Playful Architecture is Very Serious Business." *The New York Times* (January 28, 1988).

Michael Graves' office library

Lavin, Sylvia. "Interiors Platform." *Interiors* (February 1988).

Woodbridge, Sally B. "An Unfinished Harvest." *Progressive Architecture* (February 1988).

Viladas, Pilar. "Entertainment Architecture." *Progressive Architecture* (March 1988).

Hirst, Arlene. "Tempest in a Teapot." *Metropolitan Home* (April 1988).

Papademetriou, Peter. "Michael Graves, First Quarter Century." *Progressive Architecture* (April 1988).

Vogel, Carol. "Catering to the Carriage Trade." *The New York Times* (April 17, 1988).

Sutro, Dirk. "Graves, Exemplary Superstar Architect." *The San Diego Tribune* (May 27, 1988).

"Mickey the Talent Scout." *Progressive Architecture* (June 1988).

Gandee, Charles K. "The Prince of Princeton." *HG* (July 1988).

Viladas, Pilar. "The Taste of a Tastemaker." *Progressive Architecture* (September 1988).

"Plocek House." *Global Architecture Houses 24*. Tokyo: A.D.A. EDITA, October 1988.

O'Conner, John T. "Architecture: Building Corporate Symbols." *Harvard Business Review* (October 1988).

Sherman, Beth. "Art-chitecture: Designs for Living." *Harper's Bazaar* (October 1988).

Weiss, Kim. "Gods, Graves, and Scholars." *Spectator Magazine* (December 15-21, 1988).

Goldberger, Paul. "3rd Try on Expansion Design for the Whitney." *The New York Times* (December 20, 1988).

1989

Collins, Michael and Papadakis, Andreas. *Post Modern Design*. New York: Rizzoli International Publications, Inc., 1989.

Klotz, Heinrich. *New York Architektur: 1970–1990*. Munich: Prestel-Verlag, 1989.

Shoshkes, Ellen. *The Design Process*. New York: Whitney Library of Design, 1989.

"Graves, Michael." *Current Biography* (January 1989).

Goldberger, Paul. "The Whitney Paradox: To Add is to Subtract." *The New York Times* (January 8, 1989).

"Our Showhouse." *Metropolitan Home* (February 1989).

Branch, Mark Alden. "Another Try for Graves and Whitney." *Progressive Architecture* (February 1989).

"City Centre Master Plan and Office Building." *Global Architecture Document 23: GA International '89*. Tokyo: A.D.A. EDITA, April 1989.

Miro, Marsha. "Graves' Approach is a Wise Solution for the DIA." *Detroit Free Press* (April 9, 1989).

Lavin, Sylvia. "Interiors Viewpoint." *Interiors* (June 1989).

Miller, Donald. "Architect's 'Crowning' Glory." *Pittsburgh Post-Gazette* (August 15, 1989).

Menna, Christine. "The Fine Hand of Graves, Inside and Out." *Johnstown Tribune-Democrat* (September 14, 1989).

Forgey, Benjamin. "Putting a Twist on Convention." *The Washington Post* (October 7, 1989).

Courtney, Marian. "Princeton Architect Cited for 'Dominance' in Field." *The New York Times* (October 8, 1989).

Watkins, Eileen. "One Man." *Newark Star-Ledger* (October 8, 1989).

Murr, Andrew and Stoffel, Jennifer. "The (Empty) Steel Museum." *Newsweek* (October 30, 1989).

Masello, David. "Postmodern Man: Architect Michael Graves Unveils his Latest Project." *Continental Profiles* (November 1989).

Glueck, Grace. "A 'Yellow Brick Road' Brightens a Museum." *The New York Times* (November 12, 1989).

Watkins, Eileen. "The New Newark Museum." *Newark Star-Ledger* (November 12, 1989).

Fox, Barbara. "Michael Graves." *U.S. 1* (November 21, 1989).

SELECTED INTERVIEWS AND WRITINGS OF MICHAEL GRAVES

1975

"The Swedish Connection" with Caroline Constant. *Journal of Architectural Education* (September 1975).

1977

"Michael Graves: Snyderman House" with M. Perkins. *Global Architecture Houses 2.* Tokyo: A.D.A. EDITA, 1977.

"Elusive Outcome, Mental Mis-en-Scene" with others. *Progressive Architecture* (May 1977).

"The Necessity of Drawing: Tangible Speculation." *Architectural Design* (June 1977).

1978

"Porta Maggiore." *Roma Interrotta Incontri Internazionali d'Arte.* Rome, 1978.

"Toward Reading an Architecture" interview with Douglas Ely. *Nassau Literary Review* (Spring 1978).

"Thought Models." *Great Models.* North Carolina State School of Design, Fall 1978.
"Referential Drawings." *Journal of Architectural Education* (September 1978).

"Three Architects, Three Approaches to Color Use" with Peter Bohlin and Hugh Hardy. *AIA Journal* (October 1978).

1979

"Michael Graves" interview with Arthur Drexler. *Buildings for BEST Products.* New York: Museum of Modern Art, 1979.

"Referential Design: Vacation House in Aspen, Colorado." *International Architect* (Volume 1, 1979).

"Roma Interrotta," Guest Editor; "Roman Interventions," "Nolli Sector IX, Porta Maggiore." *Architectural Design* (March 1979).

1980

"Michael Graves" interview with Barbaralee Diamonstein. *American Architecture Now.* New York: Rizzoli International, 1980.

"Beyond Mere Manners and Cosmetic Compatibility" interview with Gary Wolf. *Old and New Architecture, Design Relationship.* Washington: National Trust for Historic Preservation, 1980.

"An Interview with Michael Graves" interview with Mark A. Hewitt, Benjamin Kracauer, John Massengale, and Michael McDonough. *VIA 4.* Philadelphia: University of Pennsylvania, 1980.

"Michael Graves, A Modern Architect" interview with Philip Smith. *Arts Magazine* (April 1980).

"Post Modern Expressions" interview with Ashley Harvie. *The Designer* (May 1980).

"The Value of Color." *Architectural Record* (June 1980).

"An Interview with Michael Graves" interview with Abraham Rogatnick. *Forum.* Vancouver: September 1980.

1981

"Bacchanal" with Lennart Anderson. Collaboration: Artists and Architects, ed. by Barbaralee Diamonstein. New York: Whitney Library of Design, 1981.

"Thoughts on Furniture." *Furniture by Architects.* Cambridge: Massachusetts Institute of Technology, 1981.

"The Wageman House and the Crooks House." *Idea as Model.* New York: Institute for Architecture and Urban Studies and Rizzoli International, 1981.

"Le Corbusier's Drawn References." *Le Corbusier: Selected Drawings.* London: Academy Editions, 1981.

"Michael Graves." *The Presence of the Past*, ed. by Gabriella Borsano. Venice Biennale and Electa Editrice, Milan 1981.

"Michael Graves." *Speaking a New Classicism: American Architecture Now.* Smith College Museum of Art, 1981.

"Michael Graves." *Yale Seminars in Architecture*, ed. by Cesar Pelli. New Haven: Yale University, 1981.

"Michael Graves." *Architectural Drawing: The Art and the Process*, by Gerald Allen and Richard Oliver. New York: Whitney Library of Design, 1981.

"Perspectives from the East" interview with Michael Graves and Joe d'Urso. *Designers West* (May 1981).

"Michael Graves, an Interview" interview with Ian Blair. *Revue.* Los Angeles: Summer 1981.

"Michael Graves Builds his Reputation" interview with Wilson Hand Kidde and Larz Ferguson Anderson. *Interview* (September 1981).

"Interview with Michael Graves" interview with Joanna Cenci Rodriguez. *Florida Architect* (Fall 1981).

"What is the Focus of Post-Modern Architecture?" interview with Michael McTwigan. *American Artist* (December 1981).

1982

"Representation." *Representation and Architecture*, ed. by Omer Akin and Eleanor F. Weinel. Information Dynamics, Inc., 1982.

1983

"Thoughts About Louis I. Kahn." *Architecture and Urbanism Special Issue: Louis I. Kahn* (1983).

"A Case for Figurative Architecture." *Michael Graves: Buildings and Projects 1966-1981.* New York: Rizzoli International, 1983.

"Ritual." *Princeton Journal.* New York: Princeton Architectural Press, vol. 1, 1983.

"Regional Universals" interview with William Stephenson. *Art Papers.* Atlanta: February, 1983.

"Conversation with Graves" interview with P/A Editors. *Progressive Architecture* (February 1983).

"Michael Graves on the Language of Architecture." *Architectural Digest* (April 1983).

"An Interview with Michael Graves." *Visual Merchandising and Store Design* (April 1983).

Interior landscape

Interview with Editors. *The Fifth Column*. The Canadian Student Journal of Architecture, Autumn 1983.

1984

"An Interview with Michael Graves" interview with Philip Jodidio. *Connaissance des Arts* (March 1984).

"Interview: Michael Graves" interview with Elizabeth Cowell. *Belle*. Australia, July/August 1984.

"Le Post-Modernisme serait-il un humanisme?" interview with Alain Pelissier. *Techniques & Architecture*. France, August/September 1984.

1985

Art + Architecture + Landscape: The Clos Pegase Design Competition. San Francisco: San Francisco Museum of Modern Art, 1985.

The Charlottesville Tapes. New York: Rizzoli, 1985.

"Landscape." *Princeton Journal*. New York: Princeton Architectural Press, vol. 2, 1985.

"The Met Grill" interview with Paul Goldberger. *Metropolitan Home* (January 1985).

1986

"The Formal Versus the Picturesque." *The Villas of Palladio*, by Phillip Trager. Boston: Little Brown Press, 1986.

"Museum of Art & Archaeology, Emory Museum' and Whitney Museum of American Art." *Building the New Museum*, ed. by Suzanne Stephens. New York: Princeton Architectural Press, 1986.

"The San Juan Capistrano Library." *International Lighting Review* (First Quarter 1986).

1987

"Kitchens." *Architectural Digest Supplement* (September 1987).

1988

"Newark Museum." *New Constructions: The Growth of Cultural and Educational Museums in New Jersey*. Exhibition Catalogue, 1988.

"A Case for Figurative Architecture." *Modernity and Popular Culture*. Finland: Aalvo Altar Museum, 1988.

"Has Post-modernism reached its limit?" *Architectural Digest Supplement* (April 1988).

"The New Thinking" interview with Nancy Katz. *Vogue* (June 1988).

"A Case for Figurative Architecture." *Duke University* (November 12, 1988).

1989

"Methods for Japanese Dwellings" interview at the Fukuoka International Architects' Conference. *FIAC: Architecture and the Contemporary City*. Fukuoka, Japan: Coordinating Office for FIAC, 1989.

"A Conversation with Michael Graves" interview with John R. Kirk. *Modulus: The Architectural Review of the University of Virginia*. New York: Princeton Architectural Press, 1989.

"Reading the Architecture: The San Juan Capistrano Library." *Orange County Perspective*. San Juan Capistrano Regional Library, 1989.

"Newark Museum." *New Constructions: The Growth of Cultural and Educational Museums in New Jersey*. Hunterdon Art Center, 1989.

PHOTOGRAPHY CREDITS

Except as noted below, all photographs in this book were taken by Douglass Paschall and William Taylor of Proto Acme Photo and Paschall/Taylor, or by William Taylor of Taylor Photographics.

NORBERG-SCHULZ ESSAY. Ted Bickford: 8. Keat Tan: 9.

SAN JUAN CAPISTRANO LIBRARY. © 1984 Peter Aaron/ESTO: 18, 19 top, 21 top right, bottom right, 22 top left, bottom, 23. © 1984 Hans van Stekelenburg for *International Lighting Review*: 22 top right.

ENVIRONMENTAL EDUCATION CENTER. © Cervin Robinson: 24, 26 top right, 27.

PLOCEK RESIDENCE. Norman McGrath: 28, 29 top, 30, 31, 32, 33.

THE HUMANA BUILDING. © 1985 Peter Aaron/ESTO: 38, 39, 40 top left, top right. © 1985 Peter Mauss/ESTO: 41 top.

SUNAR DALLAS SHOWROOM. Chas McGrath: 46, 47, 48 top, 49.

SUNAR CHICAGO SHOWROOM. Yuichi Idaka: 50, 51, 52 top left, top right, 53 bottom. © Rudi Janu: 53 top.

EMORY UNIVERSITY MUSEUM. Steven Brooke Studios: 58, 59 bottom, 60 top left, 61 top, 62, 63.

THE NEWARK MUSEUM. Steven Brooke Studios: 69, 70. Lizzie Himmel: 71.

SILVER TEA SERVICE. Aldo Ballo: 72.

LAMPS. © Mick Hales 1988 from *In the Neoclassic Style* published by Thames & Hudson 1988: 74 bottom right.

LIGHTING FIXTURES. Courtesy of Baldinger Architectural Lighting: 75 top left, right.

CHAIRS. Bill Kontzias: 76.

LAURA DEAN'S "FIRE." Herbert Migdoll: 79 middle right, bottom left. Keat Tan: bottom right.

GEULAH ABRAHAMS' "A SOLDIER'S TALE." Keat Tan: 80 bottom.

ALCANTARA. Aldo Ballo: 81 bottom.

RIVERBEND. © 1986 Paul Warchol: 82, 83 top, 84 bottom, 85 bottom, 86. Karen Nichols: 87.

DEUTSCHES ARCHITEKTURMUSEUM COURT-YARD. Timothy Hursley: 97 bottom.

CARRIAGE HOUSE RENOVATION. Lizzie Himmel: 110 top left, top right, 111 top left, top right.

GRAVES RESIDENCE. © Mark Darley/ESTO: 114, 115.

ERICKSON ALUMNI CENTER. © 1986 Paul Warchol: 126, 127 top, 129. Greg Ellis: 127 bottom.

CLOS PEGASE WINERY. Otto Baitz: 130 top, 134 top, middle, 135 top left, top right, 136 top left, top right, 137 bottom. Grant Mudford: 134 bottom, 136 bottom, 137 top left, top right.

DIANE VON FURSTENBERG BOUTIQUE. © 1985 Peter Aaron/ESTO: 142, 143 top right, bottom, 145 top left, top right.

STAGE CURTAIN. David Cronen: 147 top.

THE CROWN AMERICAN BUILDING. Timothy Hursley: 182, 183, 184 top left, 186, 187.

SHISEIDO HEALTH CLUB. Courtesy of Hamano Institute: 188, 190, 191.

MARDI GRAS ARCH. © 1986 Janice Rubin: 198.

SUNAR LONDON SHOWROOM. Alastair Hunter: 200, 201 top left, 202 top left. Peter Cook/Designer's Journal: 201 top right, 202 top right, bottom, 203.

VARIATION ON A THEME OF JUAN GRIS. Jesse Gerstein, courtesy of Steuben: 223 bottom left, right.

CHAMPAGNE COOLER. Courtesy of WMF: 224 bottom right.

ARCHAIC VESSELS. Robert Moore, courtesy of Steuben: 225 top left, top right.

MANTEL CLOCK. © Mick Hales 1988 from *In the Neoclassic Style* published by Thames & Hudson 1988: 228.

WRISTWATCH AND JEWELRY. Courtesy of Cleto Munari: 229 middle four images.

FLOOR TILE DESIGNS. Courtesy of Tajima: 255 bottom left, right.

LJ HOOKER OFFICE BUILDING. Brian Gassel: 258.

WALT DISNEY WORLD SWAN HOTEL. Steven Brooke Studios: 277 bottom, 278, 279 top left, top right, middle left, bottom.

LENOX STORE AT THE GARDENS. © 1988 Kim R. Sargent: 295 top left, top right, 296.

DAIEI BUILDING. Courtesy of Hamano Institute: 298 bottom.

METROPOLITAN HOME SHOWHOUSE. David Phelps: 299 top left. Michael Mundy: 299 top right. © Jeff Goldberg/ESTO: 299 bottom. All photographs courtesy of *Metropolitan Home* magazine.

MOMOCHI DISTRICT APARTMENT BUILDING. Hiroyuki Kawano: 301 top left, top right.

METROPOLIS MASTER PLAN. Mark Lohman: 309 top, middle.

METROPOLIS PHASE ONE OFFICE BUILDING. Mark Lohman: 311 bottom right.

NEW UMEDA CITY. Courtesy of Aoki Corporation: 314.

COLUMBUS CONVENTION CENTER COMPETITION. ARTOG/D.G. Olshavsky: 318 bottom.

HOTEL NEW YORK. © Walt Disney Company: 321 top, 323 bottom.

ROBERT MAXWELL ESSAY. Michael Graves: 332 top, 338 top right. Eric Kuhne: 332 center. Norman McGrath: 332 bottom. Graves office: 336 top.

Interior landscape

Interior landscape